LETTERS OF INTRODUCTION

KEVIN JACKSON is a writer, broadcaster and documentary film-maker. He wrote the abecedary-form script for a BBC documentary on the *Oxford English Dictionary*, broadcast in December 2003. His books include *Invisible Forms*, *Pyramid* and *The Verbals*. For Carcanet, he has written *The Language of Cinema* and edited the poems of Anthony Burgess and a selection from Robert Burton's *Anatomy of Melancholy*. He is a Fellow of the London Institute of Pataphysics.

T0167977

LETTERS
OF
INTRODUCTION

Kevin Jackson

CARCANET

First published in Great Britain in 2004 by
Carcanet Press Limited
Alliance House
Cross Street
Manchester M2 7AQ

The alphabet specially commissioned for this book was drawn
by Stephen Raw © 2004

A CIP catalogue record for this book is available from the British Library
ISBN 1 85754 655 5

The publisher acknowledges financial assistance from Arts Council England

Typeset in Goudy by XL Publishing Services, Tiverton
Printed and bound in England by SRP Ltd, Exeter

For Ian Irvine
Man of Letters

ACKNOWLEDGEMENTS

As noted in the Introduction, earlier and shorter forms of the Goethe, Nietzsche, Freud and Blake alphabets were originally commissioned by Ian Irvine for *The Independent*, as were the Dante and Klee alphabets. (The Blake alphabet also draws on interviews and research for a BBC Radio 3 documentary which I wrote and presented in November 2000, at the time of the Tate Britain Blake exhibition; the producer was Fiona McLean.) The Warhol alphabet was commissioned by Lawrence Earle for that paper's Features page, but rewritten into consecutive prose at very short notice in response to an unexpected shift in editorial policy; this is its first appearance in original form. The Surrealism alphabet was commissioned for a BBC website, to accompany an exhibition at Tate Modern. All the other alphabets, new to this volume, were proposed by Michael Schmidt.

My thanks for assorted facts, advice, wisdom, erudition and diversion to all the usual suspects: in alphabetical (of course) order: Alastair Brotchie, Peter Carpenter, Richard Humphreys, Robert Irwin, Tom Lubbock, Christopher Page, Simon Pettifar, Claire Preston, Michael Schmidt, Iain Sinclair, Peter Swaab, Martin Wallen, Clive Wilmer. (My apologies to anyone whose contribution to this project has been unfairly forgotten.) Ian Irvine, who one day will be recognised not merely as a great editor but as the most inspired headline writer of the last 150 years, came up with the title *Letters of Introduction*: once again, I am deeply in his debt.

Finally, Ron and Michelle Royal generously allowed me the use of their handsome house on the coast of Maine (not too far south from Marguerite Yourcenar's grave), where the bulk of this book was written and rewritten in the winter of 2002–3. Georgie Royal was an admirable hostess.

K.J. 2004

CONTENTS

LETTERS OF INTRODUCTION:
AN INTRODUCTION TO THE LETTERS

Alphabets or, to use a more exact term for the literary genre dusted down for this book, abecedaries, are among our most elementary forms of instruction and delight.

Babies, once they have progressed past their pre-verbal cooings and gurglings, are usually inducted into the mysteries and joys of written language by being shown that 'A is for Apple, B is for Bear...'

Childish as the form unquestionably is in most of its manifestations, however, there seems no good reason why one should not return to it in more mature years, and with slightly different purposes in mind.

Do not, after all, our most indispensable works of reference, from the *OED* to the telephone directory, generally adhere to the simple elegance of alphabetical arrangement?

Even as gravely austere an intellectual as Susan Sontag (greatly admired by the author, at one time a candidate for her own chapter in this book) has essayed the abecedary form for a discussion of the choreographer Lucinda Childs' work *Available Light* – see her recent collection *Where the Stress Falls*.

For me, the idea of composing critical primers in abecedarial form came about some four or five years ago, through a combination of chance and neccessity.

Goethe's 250th anniversary was imminent, and the arts editor of the *Independent* asked me to write a feature celebrating the multiplicity of Goethe's polymorphous genius.

How on earth, I fretted, was I to render so much as the most minimal kind of justice to such a vast subject in two thousand words or less?

I was, quite frankly, stumped.

Just when I was about to settle down and write something along the conventional lines of a bland encyclopaedia entry ('The greatest of all German poets, Goethe was born...'), a modest inspiration struck.

Knowing that my editor (Ian Irvine, more than deserving dedicatee of this volume) was a great admirer of Georges Perec, and of other members of the Oulipo – that wonderful French body of writers, mathematicians and fellow-travellers dedicated to the production of literary works governed by various strict restraints – I proposed a mildly Oulipian solution.

Letters were the answer – an A to Z of facts, anecdotes, asides, assessments and curiosities about Goethe's life and works which, while obviously not exhaustive or anything like, would at least evoke something of his versatility in an entertaining and succinct manner.

Much to my relief, the resulting article was well received – so much so that, whenever a subject of comparably daunting magnitude came up as potential feature fodder, I was quite often asked to see whether it could be managed in terms of the alphabetical format.

Nietzsche, for example, needed to be acknowledged on the 100th anniversary of his death; Freud, for the centenary of the *Interpretation of Dreams*; William Blake, on the occasion of a major exhibition at Tate Britain... and so all were duly alphabetised or abecedarised, and have now found their way into this present collection, a dinner-party-without-walls (to cross-breed Malraux's 'Museum Without Walls' with Judy Chicago's *The Dinner Party*) in which a dozen assorted culture-heroes – some obviously destined to be great friends, others doomed to perpetual enimity – have been sat down together (again, by a process combining chance and necessity) for fun and profit.

Obviously, the form has its limitations.

Perhaps the greatest of these is the way in which it prevents, or at any rate inhibits, the development of a linear strand of argument – usually the *sine qua non* of a good introductory piece, primer, crib or what have you.

Questions of frivolity also troubled me – an abecedary is, after all, a game of sorts, and the intrinsic lightness of the form might not, I feared, always mesh well with the occasional (attempted) *gravitas* of certain subjects.

Regardless of such potential incongruities, I pressed ahead, feeling that the pleasures of the game more than amply compensated for its minor embarrassments.

Some of the appeal was – as with all word games; indeed, as with almost all pastimes more demanding than Freud's celebrated *fort-da* routine – the pleasure of overcoming mild difficulties: not least the difficulty of finding genuninely appropriate and not merely passable entries for such unyielding letters as Z, X and – I assure you, often the hardest of all – Q.

To give just one instance, it took me hours to track down the right 'Q' for my Freud alphabet – see below.

Unlikely as it may sound, though, I often felt as though the abecedary form were in some mysterious way offering me what I might call tacit collaboration.

Very often, that is, I felt that words beginning with A, B or C readily offered highly appropriate topics for general expository statements about my subject, while X, Y and Z would either point to suitable areas of summary, or to events which came towards the end of my subject's life, so that a dying fall, a note of elegy or eulogy, came naturally.

Whether or not this happy illusion was purely a matter of fantasy, induced by too much reading about the Surrealist concept of *l'hasard objectif*, there is no doubt in my mind that writing brief introductions to these artists and thinkers in alphabetical mode forced me to explore areas that would have remained closed to me but for the need to hunt down a suitable entry.

Xymphora – a Greek word meaning 'misfortune', for example, was forced on me as an essential part of my Nietszche revisions, and but for my need to jump through those twenty-six self-imposed hoops that run from A to Z, I doubt it would ever have become part of my working vocabulary.

You will, I hope, find in these pages a number of similar curiosities from the less well-thumbed pages of the dictionary or almanac, so that by the time you reach the final Z, you will have entered into imaginative friendships not only with the twelve guests (or groups of guests) at this alphabetical feast, but also with at least a dozen z-words and z-names seldom, if ever, gathered together between the same covers:

Zorn, Zodiac, Zoas, Zelter, Zarathustra, Zweig, Zurn, Ziegfeld, 'Zweet Zurzday', Zurich, Zeno and Zen.

K.J.
Casabasciana, Italy
St George's Day, 2003

A
WILLIAM
BLAKE
ALPHABET

is for Albion

In Blake's earlier writings, the name 'Albion' is simply the familiar poeticism for England. But as he pursued his studies of world mythology and set about elaborating a dramatic mythology of his own, Blake began to use the name in a more complex way. From his readings in Spenser's *Faerie Queene* and in various English antiquarians, notably Camden, he gathered that 'Albion' was a giant who – in Ancient Time – had conquered the British Isles and given the newly subdued territories his own name. Freely cross-breeding this legend with notions he had derived from Swedenborg and the Kabbalah, Blake came up with a figure closer to the Adam of Genesis – or some still more imposing entity – than anything Camden and company had ever imagined: 'He is Albion, our Ancestor, patriarch of the Atlantic Continent, whose History Preceded that of the Hebrews & in whose Sleep, or Chaos, Creation began...' (*A Vision of the Last Judgement*). And at this point, as at so many others, Blakean cosmology becomes too complex for brisk summary. The title of Michael Horowitz's once-ubiquitous anthology of British 'underground' poetry, *Children of Albion*, was intended to sketch a lineage from Blake, understood as proto-hippy, to the new hairy men and women of English verse in the 1960s: its cover made Blake's Vitruvian image 'Glad Day' familiar to a new generation of paperback browsers.

A is also for *America, A Prophecy*, a visionary account of the colonial revolution which paid more heed to the activities of angels and demons than the more prosaic facts known to historians.

 is for Sir Francis Bacon

Often credited by historians with being the father of modern scientific method (and by tiresome cranks as the true author of the poems and plays more conventionally attributed to William Shakespeare), Sir Francis Bacon (1561–1621) was, in Blake's view, one of the three great English intellectual villains who had doomed the modern world to materialism, the gang in full being Bacon, Newton and Locke. In his prophetic poem *Milton*, Blake writes of his attempt to 'cast off Bacon, Locke & Newton from Albion's covering'. A habitual and usually irate scribbler in the margins of his books, Blake scrawled across the title page of Bacon's *Essays* 'Good Advice for Satans Kingdom', and added 'This is Certain If what Bacon says is True what Christ says Is False… I am astonish'd how such Contemptible Knavery & Folly as this Book contains can ever have been calld Wisdom by Men of Sense…' Elsewhere, he thundered that 'Bacon's Philosophy has ruin'd England. Bacon is only Epicurus over again.'

B is also for Jakob Boehme (1572–1624), the itinerant German cobbler and mystic, whose writings influenced Blake profoundly; and for **Sir Anthony Blunt**, art historian and Soviet spy, who, when not taken up with Poussin or espionage, devoted a great deal of time to the study of Blake's classical artistic sources (see *The Art of William Blake*, 1959); and, in Blakean mythology, for **the Beast**, that tyrannical power against which the poet waged his solitary, lifelong war of images and words: 'The Beast & the Whore rule without controls', he wrote in 1798.

is for Christ

As might be expected, Blake's view of Christ was robustly unconventional, from his curious belief that the Son of Man had a snub nose similar to his own ('The Vision of Christ that thou dost see/ Is my Vision's Greatest Enemy/ Thine has a great hook nose like thine/ Mine has a snub nose like to mine…': *The Everlasting Gospel*) to his angry exclamation that 'Christ died as an Unbeliever'. Adequately to explain quite what Blake believed of Christ would take a lengthy volume, as in his caricature of the doctrine of Atonement ('…a horrible doctrine. If another man pay your debt, I do not forgive it.'): 'First God Almighty comes with a Thump on the Head. Then Jesus Christ comes with a balm to heal it.' Blake's rude name for the vindictive God of the Old Testament was 'Nobodaddy'; though see also below, U is for Urizen. According to his friend Crabb Robinson, Blake once declared that Jesus 'is the only God', and then added: 'And so am I and so are you.'

C is also for Chaucer, considered by Blake to be one of the three greatest English poets, sole peer of Milton and Shakespeare. Blake made a celebrated engraving of the *Canterbury Tales*, sometimes used as the cover for modern editions of the poem, and in his 'Descriptive Catalogue' of that work wrote: 'The characters of Chaucer's Pilgrims are the characters which compose all ages and nations... As Newton numbered the stars [an unusually favourable allusion] and Linnaeus numbered the plants, so Chaucer numbered the classes of men.'

is for Dante

In his old age, commissioned by his friend John Linnell, Blake set about the huge task of illustrating the entire *Commedia* – a project still unfinished at the time of his death in 1827, though he did leave more than a hundred watercolours in various stages of completion, as well as seven engravings. Always a quick study when it came to foreign languages, Blake taught himself enough Italian in a few weeks to be able to appreciate at least some of Dante's poetry in the original. It's likely that he already knew it well in translation, since a passage in *The Marriage of Heaven and Hell* makes Dante the peer of Shakespeare, and Blake was not, to put it gently, a man given to parroting received wisdom. Sincere as his admiration undoubtedly was – he considered the Italian poet inspired by the Holy Ghost – he could also be scathing about what he regarded Dante's excessive regard for the tyrannical 'Caesars' of this world (according to Crabb Robinson, 'Blake declared [Dante] a mere politician and atheist, busied about this world's affairs...') and his false visions of other worlds: 'Dante saw Devils where I see none.'

D is also for Deism, the would-be rational form of Natural Religion modish in the intellectual circles of Blake's time, which he despised and railed against throughout his life; and for **the Druids**, much talked about in the eighteenth century, and crucial to Blake's version of English history; he believed that they carried out human sacrifices on the 'slaughter stone' of Stonehenge. (This seems an appropriate place for the author to add that he has, by chance rather than design, made contact with a present-day group of Druids who claim Blake as one of their earliest Lodge Masters, and insist that there is documentation for their claim. To date, the author has been too lazy and timid to pursue this matter any further.)

E is for the *Songs of Experience*

Experience and Innocence are, as Blake's subtitle puts it, the two 'contrary states of the human soul': the latter term includes, among other things, the condition of Man before the Fall and the unblighted world of childhood; the former denotes the postlapsarian and adult worlds. Blake's illustrated books *Songs of Innocence* (1789, Year of Revolution) and *Songs of Experience* (1794) are his complementary accounts of these two states, and remain the most readable and widely loved of all his works. At their best, they have the eerie force and immemorial authority of great anonymous folk poems and ballads; brief and superficially simple, they invite and sometimes reward prolonged exploration of their most recondite meanings. Among the best known of the *Experience* songs are 'The Tyger' ('Tyger, Tyger, burning bright/ In the forests of the night…'), 'London' ('I wander thro' each charter'd street,/ Near where the charter'd Thames does flow…') and 'The Sick Rose':

> O Rose thou art sick.
> The invisible worm,
> That flies in the night
> In the howling storm:
>
> Has found out thy bed
> Of crimson joy:
> And his dark secret love
> Does thy life destroy.

F is for the French Revolution

Only a small fragment of Blake's epic poem on the French Revolution has survived. It seems that he wrote the piece in seven books, all but the first of which have gone missing. Even that relatively brief fragment (despite the optimistic declaration on the title page that it was 'Printed for J. Johnson, No. 72 St. Paul's Church-yard MDCCXCI') remained unpublished until 1913 – possibly because Mr Johnson, radical though he was, thought it best not to bring charges of sedition down on his head, or possibly because the Revolution itself did not develop quite as Blake had foreseen. In the words of one of his earliest biographers, Gilchrist, Blake 'was himself an ardent member of the New School, a vehement republican and sympathiser with the Revolution, hater and contemner of kings and king-craft... To him, at this date, as to ardent minds everywhere, the French Revolution was the herald of the Millennium, of a new age of light and reason. He courageously donned the famous symbol of liberty and equality – the *bonnet-rouge* – in open day, and philosophically walked the streets with the same on his head.' But when he came to hear of the Terror, Gilchrist continues, he tore the red bonnet off and never wore it again.

F is also for Felpham, the small coastal resort near Bognor where Blake lived, worked and saw visions from 1800 to 1803 – his longest period of residence outside London. It was here that he had his most potentially dangerous encounter with authority: see below, S is for Scofield.

G is for Allen Ginsberg

The American Beat poet worshipped Blake to the point of idolatry, and dated the true beginnings of his own poetic career to an auditory hallucination he experienced in New York as a young man: the voice of Blake addressed him directly. Though it would be an exaggeration to say that all of Ginsberg's poetry was written under the spell of Blake (one of the under-rated virtues of Ginsberg's poetry was a kind of demotic and occasionally knockabout comedy, quite distinct from the Blakean sublime), it is plain that Blake's example both as a writer and a self-appointed prophet stayed with him to the last. He was fond of singing Blake's lyrics to the accompaniment of acoustic guitar and his own squeeze-box, and it has been pointed out (by the critic Peter Swaab) that one of his last publications can be seen as a kind of updating of the 'Proverbs of Hell'. Ginsberg's advocacy of Blake helped establish the English poet as a kind of benign great- great- great- grandfather figure for the counter-culture of the 1960s and 1970s – a period in which Blake's words and images, which until that point had remained obscure, wormed their way out of learned tomes and onto the covers of rock albums (a suitably embarrassing example would be Atomic Rooster's *Death Walks Behind You*, which reproduced the grim portrait of Nebuchadnezzar insane and on all fours). Blakean maxims appeared on posters, in the underground press, on walls: 'The Tygers of Wrath are wiser than the Horses of Instruction'. And in Adrian Mitchell's musical play for the National Theatre, *Tyger*, Blake was shown embracing Ginsberg as a kindred spirit and rare peer.

G is also for Golgonooza, a city of 'Art & Manufacture' in Blake's two prophetic works *The Four Zoas* and *Milton*; and, more recently, the name of a small, idealistic publishing house inspired by Blake and specialising in poetry and prophetic criticism by, among others, Kathleen Raine.

H is for *The Marriage of Heaven and Hell*

A brief and extraordinary (even by his standards) early work of Blake's, first issued in 1793. It is an almost unexampled mixture of satire and abstruse philosophy, conceived partly as a rebuke to a work by his former mentor Swedenborg, *Heaven and Hell*. Blake's admirers have lavished extravagant praise on the text: the American critic S. Foster Damon, for example, claimed that it is 'Blake's *Principia*, in which he announced a new concept of the universe', and that it is also 'the first manifesto of modern psychology.' For Blake, Heaven and Hell are not so much our possible destinations in the next world as opposed states of mind within every one of us – corresponding, perhaps, to what early generations of psychoanalysts would term as the super-ego and the id. At the same time, *The Marriage of Heaven and Hell* offers some tantalisingly oblique glimpses of Blake's everyday life, including – or so one ingenious scholar of Blake's visual work has recently suggested – a coded allusion to the precise technical process he was using to manufacture its plates: 'the notion that man has a body distinct from his soul is to be expunged; this I shall do by printing in the infernal method, by corrosives, which in Hell are salutary and medicinal, melting apparent surfaces away, and displaying the infinite which was hid.' In more prosaic terms, Blake appears to be stating that he creates his plates not by scratching into them with engraving tools, but by using acids to eat into them, presumably by covering the surfaces which are meant to stand proud with some kind of waxy protective covering. There may also be some hint of Blake's philosophy of mind here: rather than being the passive, Lockean *tabula rasa* which receives impressions from the outside world via the senses, Blake considers that the human mind comes into the world filled with innate ideas, latent riches which can be recovered by a kind of healthy stripping away. (Compare the often-heard notion that what a sculptor does with a piece of stone is not to shape it in accordance with some preconceived pattern, but to clear away clutter and 'release' its true, hidden form.) At any rate, Blake continues this passage with some of the most frequently cited of his credos: 'If the doors of perception were cleansed every thing would appear to man as it is, infinite. For man has closed himself up, till he sees all things through narrow chinks of his cavern.' It was this passage which gave Aldous Huxley the title for his account of the mescaline experience, *The Doors of Perception*, and so, in turn, inspired Jim Morrison to name his 1960s rock band The Doors.

is for the *Songs of Innocence*

This was the first complete work of Blake's to have been produced by his personal method of illuminated printing (see H, above), in which the text and designs were etched on copper in relief, and the prints from these plates then coloured by hand. To judge by the relatively few copies known to have survived – about twenty – it did not enjoy a very wide readership, but posterity has made recompense by ensuring that the complementary volumes of *Innocence* and *Experience* have been familiar to generation after generation of schoolchildren – an appropriate readership, especially if it is true that Blake wrote some of the *Innocence* poems when not much more than a child himself. Adult readers, even those fond of Blake's later work, have sometimes found the first group of poems a little sickly for their digestion – too redolent of Sunday School pieties, too jingling in their facile rhymes – and may need the assurance of the learned that this is, in fact, intensely serious stuff. Hence, say, Harold Bloom in *The Visionary Company*: '"The Lamb", usually considered a fine example of namby-pamby, is a poem of profound and perilous ambiguity…' For dubious readers, the best advice may be to reflect that each of the *Innocence* poems is qualified by its counterpart in *Experience*, and that the otherwise dismaying cuteness of the former reads very differently in the harsh light cast by the latter.

I is also for 'An Island in the Moon', Blake's weird and farcical satire of contemporary intellectuals, including himself (see below, Q is for Quid the Cynic); oddly, given its coarse tone, its final version includes three of the 'Songs of Innocence'.

J is for Jerusalem

The poem or song or anthem or hymn that every British subject or citizen thinks of when the name 'Jerusalem' is mentioned ('And did those feet in ancient time/ Walk upon England's mountains green' – and see below, T is for E.P. Thompson) was not entitled 'Jerusalem' by Blake himself, but was part of the prefatory material of the much longer work *Milton* (1804–8). The poem which Blake called *Jerusalem* – or, more completely, *Jerusalem: The Emanation of the Giant Albion* (1804-20) – is a tyger of quite a different stripe, and the largest of all his published works, encompassing not only a weighty text but a hundred plates. In Blake's own summary: 'it is voluminous and contains the ancient history of Britain, and the world of Satan and Adam'. Would it were really that simple. Something of what the poem is more precisely about may be glimpsed from reviewing what the term or name 'Jerusalem' means elsewhere in Blake. Broadly speaking, 'Jerusalem' is, at various times, a (female) personification of Liberty; the 'Emanation', or feminine manifestation of the Giant Albion; a Holy City of Peace, and thus an image of the perfect society on Earth; the spirit of divine inspiration in every human heart; and the Bride of the Lamb. So far, so polyvalent. Thus, as *Jerusalem* begins, there is a conflict between Albion and the Lamb over her possession. Albion hides Jerusalem inside his breast, turning his back on the Divine Vision and then, by some process of metaphysical controtion, fleeing guiltily after her… The rest is for the intrepid reader to discover unaccompanied.

J is also for the Book of Job, magnificently illustrated by Blake at the end of his life.

 is for *King Edward the Third*
Though much of Blake's writing takes the form of dramatic exchanges between various entities or embodied principles, his only true attempt at a work for the stage was his early, uncompleted *King Edward the Third*, a pseudo-Shakespearean account of the English preparation for the battle of 'Cressy' (i.e. Crecy) in 1346. For many years, it was assumed that Blake's play was straightforwardly patriotic, a bellicose piece of warming-up propaganda for Britain's imminent war with France in 1778, but more recent critics have suggested that it was always intended ironically, as a tacit condemnation of Edward's bloodthirstiness and imperial greed. Certainly, some of the more memorable lines of this otherwise largely unmemorable piece evoke the horrors of battle rather than its glory:

> I seem to be in one great charnel-house,
> And seem to scent the rotten carcasses!
> I seem to hear the dismal yells of death,
> While the black gore drips from his horrid jaws…

Blake may have written himself into the piece in the person of 'William', the *idiot savant* servant of Sir Charles Dagworth. In the course of a discussion about Ambition, William declares: 'I have a great ambition to know every thing, Sir.'

K is also for Sir Geoffrey Keynes, the most distinguished editor of Blake's works.

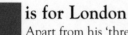 **is for London**
Apart from his 'three years' slumber on the banks of the Ocean' –
that is, in his cottage at Felpham – Blake lived and worked in
London almost all his life. (A recent historian of London, Stephen
Inwood, makes the amusing and just observation that in the course of 'sixty-
seven years in London, his eccentric genius brought him little public success,
but no repression. His three years in Sussex ended in his arrest and trial for
treason' (*A History of London*, 1998, p. 296). See below, S is for Scofield.) While
he may not be the greatest poet ever to have lived in London, he is none the
less *the* great London poet – the poet who saw the city most richly and strangely
and with the most far-reaching penetration. If we can bracket out its over-famil-
iarity for a moment, the early lyric from *Songs of Experience* is perfectly chilling:

> I wander thro' each charter'd street
> Near where the charter'd Thames does flow,
> And mark in every face I meet
> Marks of weakness, marks of woe…

And – for lifelong Londoners in particular – there is a uniquely Blakean thrill
that comes of stumbling across the prosaic names of streets and landmarks as
they crop up in the intricate labyrinths of his long prophetic books:

> From Golgonooza the spiritual Four-fold London eternal,
> In immense labours & sorrows, ever building, ever falling,
> Thro' Albion's four Forests which overspread all the Earth
> From London Stone to Blackheath east: to Hounslow west:
> To Finchely north: to Norwood south…
>
> (*Milton*, Section 6)

L is also for Los, Blake's personification of the spirit of poetry, 'Prophet of
Eternity' and also, by some accounts, his alter ego.

M is for Marginalia

The Romantic period of English literature produced two major writers who were also major scribblers – that is to say, chronic defacers of the title-pages, endpapers and margins of the books they owned or borrowed: Coleridge and Blake. Some of Blake's marginalia are so pungently phrased that they have achieved an immortality to rival many of his poems: 'The Enquiry in England is not whether a Man has Talents & Genius, but whether he is Passive & Polite & a Virtuous Ass & obedient to Noblemen's Opinions in Art & Science. If he is, he is a Good Man. If not, he must be Starved.' Thus his commentary on the pages of Sir Joshua Reynold's *Discourses*. ('This man was hired to depress art', he snarled on its title page.) And some of his marginalia actually took the form of poems:

> When Sir Joshua Reynolds died
> All Nature was degraded;
> The King drop'd a tear into the Queen's Ear,
> And all his Pictures Faded.

M is also for John Milton, in Blake's view the greatest of all English poets, and in the view of many the greatest influence on his own poetry. ('Milton was to Blake's poetry what Michelangelo was to his painting': S. Foster Damon). *Milton* (1804–8) is, again, Blake's immensely complex, semi-autobiographical prophetic work, which he once claimed to have taken down from the dictation of the long-dead Milton himself.

N is for Newton

Though Blake acknowledged the scientist's unparalleled genius, he considered Sir Isaac Newton guilty of an appalling crime: the creation of a materialist vision of the universe which excluded both God and the divine element in Man. Together with Locke and Bacon (see above), Newton had, he thought, sought to 'Deny a Conscience in Man & the Communion of Saints & Angels, Contemning the Divine Vision & Fruition,

Worshiping the Deus of the Heathen…' Hence the pious appeal at the conclusion of a short poem he included in a letter to his friend Thomas Butts:

> Now I a fourfold vision see,
> And fourfold vision is given to me;
> 'Tis fourfold in my supreme delight
> And threefold in soft Beulah's night
> And twofold Always. May God us keep
> From Single vision and Newton's sleep!

It is important to stress, though, that his attitude to Newton was not always satirical in any obvious sense, and certainly not derisive. One of Blake's most striking visual works is his portrait 'Newton', which shows a naked youth of heroic proportions, apparently seated on a rock at the bottom of the sea, and drawing a set of geometrical figures with a compass. The critical element here is so cryptic as to be imperceptible to many viewers, and it is hardly surprising that Sir Eduardo Paolozzi should have taken 'Newton' as the basis for his giant sculpture outside the new British Library near King's Cross. (A very Blakean district, as readers of contemporary English poetry have been reminded in the last decade or so by the publication of Aidan Dun's neo-Blakean epic *Vale Royal*.)

O is for Orc

In Blake's private mythology, Orc is the personified spirit of Revolution, first-born son of Los and Enitharmon; his name was probably coined as an anagram of *cor*, 'heart', since he springs from Enitharmon's heart, though it may also be related to *orca*, because in one of his manifestations he becomes a whale in the South Seas. Weird and many as Orc's adventures are – at one point, he is bound on a mountain top like Prometheus – it is not too misleading to say that whenever Blake writes about him, he is generally brooding on the causes, development and eventual corruptions of the American and French Revolutions in particular and of revolutionary movements in general. (A mildly Freudian reading of one of Orc's less happy experiences has also been read as an account of a classic Oedipal rebellion against the Father.) Blake, one might note, had something of a penchant for the letter O when it came to inventing or borrowing mythic figures. Among the other beings in his prophetic verses are: Ocalythron, Orc's sister, and first-born daughter of Los and Enitharmon; Ochim, their seventeenth son; Ololon, the spiritual form of Milton's Sixfold Emanation (or, in slightly plainer terms, the embodiment of everything Milton didn't understand about women); Ona, daughter of Urizen; Oothoon, the main character in the *Visions of the Daughters of Albion*; Ozoth, father of eight million and eight sons; and so on, and on.

P is for the *Proverbs of Hell*

One of the central sections of *The Marriage of Heaven and Hell*, the 'Proverbs' include some of Blake's most memorable and pithily expressed doctrines, aperçus, maxims and provocations. In the 1960s, when (see above) hippies loved to scrawl Blakean graffiti on the walls (a practice far from dead, as a stroll around present-day Stoke Newington will confirm), it was the 'Proverbs' which proved the most fruitful source of palatable paradoxes. A sampling will show why:

'The road of excess leads to the palace of wisdom.' (Much favoured by heavy drinkers and druggers.)

'The tygers of wrath are wiser than the horses of instruction.' (Much favoured by student revolutionaries about to burn down the canteen and occupy the Senate House.)

'Sooner murder an infant in its cradle than nurse unacted desires.' (Much favoured by philanderers, and anyone who followed the Crowleyan injunction that 'Do what thou wilt shall be the whole of the Law.')

'If the fool would persist in his folly, he would become wise.' (Much favoured by persistent fools.)

And

'The cut worm forgives the plow.' (Not so much favoured. By anybody.)

P is also for Plato, the Greek philosopher Blake found most interesting, despite the 'most Pernicious Falsehood' of many Platonic doctrines; and for the **Prophets**, who to Blake's mind were not seers of the future, but revealers of eternal truth – 'Every honest man is a prophet'; and for **Poetry**, **Painting** and **Passion**.

is for Quid the Cynic

A character in Blake's zany satire of his intellectual contemporaries, 'An Island in the Moon', who appears to be based, at least in part, on the author himself. 'In this Island dwells three philosophers – Suction the Epicurean, Quid the Cynic, & Sipsop the Pythagorean… The three Philosophers sat together thinking of nothing…' Suction has been identified with Blake's younger brother Robert, and Sipsop with Thomas Taylor, a Platonist, though the evidence is inconclusive. Quid the Cynic sings many of the songs scattered throughout this prose fragment, including a rude one about Samuel Johnson:

> 'Oho', said Dr Johnson
> To Scipio Africanus,
> 'If you don't own me a Philosopher,
> I'll kick your Roman Anus.'

One of the details that has held critics back from a complete identification of Blake and Quid is that the latter derides some of the writers that Blake most admired: 'I think that Homer is bombast, & Shakespeare is too wild, & Milton has no feelings: they might easily be outdone. Chatterton never writ those poems!…'

Q is also for the Quatrain, the verse form frequently used by Blake in his earlier writings, and that which gave shape to some of his most unforgettable and magnificent lines:

> When the stars threw down their spears
> And water'd heaven with their tears
> Did he smile his work to see?
> Did he who made the Lamb make thee?

R is for *Red Dragon*

The thriller by Thomas Harris which introduced the modern world to its favourite bogeyman of recent years, Dr Hannibal Lecter, takes its title from a powerful watercolour by Blake, *The Great Red Dragon and the Woman Clothed with the Sun*. When the director Michael Mann first brought Harris's fiction to the big screen as *Manhunter* – a greatly over-rated work – he foolishly trimmed it of virtually all its Blakean trappings, including, criminally, the delightfully mad scene in which the serial killer Francis Dolarhyde (a.k.a. 'The Tooth Fairy'), having insinuated himself into the Brooklyn Museum in the guise of a scholar researching the life of Blake's patron 'William Butts' (is this perhaps meant to be Thomas Butts?), coshes the curator, tears the watercolour from its case… and eats it. The second version of the film, which returns to the original title *Red Dragon*, replaces this fine scene – and quite well, though the film was largely dismissed by reviewers. Harris's novel, by the way, also has two epigraphs from Blake, of which the second seems the more pointed:

> Cruelty has a Human Heart,
> And Jealousy a Human Face,
> Terror, the Human Form Divine,
> And Secrecy, the Human Dress…

On the subject of museums and galleries, **R is also, of course, for Sir Joshua Reynolds**: see above, M is for Marginalia.

S is for Scofield

The private soldier who brought a charge of sedition against Blake after the poet threw him out of his garden at Felpham on 12 August 1803. According to Scofield, Blake had shouted 'D——n the King, d——n all his subjects, d——n his soldiers, they are all slaves; when Bonaparte comes, it will be cut-throat for cut-throat, and the weakest must go to the wall; I will help him...' Since the nation was terrified by the possibility of an imminent French invasion, these were highly dangerous charges, and Blake stood trial for High Treason on 16 January 1804. The poet drew up a *Memorandum* in his own defence: 'If such a Perjury as this can take effect, any Villain in future may come and drag me and my Wife out of our House, and beat us in the Garden or use us as he please or is able, and afterwards go and swear our Lives away...' Thanks to the eloquence of this document, to Blake's hearty and authoritative bellows of 'False!' throughout Scofield's less articulate deposition, and to the poet's popularity with the locals, who all spoke of his habitual gentleness and good nature, Blake was acquitted to wild cheers. But this was not the last of his dealings with Scofield: Blake put him into the verses of *Jerusalem* as a villain – the accuser, the spirit of hate.

S is also for Emmanuel Swedenborg (1688–1772), the mystic writer whose works made a great impression on the young Blake, though he later came to ridicule his one-time mentor; and for **Satan**, who in Blake's cosmology is the God of This World.

T is for E.P. Thompson

The most eminent English Marxist historian of the later twentieth century, and one of that conflict-ridden tradition's most humane thinkers and resourceful prose stylists. Thompson's posthumous work *Witness Against the Beast* takes Blake's work out of the hands of his more mystical and airy-fairy admirers and places it in the context of popular English radical traditions that originated at the time of the Civil War. To be exact, Thompson proposes that Blake might have been heir to the charmingly named Muggletonian heresy – an argument now, according to more recent researchers in the same murky areas, discredited in its particulars but respected for its general tendency. *Witness Against the Beast* was obviously a heartfelt and urgent book for Thompson, who throughout his intellectual and political careers had tried to revive the Romantic, imaginative and generous traditions of English socialism – his first major work was a biography of William Morris – in place of the continental or Asian systems of socialism hero-worshipped by other thinkers of the left. As early as his classic *Making of the English Working Class*, in 1963, Thompson had noted that 'Against the background of London Dissent, with its fringe of desists and earnest mystics, William Blake no longer seems the cranky untutored genius that he must seem to those who know only the genteel culture of the time. On the contrary, he is the original yet authentic voice of a long popular tradition.' Despite the best efforts of Thompson and other independent-minded socialist scholars, it would be a sorry exaggeration to say that the British left has whole-heartedly embraced Blake as a founding father – there is still too much of the 'cranky' about him, no doubt. Still, there have been times when the flirtation has looked promising, since:

T is also for 'Tygers of Wrath' (see above, P is for the *Proverbs of Hell*), a concert in celebration of Blake's legacy at London's Queen Elizabeth Hall in February 2001, co-organised by the art historian Richard Humphreys and the present author. The concert began with a set by Billy Bragg, the singer, song-writer and articulate proponent of a 'socialism of the heart'. Bragg, who has recorded a moving version of 'Jerusalem' and – on the splendidly named CD *William Bloke* – a tribute to Blake called 'Upfield', has lobbied for 'Jerusalem' to become what for many British people it already is: our true National Anthem.

U is for Urizen

One of the most important figures in Blake's cosmology, Urizen (possibly a play on the words 'Your Reason') is the embodiment of law-making, of the avenging conscience, and of the limitation of Energy – as well, of course, as Reason itself. He also seems to be a version of the Jealous God of the Old Testament, who creates the world, plants the garden of Eden, and issues the Ten Commandments. On the other hand, there are also times when his career seems to parallel that of Satan in *Paradise Lost*. It has been argued that he first appears, unnamed, in *The Marriage of Heaven and Hell*, and as the off-stage Creator in 'The Tyger', but his first unambiguous and credited appearance is in the *Visions of the Daughters of Albion*: 'O Urizen! Creator of men! Mistaken Demon of Heaven…' Thereafter he plays a major role in almost all Blake's poems, and particularly in *The Four Zoas* (1795–1804). Sample:

'Am I not God?' said Urizen. 'Who is Equal to me?
'Do I not stretch the heavens abroad, or fold them up like a garment?'
He spoke, mustering his heavy clouds around him, black, opake.
Then thunders roll'd around & lightnings darted to & fro;
His visage chang'd to darkness, & his strong right hand came forth
To cast Ahania to the Earth…

V is for Varley

John Varley, an interesting man who combined the callings of watercolour painter, landscape designer and astrologer, was a good friend to Blake in the poet's declining years. It is thanks to Varley's encouragement that Blake now began to make sketches of the Spirits who came to visit him on a daily basis. The resulting series, now known as the 'Visionary Heads', includes portraits from the life – or the ectoplasm? – of Edward I, Edward II, William Wallace and 'The Man Who Built the Pyramids', who was, it seems, a bit of a Hooray Henry, all receding chin, plump cheeks and inbred pointy nose. Moses, Julius Caesar, Richard the Lionheart and other historical notables would also drop by of an evening when Blake was busy with his pencil, and it is to the sessions with Varley that we owe perhaps the most frightening of all Blake's images, the 'Ghost of a Flea' – a huge and ghastly thing, part humanoid with the hypertrophied musculature of a comic-book hero, part reptilian predator, holding a bowl full (presumably) of blood. Varley has left us an account of the evening this dread apparition arrived: 'I felt convinced, by his mode of proceeding, that [Blake] had a real image befire him; for he left off, and began on another part of the paper to make a separate drawing of the mouth of the Flea, which the spirit having opened, he was prevented from proceeding with the first sketch till he had closed it…'

V is also for *Vala, or the Four Zoas* – see Z, below; and for **A Vision of the Last Judgement**, a text which describes a lost painting by Blake on a grand scale, with more than 1,000 figures.

W is for Wordsworth

The two English poets never met, though Crabb Robinson tried several times to bring them together, but each man expressed both admiration and misgiving about the other. Blake, on reading one of Wordsworth's shorter poems, scribbled in its margin that 'This is all in the highest degree imaginative & equal to any poet, but not Superior. I cannot think that Real Poets have any competition. None are greatest in the Kingdom of Heaven; it is so in Poetry.' In darker vein, he considered that Wordsworth – who, as a worshipper of Nature, was thus, to Blake's mind, no better than an Atheist or indeed Satanist – represented '…the Natural Man rising up against the Spiritual Man Continually, & then he is No Poet but a Heathen Philosopher at Enmity against all true Poetry or Inspiration'. More dramatic to record, it seems that reading Wordsworth's 'Preface' to *The Excursion* 'caused him a bowel movement which nearly killed him'. For his part, Wordsworth, on reading the *Songs of Innocence and of Experience*, remarked: 'There is no doubt this poor man was mad, but there is something in the madness of this man which interests me more than the sanity of Lord Byron and Walter Scott!'

W is also for War, about which Blake had much to say. Among his more idiosyncratic beliefs on the topic was the opinion that the European tendency to bellicosity could be traced back to Homer and Virgil, who had been immoral enough to represent armed combat in a glorious light.

X is for Catherine Blake

Why? Because, in a sense, that was her name. Blake's biographer, Gilchrist, tells us, when 'by-and-by, her turn came, as bride, to sign the Parish Register, she, as the same yet mutely testifies, could do no more than most young ladies of her class then... and magistrates of the land four centuries before could do – viz., make an X as "her mark"...' Catherine Sophia Boucher, of Battersea, married William Blake on 18 August 1782; the groom was twenty-five, the bride twenty-one. Their courtship, apparently a brief one, had begun when Catherine heard Blake complaining about his disappointments in love. 'His listener, a dark-haired, generous-hearted girl, frankly declared "She pitied him from the heart." "*Do* you pity me?" "*Yes!* I do, most sincerely." "Then I love you for that!", he replied, with enthusiasm...' Their marriage was long – almost exactly forty-five years – and, despite long periods of poverty and domestic discomfort, by most reliable accounts an unusually happy one, though they remained childless. Over the years, William taught Catherine to read, write and draw, as well as something of his own art of engraving, and she eventually became skilled enough to work side by side with her husband, on at least some footing of equality. On his deathbed, William cried out to her: 'Stay! Keep as you are! *You* have ever been an angel to me: I will draw you!' And so he executed his last sketch. Blake died just a few days later, singing songs of his own composition about the nature of Heaven, which was already visible to him.

Y is for Young's *Night Thoughts*

One of Blake's earliest full-scale commissions came from Richard Edwards of New Bond Street, who in 1796 engaged Blake to illustrate a lavish edition of the immensely popular poem *Night Thoughts*, by Edward Young. Almost entirely forgotten by the readerships of subsequent centuries (though the Surrealists had a kind word or two for him), Young was in his day considered one of the greatest of all poets, and *Night Thoughts* – largely a collection of versified pieties about mortality and immortality – was an international hit, giving rise to an entire poetic movement, the so-called 'Graveyard School'. Privately, Blake had no time whatsoever for most of Young's beliefs, but these reservations did not seem to cramp his style or dampen his energies: he produced some 537 water colours for the project, though only 43 of these reached the engraving stage: the first instalment of the edition did not sell very well, so Edwards discontinued it. Critical opinion of Blake's *Night Thoughts* work has varied considerably, some comparing it favourably with Raphael, others finding it monotonous.

Y is also for W.B. Yeats, who as a young man spent many hours in the British Library editing a ground-breaking, if somewhat high-handed edition of Blake's poems – Rossetti and Swinburne were among the other poets who had whipped up a Blake revival – including a number of Yeatsian 'improvements'. Yeats amended 'shuddering fears' to 'shadowy tears', changed 'throw the sand against the wind' to 'throw the dust against the wind…'

Z is for the Zoas

These beings, which stalk through Blake's prophetic works, seem to have been derived from the poet's autodidactic readings in the Book of Revelations, where John the Divine sees four creatures standing around the throne of the Lamb. The Greek word *zoa*, usually translated as 'beasts', is a plural; whether from grammatical ignorance or some subtler cause, Blake treated it as a singular, and his four Zoas are made to stand for the four essential attributes of man, as well as the four points of the compass: body (Tharmas, the West), emotions (Luvah, the East), reason (Urizen, the South) and imagination (Urthona, the North). But, as one would expect of Blake, the larger picture is a good deal more complicated. For a time, Tharmas is also equated with God the Father; Luvah with God the Son; Urthona with the Holy Ghost; and Urizen with Lucifer. Well, that will pass as an approximation. Then the mutations begin. Urthona becomes Los, Blake's spirit of poetry; Luvah splits like an amoeba from his feminine form – or 'Emanation' – Vala, to be reborn as Orc; Urizen also splits, and turns into a dragon, as does Tharmas, who dwindles to the merely material plane. In their course of their evolutionary exploits, each entity comes to the conclusion that He, She or It must be the Supreme Being – a gross mistake, though the whole story appears to reach a happy end in the bosom of Albion... At which point, this Blakean alphabet may finally return to its point of departure, swallowing its tail like the mythological serpent.

A
DANTE
ALPHABET

A is for Alighieri

Dante Alighieri (1265–1321): leading Florentine politician, ambassador, alleged criminal, exile; author of a number of prose works on philosophical, literary and political themes, including the *Convivio, De Vulgari Eloquentia*, the *Epistle to Can Grande* and the *Monarchia*, as well as a strange, autobiographical love story in prose and verse, the *Vita Nuova*; by some (sober) accounts the man who founded the modern Italian language; early and major theorist of Europe as a political entity; self-mythologiser and grudge-bearer on a heroic scale; polymathic genius; religious thinker and mystic; 'the central man of all the world' (Ruskin); author, narrator and main human character of the *Commedia* or *Divine Comedy* – almost certainly the most influential poem of the last 2,000 years; by some (also fairly sober) accounts, the greatest of all poets.

B is for Beatrice

The heroine and central figure of both the *Vita Nuova* and the *Commedia*; traditionally identified, on the authority of an early *Vita di Dante*, as Beatrice Portinari, daughter of Folco Portinari: born 1266, married (to Simone de' Bardi) in 1287 and died in 1290, *aetat.* twenty-four. Dante first saw her, on his own account, in 1274 when he was nine – for some reason, T.S. Eliot thought he must have been even younger – and then again when he was about eighteen. He was more than commonly smitten. On this slender acquaintance was raised a vast and almost unfathomably complex literary edifice. At the most modest level, Beatrice's role in the *Commedia* is to conduct Dante from the Terrestrial to the Celestial Paradise; but her presence inspires and permeates the entire work. History does not record what Dante's wife, Gemma Donati, who bore him four children, made of this undying infatuation with a dead woman; hard to believe she was flattered.

C is for *Commedia*

The Russian poet Osip Mandelstam, one of many twentieth-century writers who revered the work, described the *Commedia* as a single crystal with 13,000 facets. The poem can, in fact, be described in a variety of ways, most straightforwardly as an epic journey through Hell (*Inferno*), Purgatory (*Purgatorio*) and Heaven (*Paradiso*) modelled in some respects on classical epics such as Virgil's *Aeneid* – Virgil himself acts as Dante's tour guide through Hell; as the account of an actual mystical experience undergone by the poet in Holy Week, 1300; as a quest for divine Love through the experience of human love; as an encyclopaedia-cum-cosmology encompassing or at any rate touching every significant branch of art and science known to Dante's time…

Among other things, the poem showed that topical events and contemporary figures could be incorporated into a work of the highest art; hence:

D is for the Damned

In Dante's progress through the infernal regions, he encounters any number of souls who were once living, and engages in lively (and deathly) dialogues with them. Some, as you might expect, are his old enemies, but not all: in *Inferno* XV, for example, he encounters his old mentor, the Florentine notary Brunetto Latini – *'Siete voi qui, ser Brunetto?'*; 'Are *you* here, ser Brunetto?' – who has unfortunately been pitched into the circle of the Violent Against Nature for the crime of sodomy. The finale of the encounter (*'Poi si rivolse…'*) is one of the most celebrated passages in the poem: 'Then he turned back, and seemed like one of those who run through the field for the green cloth at Verona; and of them seemed like one who wins, not he who loses.' Many modern poets – Robert Lowell for one – have made translations of this moving episode.

E is for Exile

In 1302, Dante and three of his political allies were charged with bribery and other crimes, including conspiracy against the Pope, and sentenced to fines and two years of banishment; a sentence soon revised to death by burning. (The charges were almost certainly trumped up: see G is for Ghibellines and Guelphs.) For the rest of his life, Dante was an exile from his native city, separated from his family and his funds; in the *Convivio* he speaks of travelling 'through almost every region to which this tongue of ours extends, a stranger and almost a beggar.' He may also have gone as far afield as Paris and, according to a legend which delighted one of his English fans, Gladstone, to Oxford. The *Commedia*, then, is a poem written in exile.

F is for Francesca

The episode of Paolo and Francesca is one of the miniature narratives from the *Commedia* that is sometimes known even to those who have never tackled the poem itself. (And Francesca's lament is, perhaps, still more widely known – as a traditional wisdom if not word for word: '*Nessun maggior dolore…*': 'There is no greater pain than to recall a happy time in wretchedness.') In the circle of the Lustful, Dante sees, and questions, two intertwined figures blown about by hellish winds; Francesca tells him how her adultery began when she and Paolo were reading together from a book about the loves of Sir Lancelot: '*Galeotto fu il libro…*': 'That book was a Galeotto [a pandar], and so was he who wrote it; that day we read in it no farther.'

G is for Ghibellines and Guelphs

The two political factions in Dante's Florence. The Guelphs, who by 1295 had recovered their ancestral control of the city, had traditionally supported the power of the Pope in central Italy; their opponents, the Ghibellines – many of them sent into exile – supported the claims of the German Emperor. But the Guelphs themselves were split into two wings, the Black and the White, associated respectively with the families of

Corso Donati and Vieri de' Cherchi; Dante adhered to the White Guelphs, so that when the Blacks staged a *coup d'état* in 1301, he was one of the many Whites charged with all manner of heinous crimes and sent into banishment.

is for Hannibal Lecter

The most notorious of modern Dante scholars, who in the guise of 'Dr Fell' delivers a substantial Lecter-lecture on the *Commedia* in Thomas Harris's novel *Hannibal*; an exercise, sad to relate, much trimmed down in the screen version. To spare readers the trouble and expense of securing that text, here is a swift and somewhat modified summary:

Dr Fell takes for his principal text Dante's encounter with Pier delle Vigne, *Inferno* XIII, lines 31ff., in the wood of the Violent Against Themselves – that is, the suicides, who in punishment for their offence against the Holy Spirit have all been transformed into bushes and trees; trees which can shriek with pain and tell their mortal stories when, as Dante does at Virgil's instruction, their branches are snapped off. Fell claims that Dante represents Pier (c. 1190–1249) – minister of Frederick II and Chancellor of the Two Sicilies – as a figure of avarice, and thus associated with Judas Iscariot, who also hanged himself. It is always dangerous to disagree with Dr Lecter, but honesty obliges one to say that there does not seem to be any warrant for this charge of avarice either in the text, in which Pier is allowed to stress that he was driven to suicide by a campaign of malice and his own pride:

> L'animo mio per disdegnoso gusto,
> > credendo col morir fuggir disdegno,
> > ingiusto fece me contra me giusto.

(My soul, in its disdainful mood, thinking to escape disdain by death, made me, though just, injust against myself.)

or in the traditional historical accounts of Pier, whose actual offence seems to be that he plotted, or was accused of plotting, with Pope Innocent IV against Frederick. (Incidentally, 'Fell' also seems to confuse the un-named Florentine speaker, another suicide, at the end of Canto XIII – '*Io fei giubbetto a me delle mie case*' (I made a gibbet for myself of my own house) with Pier delle Vigne.) Probably the most memorable part of the lecture comes when Dr Fell recites some of Pier's testimony, hamming it up to accentuate the 'strained hisses and coughing sibilants' he hears in the words, and regards as one of Dante's dramatic coups: Pier's voice is that of a man being strangled:

> *Qui le strascineremo, e per la mesta*
> *selva saranno i nostri corpi appesi,*
> *ciascuno al prun dell' ombra sua molesta.*

> (Here we shall drag them, and through the mournful wood our bodies shall
> be hanged, each on the thorny tree of its tormented shade.)

Oddly, Dr Fell's audience – a group of the most ferociously learned medieval and Renaissance scholars in the world, we are told – find this hugely impressive. Perhaps you had to be there. One might add that it is easy to see why Dr Lecter would have a taste for the more sanguinary elements of the *Inferno* (a point we will examine in U is for Ugolino, below), which does not stint its horrors, but it's also possible that his vanity might have been tickled by Dante's various explicit and veiled references to the original Hannibal. See, for instance, *Inf.* XXVIII, 11; and *Par.* VI, 50: '*Esso atterrò l'orgoglio…*': 'It cast down the pride of the Arabs that followed Hannibal across the Alpine rocks…' (This is the second of three entries for Dr Lecter in these dozen alphabets; *caveat lector*.)

I is for *Inferno*

Religious and literary purists alike insist that the *Commedia* must be read as a whole; or, that if one has to be so perverse as to read only a fragment, then it is the *Paradiso* which really matters. For the mass of unregenerate readers, however, it is the torments, the monsters, the voices howling from the pit which count; and when Keats joked that he found going to a bank an experience out of Dante, he meant the *Inferno*, not the ecstatic parts. (Similarly, the phrase 'Dante's Inferno' comes readily enough to the lips of thousands who may have little idea that the poet also voyaged through Purgatory and Heaven: at any rate, you seldom hear the joyful exclamation that 'it was like something out of Dante's *Paradiso*!') And the one line from Dante that almost everyone can quote – in English – is the inscription above the gates of Hell: '*lasciate ogni speranza, voi ch'entrate*'. Oddly enough, it is Longfellow's slightly loose translation which has entered our common speech: 'Abandon hope, all ye who enter here'.

J is for Jesus

According to some scholarly accounts, the name 'Christ' occurs no fewer than thirty-nine times in the *Commedia*, but 'Jesus', on its own, only once: at *Par.* XXV, 33: '*quanto Jesù ai tre fe' piu chiarezza*' (as Jesus gave more light unto the three).

K is for Kingship

The subject of Dante's most substantial Latin prose work on political theory, *De Monarchia*, an analysis of the relationship between the Empire and the Papacy which argued the case for a universal temporal monarchy, as a precondition of that state of peace and justice in which humanity might make real the intellectual potential bestowed on us by God. In Dante's view, the supreme king would be qualified for his office by a unique capacity for love; he would be at once elected and divinely ordained. Modern commentators have pointed out how much this vision owes to the wise monarchs of history, legend, and legendary history: Barbarossa, Prester John, and, above all, King Arthur – Dante was a great admirer of the Arthurian tales. (The *Monarchia*, incidentally, was a completed work: Dante's other philosophical treatises, the *Convivio* and the *De Vulgari Eloquentia*, remained fragmentary.)

L is for Limbo

Dante's Limbo, the first circle of Hell (*Inf*. IV), is populated by the spirits of those who lived without baptism or Christianity; the only pain suffered here is the knowledge of never knowing God. Among the distinguished tenants of this circle are the great pagan poets Homer, Horace and Ovid; Greek philosophers such as Socrates, Plato, Democritus, and Roman thinkers including Cicero and Seneca; even some heterodox Arabian commentators on Aristotle, notably Averroes (Ibn al Rushd). Virgil, as he admits, usually resides with them – '*e di questi cotai son io medesmo*' – but has been let out on special leave for this mission.

M is for Modernism

Dante's influence on literary modernism was, one can plausibly argue, far greater than that of any other writer in the Western canon. The Florentine master haunts *The Waste Land*, from the crowd of lost souls passing over London Bridge in Book I to the fragment from the *Purgatorio* ('*Poi s'ascose nel foco che gli affina*') at the finale of Book V; T.S. Eliot also wrote some of the last century's most profound Dante criticism, and returned to the *Commedia* for the second section of 'Little Gidding', composed in an English version of *terza rima*, in which the narrator, wandering alone through the empty streets of wartime London, encounters a Virgilian 'familiar compound ghost' who imparts lacerating wisdoms. Eliot's friend, editor and fellow poet Ezra Pound was also a lifelong Dantescan; his *Cantos* pass through a twentieth-century Hell (a Hell to which Pound, it might be said, added his own peculiar mite of evil) and Purgatory before arriving at a chastened and tentative glimpse of Paradise. James Joyce was another member of the Dante faction, as was his younger friend Samuel Beckett, who wrote an essay about Joyce's debt to Dante in the writing of *Finnegans Wake*, devoted his first collection of semi-autobiographical stories to a character named Belacqua (*Purg*. IV: his sin was sloth) and went on to make his own surveys of the damned. Add to this quartet the names of Yeats, Wyndham Lewis, Auden, Wallace Stevens, Thomas Mann, George Santayana, Anna Akhmatova and Osip

Mandelstam, and then still more recently Robert Lowell, Seamus Heaney, Geoffrey Hill and Robert Pinsky, and one can begin to appreciate the extent to which modern literature is a series of footnotes to Dante.

N is for Numerology

The *Commedia* is composed in accordance with a system of numerology – partly traditional, partly invented – so complex as to inspire awe even in those immune to the poem's literary merits. To scrape the surface of this topic, let's begin with the numbers 3, 9 and 10. In honour of the Trinity, the *Commedia* is divided into three parts, and each of its three sections is made up of thirty-three cantos, except for the *Inferno*, which has an introductory canto, bringing the total to a hundred. (Ten being, in some mystical traditions, the number of perfection, and a hundred being ten squared.) The poem's rhyme scheme, *terza rima*, is also based on threes, and in such a way that each canto is divisible by three with one left over – a return to unity. So far, so good. Now, we learn from the *Vita Nuova* that Beatrice is mystically identified with the number 9 – three squared. Each of the poem's afterworlds is divided ninefold or tenfold, depending how you look at it. (Paradise, for example, is made up of the nine heavens plus the Empyrean.) Beatrice is mentioned by name sixty-three times (6 + 3 = 9), and her name is used as a rhyme on nine occasions. She appears to Dante in the sixty-fourth canto of the *Commedia*, i.e. with sixty-three cantos behind her (6 + 3 = 9) and thirty-six ahead (3 + 6 = 9); canto 64 contains 145 lines (1 + 4 + 5 = 10), and she appears in its seventy-third line (7 + 3 = 10). Then it really starts to get complicated...

For further enlightenment, try the appopriate section of William Anderson's *Dante the Maker*.

O is for Odysseus

Or, as Dante calls him – not having access to Homer in the original – *Ulisse*, Ulysses. In Dante's version (*Inf.* XXVI), Odysseus appears in Hell as an ageing man who, content neither with the sum of his exploits nor the pleasures of domesticity, had determined to set off on a final voyage beyond the Pillars of Hercules. Rallying his retired veterans, he had uttered the magnificent lines: '*Considerate la vostra semenza:/fatti non foste a viver come bruti,/ma per seguir virtute e conoscenza*' (Think of the seed from which you sprang: you were not made to live like beasts, but to follow virtue and knowledge.) They sailed on and on past the equator, till they came in sight of Mount Purgatory, from whence a storm blew up and drowned them all. It is Dante's tale, not Homer's, which inspired Tennyson's dramatic monologue 'Ulysses'.

P is for *Paradiso*

For neophytes the most difficult, for initiates the most invaluable part of Dante's poem, the *Paradiso* is something like a cross between an epic journey into space and an advanced postdoctoral seminar in theology and cosmology. Beatrice conducts Dante up through the various heavens, outlining to him the nature of each level of the universe from the moon onwards; en route, her efforts are supplemented by the likes of Justinian, St Thomas Aquinas, Solomon, an eagle, St Benedict, St John, St Peter and St Bernard of Clairvaux, who takes over Beatrice's tutorial duties. It all ends in light, and a vision inexpressible in words – even the words of a Dante.

Q is for Quadrivium

The Seven Liberal Arts of the Middle Ages, pursued by young men on their path to a Master's degree, were divided into two blocks: the *trivium* of grammar, rhetoric and dialectic (or logic), studied for the first four years, and the *quadrivium* of music, arithmetic, geometry and astrology, studied for the last three. In the *Convivio*, or 'Banquet of

Knowledge', Dante maintains (II, xiv) that these seven arts correspond to the seven lowest heavens, though he gives them in a slightly idiosyncratic order. Hence, grammar is like the moon; Mercury like dialectic; Venus like rhetoric... These were Dante's sciences, and the sciences which shape and are expounded in the *Commedia*, especially the *Paradiso*.

R is for Rose

'*In forma dunque di candida rosa/mi si mostrava la milizia santa/che nel suo sangue Cristo fece sposa...*' (In form, then, of a white rose displayed itself to me that holy militia which in His blood Christ made His spouse...; *Par*. XXXI). Dante's vision of ultimate reality on reaching the Empyrean – an experience he compares to the stupefaction of barbarians on first seeing Rome – takes the form of a giant rose, thousands of angels darting in and out of it like bees ('*Sì come schiera d'ape...*'), the souls of the blessed among its petals, and – once St Bernard has drawn his attention to Her presence – the Virgin Mary in its heights.

S is for Satan

Hell is shaped like a cone, and Satan is trapped at its very lowest point. The Arch Traitor, he is, like lesser traitors, being punished eternally for his sin. An immeasurably huge, unutterably hideous giant, he has three heads – red, yellow and black – three sets of bat's wings ('*di vipistrello*'), and in each of his bloodily foaming mouths he chomps eternally on the three most heinous of all mortal traitors – Judas, Brutus and Cassius. Virgil and Dante swarm down Satan's hairs until suddenly, to Dante's bafflement, he appears to have turned upside-down and have his legs stuck in the air: they have passed through the centre of the earth, and are ready to climb up into the opposite hemisphere, where Mount Purgatory awaits them.

T is for *Terza Rima*

The rhyme scheme of the *Commedia*, founded on a three-line unit (see N is for Numerology) in which the word ending the middle line of one tercet becomes the main rhyme of the next: ABA/BCB/CDC/ and so on. Hence: '*Nel mezzo del cammin di nostra VITA/mi ritrovai per una selva OSCURA/che la diritta via era SMARRITA.///* Ahi quanto a dir qual era è cosa DURA…' Though it is much harder to handle in English than in Italian – since our language, though richer in total number of words, is poorer in true rhymes – a number of English poets have ventured to use in for Dantescan themes, notably Shelley in 'The Triumph of Life'.

U is for Ugolino

The most harrowing of all the dramatic sololiquies of the damned comes in *Inf.* XXXII and XXXIII: Dante encounters two sinners trapped together in a hole: '*ch'io vidi due ghiacciati…*': 'I saw two frozen in one hole so closely, that the one head was a cap to the other; and as bread is chewed for hunger, so the uppermost put his teeth into the other there where the brain joins with the nape.' The chewed is Archbishop Ruggieri, the chewer Count Ugolino, and both men are traitors: Ugolino, a Guelf sympathiser from Pisa, had formed a treacherous alliance with the Ghibelline Ruggieri, who had repaid Ugolino with equal treachery by then having him and his two sons nailed up in a tower. Ugolino breaks off from his infernal snack on Ruggieri's skull just long enough to tell the horrific end of the tale: before long, his boys had died of starvation. Ugolino had mourned over their bodies for a while; then 'fasting had more power than grief'. Hannibal Lecter has, as noted above, a particular interest in this passage.

V is for Virgil

Dante's guide and instructor through the depths of Hell and the slopes of Purgatory, where he hands his task over to Beatrice (*Purg.* XXX): as a pagan, however virtuous, Virgil can never be permitted entry into Paradise. Why Virgil? As so often with Dante, there are many reasons, including these and more: (1) the *Inferno* echoes Aeneas' journey into the underworld in *Aeneid* Book VI – Dante's underworld has a number of points in common with Virgil's; (2) Dante hails him as his supreme literary mentor: '*To se' lo mio maestro...*': 'you are my master and my author; you alone are he from whom I took the beautiful style that has won me honour' (*Inf.* I, 85–7); (3) he also regarded Virgil as a political mentor, whose triumphalist vision of Rome's destiny was crucial to his own view of European history; (4) he was well aware of the tradition that Virgil had prophesied the Incarnation in his Fourth Eclogue; (5) in terms of the *Commedia*'s intricate system of figurative meanings, Virgil has often been understood to represent human reason, where Beatrice embodies divine grace. The simplest answer involves a brag: Dante is implicitly placing himself in the same league as '*degli altri poeti onore e lume*', the glory and light of other poets.

W is for Women

As should be clear by now, the two most important female presences in the *Commedia* are Beatrice and the Virgin Mary – '*Vergine Madre, figlia del tuo figlio,/umile ed alta più che creatura,/termine fisso d'eterno consiglio*': 'Virgin Mother, daughter of thy son, lowly and uplifted more than any creature, fixed goal of the eternal counsel...' (*Par.* XXXIII, 1–3). Though much of the poem's supporting cast list is masculine, however, it is far from exclusively so, and Dante meets up with quite a few Bad Girls in Hell – besides Francesca da Rimini, he also bumps into Semiramis (*Inf.* V) and Myrrha (*Inf.* XXX), both of whom are guilty of incest. Feminist critics have had a lot of fun with that juxtaposition.

X is for Xerxes

Or, as some editions spell the name, *Serse* or *Xerse:* son of Darius, King of Persia (485–465 BC). He is mentioned in *Par.* VIII, 124–5, and in *Purg.* XXVIII, 71, apparently as a type of humbled warrior-hood, when Dante alludes to his crossing of the notoriously invincible Hellespont: '*ma Ellesponto, dove passò Xerse/ancora freno a tutti orgogli umani*' (but the Hellespont, where Xerxes crossed, to this day a curb to all human pride…). When he invaded Greece by constructing a bridge of boats, Xerxes was accompanied by more than a million soldiers; on his return, in a fishing boat, he had just a handful of men with him.

Y is for Ytalia

Dante's term both for the Ancient Romans (*De Monarchia* II, x, 7) and for the modern Italians, especially in *De Vulgari Eloquentia*. Italy did not exist as a political unit in Dante's day. His place in forging the modern nation, and its language – '*del bel paese là dove il "sì" suona*' (of the beautiful land where '*sì*' is heard; *Inf.* XXXIII, 80) – is hard to assess, but not to be slighted.

Z is for Zodiac

'*Tu vederesti in Zodiaco rubecchio…*' (You would see the glowing Zodiac revolve yet closer to the Bears…; *Purg.* IV, 64–5). Astrology was one of the seven pillars of medieval wisdom (see Q is for Quadrivium), and Dante was profoundly learned in the subject. Astrological lore permeates the *Commedia*, above all in the astral ascent of the *Paradiso*. In the Circle of Venus (*Par.* VIII–IX), for example, Dante meets his friend Carlo Martello, who explains how it can be that degenerate children may be born of noble parents: God, through the celestial influence of the planets, has arranged for the possibility of variety in human characters; otherwise, each child would be a mere copy of its father. Something of the importance of astrology to Dante's work may be inferred from the well-known fact that each of its three books ends with the word *stelle*, 'stars'. Its very last line – which can be overwhelmingly moving when read in context – evokes *'l'amor che move il sole e l'altre stelle'*, the Love that moves the sun and the other stars.

AN
ELLINGTON
ALPHABET

A is for Armstrong, or Ellington?

No introduction to the life and music of Duke Ellington (1899–1974) could justly pass without paying homage to the one man who, above all, made his career possible. Indeed, there are some purists who would want to argue that Louis Armstrong was a far greater artist than Ellington: not only the all-but-undisputed Founding Father of Jazz, but one of its outstanding instrumentalists (and not even his most ardent supporters claim that Ellington was a true virtuoso of his chosen instrument, the piano) as well as one of its most astonishing and resourceful vocalists (and Ellington was not a singer, barely recording so much as a few minutes of his own voice raised in song). Armstrong overcame more obstacles, reached across wider barriers, created more joy, inspired more love. It is a forceful argument.

There is an equally strong argument, though, which would point out that it was Ellington who had the greater world-historical presence and recognition; Ellington who – like Goethe, or (that noted Duke fan) Stravinsky – repeatedly and tirelessly re-invented himself, thus pushing back the boundaries of his art time after time; Ellington who was a prodigy of creative energy, with well over three thousand compositions to his credit; Ellington who took over a still-novel art form and made it do previously unimaginable things. As a French critic neatly put it: Armstrong created Jazz; Ellington created Form in jazz. As many others have said: Ellington is Beyond Category – not, that is, too large for his chosen art, but a man who made his chosen art large enough to accomodate his varied genius.

Born into a self-consciously proud and respectable middle-class family in Washington DC, on 29 April 1899, Ellington lived in his nation's capital for the next twenty-four years – a marked contrast to the extreme nomadism of his later life, spent largely on trains (no penance: he loved trains, and wrote many of his compositions between station stops) and in hotels. He married young, in 1918, and his son Mercer was born in 1919; he toyed with idea of a career as a graphic designer, and won a scholarship to pursue studies in that area, but abandoned that ambition in favour of a career in music. On the face of it, this was a risky choice, since, unlike many musicians, Ellington had showed few signs of precocity, and even when he first went to New York in 1923 he lacked obvious distinction either as a performer or a composer. The next three years changed that. By 1926, his band – the Washingtonians – had begun to produce music of an originality, wit, mordancy and drive that the world had never heard before. In the three or four following years, Ellington became a real composer, and became famous. He was well on the road to being – as many have asserted – the most important American musician of the twentieth century.

The novelist Ralph Ellison called him the 'most outstanding creator' in America's 'most important indigenous art form'.

B is for *Black, Brown and Beige*

The first Ellington composition on a major scale, *Black, Brown and Beige* had its premiere on 23 January 1943 – a date intended by the Duke to commemorate his twenty years as a professional band leader, which began when he arrived in New York in 1923. He had been preparing for the piece for at least ten years, and not just in musical terms. On his return from his triumphant English tour of 1933, Ellington had begun to collect a personal library of books and articles on Africa, slavery, the Civil War and related subjects. (By the time of his death, this section of his library ran to over 800 volumes.) His intention was to create a musical work which would reflect the African-American experience from capture to slavery to the present day, and his medium of choice was an opera in five parts, to be entitled *Boola*. This work was never completed, but from the early months of 1942 onwards, Ellington set himself to composing, in fits and starts, a different kind of work on exactly the same theme. According to some acounts, he was still composing parts of the final section on the day of the concert. Apart from Gershwin's *Rhapsody in Blue* and Ferde Grofé's *Grand Canyon Suite* – themselves ambiguous cases – there had had never been a jazz piece conceived and executed on such a grand scale. Briefly, the three sections of Ellington's piece addressed (1) slavery, reflected in musical themes derived from work-songs and spirituals; (2) the black presence in the American revolution and the Civil War, enacted with quotations from 'Yankee Doodle' and 'Swanee River'; (3) the coming to the cities, inflected with blues themes. *Black, Brown and Beige* was greeted with almost unanimous hostility, condescension and disdain, even by writers who had championed Ellington's earlier work. It was not, they chorused, 'real jazz'. (Musical historians note that Scott Joplin's *Treemonisha* was met with similar purist objections, and charged with not being true ragtime.) This unexpected slap in the face made Ellington grow quiet and withdrawn, and discouraged him from working in longer forms for many years. Much of the criticism was unfair: as one of Ellington's biographers put it, the piece is 'awash with gorgeous music', and parts of it – including the spiritual 'Come Sunday' – are piercingly fine.

B is also for Johann Sebastian Bach, to whom Ellington was sometimes compared by his 'long-haired' admirers. According to some accounts, it was the seldom less than eccentric Australian composer Percy Grainger (1882–1961) who helped get the ball rolling by declaring, in 1932, that the three greatest composers in the history of music were Bach, Delius and Ellington. Another version is more modest: on hearing 'Creole Rhapsody', Grainger made the casual observation that the Duke was comparable to Bach and Delius in terms of melodic inventiveness. Whatever the truth of the yarn, Grainger's idea became an *idée reçue*, so that when the *New Yorker* published a three-part profile by Richard O. Boyer in the summer of 1944, it seemed natural that it should be titled 'The Hot Bach'. Boyer's piece, one might add, is a model, even a classic of its kind, and the most evocative account of what life on the road was like for the Ellington Band in the strange days when as Boyer points out, they were hailed as transcendental geniuses in Europe but still had to shout 'Yes, suh!' in Texas and other parts of the States.

Ellington used to enjoy citing the wisdom of Bach; well, his private version, anyway: 'As Bach says, if you ain't got a left hand, you ain't worth a hoot in hell!'

After Percy Grainger, the deluge:

C is for Classical Music

From the early 1930s onwards, it became almost routine for the Duke's intellectual fans to compare him with various classical composers: after Grainger with Bach and Delius came Constant Lambert with Liszt, Ravel and Stravinsky (see L and S, below), and others with Rimsky-Korsakov and Richard Strauss. Some of the greatest and/or most celebrated of modern composers and conductors paid tribute to Ellington at one time or another: Stravinsky, Milhaud, Beecham, Bernstein, Toscanini, and Stokowski. Ellington loved this kind of flattering attention, though he often received it with diffidence or sceptical wit. Often, but not always. One of the less well reported encounters between the Duke and the classical music establishment came during his visit to the Soviet Union in 1971. After a successful session with the Radio Moscow Jazz Orchestra, which was directed by Maxim Shostakovich, Ellington was asked by Maxim if he would be willing to pay a visit to his invalid father Dmitri, who was in hospital but anxious to meet Ellington if possible. 'I'd be honoured,' said the Duke, and the visit was paid. We do not know what was said, but Ellington was greatly moved by the encounter.

C is also for the Cotton Club; see the Harlem Renaissance Alphabet.

And for the Surrealist poet **Blaise Cendrars**, who said, on hearing Ellington play in Paris, 'Such music is not only a new art form, but a new reason for living.'

D is for 'Duke'

The nickname was coined when he was just twelve, in response to a precocious elegance which, later in life, blossomed into full-blown dandyism. (In public, anyway. In private, the Duke enjoyed lounging in old clothes as much as the next man.) In the early 1940s, he was said to own forty-seven suits and well over a thousand ties; his hats, shirts and shoes were all custom-made – one of the reasons he liked coming to London was his penchant for Turnbull and Asser – and he favoured a blend of toilet water blended to his own requirements, named 'Warm Valley' after one of his compositions. Other notable nicknames in the Ellington circle: Rabbit (Johnny

Hodges), Nasty (Sonny Greer), Fatstuff (Rex Stewart), Tricky Sam (Joe Nanton) and Professor Boozay (Otto Hardwicke).

D is also for Frederic Delius – the classical composer to whom Ellington was most often compared, partly because of similiarities in the way the two men used chord progressions. It seems likely that Ellington did not hear Delius until his trip to England in 1933, when the jazz critic Spike Hughes brought his American hero a thick pile of Delius records, to which the two men sat up all night listening while talking and drinking. Ellington was particularly taken with 'On Hearing the First Cuckoo in Spring'…

And for another Delius devotee, the American classical music critic **R.D. Darrell**, who at twenty-eight became the author of the earliest important critical assessment of Ellington, the essay 'Black Beauty'.

E is for 'East St. Louis Toodle-Oo'

Recorded in November 1926, this miniature gem – at once jaunty and melancholic, lyrical and coarse – became the Ellington band's radio signature tune. The title, Ellington explained to an interviewer, was a printer's error. It was originally called the 'Todalo', meaning a broken walk. Like many of his compositions, it was meant to summon up a mental picture – in this case, an old man heading home, exhausted after his day's labours in the fields, but still strong enough to be able to walk determinedly towards the hot dinner waiting for him.

As Ralph Ellison recalled in 1969: 'During the Depression whenever his theme song "East St. Louis Toodle-Oo" came on the air, our morale was lifted by something inescapably hopeful in the sound. Its style was so triumphant and the moody melody so successful in capturing the times yet so expressive of the faith which would see us through them…'

E is also for England, which the Ellington band first visited in the summer of 1933 – mainly for professional reasons, of course, but also partly by way of therapy for a mood of gloom into which Ellington had recently fallen. The incentive to cross the ocean had to be very strong, since the Duke was petrified of sailing, a genuine phobia which he attributed to having read a harrowing account of the *Titanic* at a tender age. (When he heard that the ship was piloted automatically at night – which meant that no one was looking out for icebergs – he would stay up until daybreak, drinking brandy to control his nerves.) Fortunately, the trip was wildly successful: the musicians were lionised, the concerts were packed with eager and – still better – knowledgeable fans, the doors of high society were thrown open so wide that the Duke ended up hob-nobbing with real dukes, not to mention a prince. For many of the orchestra, it was an unprecedented experience – suddenly, they were being treated by large numbers of friendly but polite white people as artists and gentlemen. (And Paris, their next destination, was even more racially open.) Most important of all, Ellington suddenly found himself surrounded by a crowd of artists and intellectuals who treated him with grave respect. It was a turning point. As Billy Strayhorn said, when the English press mentioned him in the same sentences as Ravel and Stravinsky, he took it earnestly, and from that point on thought of himself as a serious composer. Even so, the Duke could be level-headed enough when it came to English praise. 'Don't those London fellows push a mean pen?' was Ellington's response when read one critic's account of how his work recalled 'the opalescent subtleties of Debussy'.

is for Film Music

The Ellington band's involvement with film began almost as soon as the era of talkies was born. It was Dudley Murphy, a sometime expatriate in the Parisian avant-garde community of the 1920s, who introduced them to film. With the help of Carl Van Vechten, Murphy (now under contract to RKO) had the idea of making a series of short musical films featuring Harlem's finest. The second of these, *Black and Tan*, was shot in 1929, and features Ellington in the not too challenging role of a young band leader – the most substantial dramatic part he was ever to play. Its plot was a somewhat ramshackle affair, involving a tragic young woman, the Duke's love interest, who literally dances herself to death, but the film was unusually accomplished at the level of its visuals, and was a rare example of a drama which integrated jazz into its plot. Numbers featured in the film included 'Black and Tan Fantasy',

'The Duke Steps Out', 'Cotton Club Stomp' and 'Flaming Youth'.

The Ellington band went on to appear in, among other productions, *Murder at the Vanities* (1934) and *Belle of the Nineties* (also 1934), before moving on to make a short of their own, *Symphony in Black* (1935) – which also featured a young Billie Holiday. They performed as the Paradise nightclub's house band in the all-black musical *Cabin in the Sky* (1943), and contributed a version of 'Take the A-Train' to *Reveille with Beverly* (1945). It was not until Otto Preminger's *Anatomy of a Murder*, however, that Ellington finally composed a full-length movie score; the result won three Grammies and was nominated for an Academy Award. (Ellington also had a bit part in the film, playing four-hand with Jimmy Stewart.) No other jazz composer had ever written a full film score and had it performed by his own orchestra; some critics have ranked it among the Duke's outstanding accomplishments. Unsurprisingly, he went on to compose other scores, including those for the Paul Newman/Sidney Poitier vehicle *Paris Blues*, and for the mediocre hijack thriller *Assault on a Queen*, the Queen in question being the *Queen Mary*.

F is also for Food. Ellington was an Olympic-standard trencherman, even when – as often – he was officially watching his weight. One of his most legendary stunts was eating thirty-two giant melted-cheese hot dogs in a single brief session. Seeing the inevitable effect on his waistline, he would intermittently announce his intention of going on a strict diet. The comedy of self-deception involved in these short-lived stabs at asceticism was enjoyed by all. Swearing to eat nothing but Shredded Wheat and black tea, Ellington would solemnly say grace over his lenten spread and munch and sip his way through it with an air of righteous martyrdom. Then, after seeing another band member tearing happily into a rib-eye or t-bone, he would relent a little and order himself just the one steak. And then another, this time slathered in fried onions. And then a double order of french fries, with green salad and tomato salad... and then a giant lobster drenched in molten butter, and then one of his trademark multiple desserts, usually composed of cake and pie and ice-cream and custard and fruit and jelly and maybe just a little cheese. Then, getting into his stride, he would demolish some ham and eggs, some pancakes, waffles with maple syrup and the scone-like American pastries known as 'biscuits'. Then, to reaffirm his credentials as a weight-watcher, he would conclude with more Shredded Wheat and black tea.

He mapped out the United States, and the world, in terms of the restaurants he knew, and their speciality dishes, be it chow mein with pigeon's blood in San Francisco or gumbo file in New Orleans or devilled crabs in Washington DC… or octopus soup in Paris, smorgasbord in Sweden or roast mutton in London. The Duke's metabolism must have been like a furnace, for despite these heroic plyings of fork and spoon, he never appeared truly obese – 'bear-like' was the usual description, where one might easily have expected 'whale-like'.

G is for Sonny Greer

William 'Sonny' Greer (c. 1895?–1982), flamboyant percussionist, singer, and long-term member of the Ellington entourage, from the Washingtonians line-up in 1920 until his somewhat ignominious departure in 1951 – his heavy drinking had become full-blown alcoholism, and he was quietly asked to leave. Ellington was saddened by this end to a working relationship, which had begun in a close friendship and mutual admiration. Greer was a natural-born showman who loved to stage simple but effective tricks like hitting swift rim shots while opening and closing his jacket in time.

H is for Harlem

Not merely a launch pad for Ellington's career, but a spiritual home and the inspiration for many pieces: 'Harlem Twist', 'Harlem Airshaft', 'Harlem River Quiver' and so on. Arturo Toscanini commissioned a *Harlem Suite* from Ellington for the NBC Orchestra in 1950; the work was premiered in 1951. (See also the Harlem Renaissance Alphabet *passim*.)

And for **Johnny Hodges** (1907–70), alto saxophonist. He joined Ellington in 1928 and, on and off, stayed with him for four decades. A short, slight, taciturn, insouciant figure, almost entirely inexpressive in his stage performances, he produced sounds which were the envy and despair of his fellow musicians.

Benny Goodman, for one, thought that he was simply without peer on his instrument. In 1936 – when Hodges was twenty-nine – a journalist wrote that he 'has an unlimited musical imagination, the manner in which he employs his knowledge of harmonic structure is amazing, his every phrase swings, and his intonation is superb...' In Paris, the conductor of a symphony orchestra, chancing across Hodges in the street, bowed low and asked him in awed tone how he achieved his artistry. 'I just lucked up on it, Bubber, I just lucked up on it,' Hodges replied.

I is for 'It Dont Mean a Thing...

if it ain't got that swing'. The song was inspired by a favourite maxim of one of the Ellington band members, 'Bubber' Miley: 'If it ain't worth singing, it ain't worth swinging, and if it ain't worth swinging, it ain't worth playing.' (**I is also for Ivie Anderson**, who recorded the song's vocal as her debut in February 1932.) The phrase soon entered the English language; Ellington would explain that 'swing' was a Harlem term for 'rhythm'.

And for **Irving Mills**, who signed Ellington to a management and publishing contract in November 1926. He was not, on the whole, regarded fondly.

And for **'Mood Indigo'**, the great standard, said to have been effortlessly written during a few minutes one evening late in 1930. Ellington inverted the standard scorings of clarinet, trumpet and trombone for the piece, with the result that, as the critic Gunther Schuller wrote, '[these] tonal colours had never been heard before in all of music history'.

J is for Jazz

Ellington often said that he disliked the term: 'I don't write jazz. I write Negro folk music.'

J is also for Jump for Joy, Ellington's first musical, which opened in Los Angeles on 10 July 1941. A lavish production, with a cast of sixty actors headed by Dorothy Dandridge (one of the best-known black actresses of the day), Ivie Anderson and Herb Jeffries. Most of the music was written by

Ellington, in collaboration with his son Mercer and Billy Strayhorn; a diverse crew of talents, from Langston Hughes to Mickey Rooney, helped out with lyrics and ideas. Fizzing with wit and dry insolence, the show was widely seen as a milestone in American theatre, being the first all-black musical to avoid cheap and silly racial stereotyping. One typical sketch showed the king and queen of an ancient African tribe relaxing with brandies, His Majesty in a tuxedo, Her Majesty in a Parisian gown. The telephone rings: an expedition is on its way from America, in search of the sources of jazz. Wearily, the regal couple conclude that they are going to have to pull out their leopard-skins again… The show ran to enthusiastic houses for 101 performances, but generated only modest profits, and gave birth to only one standard: 'I Got It Bad (and that ain't good)'.

 ## is for 'Ko-Ko'

A short, mysterious, compelling piece, which has been compared by one over-heated critic to Goya's macabre pictures of witches' Sabbaths and Satanic monstrosities. Ellington once said that the cryptic title alluded to Congo Square in New Orleans, 'where jazz was born'. (It was not.) 'Ko-Ko' was composed as part of the uncompleted *Boola*, and thus forms part of the deep background to *Black, Brown and Beige*. Written and recorded in 1940, it has the basic underlying form of a twelve-bar blues in E flat minor, but that simple base is the foundation for an immensely complex superstructure, including dissonances so bold as to risk cacophony. Some think it the greatest three minutes Ellington ever recorded, and Gunther Schuller declared it unequalled by anything in modern music save, perhaps, Stravinsky's 'Symphony of Psalms'; which is why a far less spirited version, recorded in 1956, was greeted with shock and dismay. The French writer André Hodeir saw it as evidence of terrible fatigue and decline; others concluded that the older Ellington lacked any real sense of his own classics.

And for **Martin Luther King**. The Duke was a long-time admirer of the Reverend King, but they did not meet until 1963, and then only by chance. King was sitting in his car on a street in Chicago when he saw Duke walking past; he jumped out, and the two embraced as if they were old friends. It was happy timing, since Ellington had just dedicated his musical pageant *My People*, staged as part of Chicago's 'Century of Negro Progress' exhibition, to Dr King.

L is for Constant Lambert

The English composer, critic and musical director of the Sadler's Wells Ballet, who was among the early highbrow champions of the Duke's music, albeit in terms which now seem more than a trifle patronising. In *Music Ho!*, Lambert wrote that 'Ellington… is a real composer, the first jazz composer of distinction, and the first Negro composer of distinction.' He went on: '…I know of nothing in Ravel so dextrous in treatment as the varied solos in the middle of the ebullient *Hot and Bothered* and nothing in Stravinsky more dynamic than the final section.' Ellington, who generously recalled Lambert and other English intellectuals as 'nice fellows', was pleased by praise of this order: 'Hot damn! I guess that makes me pretty good, doesn't it?' It is not known how he reacted to the much cooler water of Lambert's final verdict: '[Ellington] is definitely a petit maître, but that, after all, is considerably more than many people thought either jazz or the coloured race would ever produce…'

L is also for the *Liberian Suite*, commisioned by its government for Liberia's centenary in 1947.

M is for *Music is my Mistress*

Ellington's famously guarded autobiography, produced in collaboration with his friend Stanley Dance, which has not a bad word to say for anyone.

And for **his Mother**, Daisy. The Duke's bond with his mother was of such singular intensity as to have the least Freudian of biographers reaching for the term 'Oedipal'.

N is for the Newport Jazz Festival

The most sluggish period in Ellington's career lasted almost an entire decade, from 1947 to 1956. Big bands were going out of style, ballrooms were closing and television was becoming the dominant form of American entertainment. Even inside the jazz world, the perpetually self-renewing Ellington was starting to seem like old hat, as the bebop generation of Miles Davis, Charlie Parker, Thelonious Monk and others began to replace the swing bands. Ellington kept on composing, but many felt that the excitment was gone, and there was more than one article suggesting that the band should call it a day before they soured the memory of past glories. All of that was turned around in one evening, 7 July 1956. It was almost midnight when the band took the stage, and their first few pieces were treated with respect but little more. Then, with 'Diminuendo and Crescendo in Blue', Ellington called Paul Gonsalves forward for a saxophone interlude. He was electrifying. Gradually, then more rapidly, the crowd began to realise that they were witnessing something out of the ordinary. Within minutes, the entire crowd was on its feet and everyone was dancing wildly. They had to play four encores. Ellington later said: 'I was born in 1956 at the Newport Jazz Festival.'

N is also for Joseph 'Tricky Sam' Nanton (1904–46), who played trombone with Ellington from 1926 until his early death. Among his signature effects was the ability to produce quasi-vocal effects from his instrument.

O is for the Ellington Orchestra

'Duke plays the piano, but his instrument is the orchestra': Billy Strayhorn. Exactly. At the time of their Cotton Club residency in the late 1920s, Ellington was the only band-leader to be the composer, arranger and director of an orchestra he had created for and by himself. The combination of economic freedom (thirty-eight months of straight employment, a wonderful liberation from money problems) and artistic discipline (maintain the output of new work to keep the customers dancing and the musicians interested) was invaluable. That residency, it is said, turned Ellington from a songwriter into a composer.

P is for *Porgy and Bess*

… which Ellington – a rare crack in his otherwise almost flawlessly diplomatic and emollient persona – criticised harshly for, among other things, its lack of fidelity to Negro life. Or did he? The remarks appeared in an interview by Ed Murrow for the left-wing *New Theater* (December 1935), and Ellington is said to be have been upset at being reported inaccurately.

And for **the Pulitzer Prize commitee**, whose advisory board turned down a suggestion that Ellington be given a special composition award. (He was sixty-six. It is hard to avoid the conclusion that snobbery, or worse, was behind the insult.) His typically suave reply: 'Fate is being kind to me. Fate doesn't want me to be famous too young.' But he was hiding his disappointment and anger. In the blundering way of committees, the Pulitzer people later tried to make recompense for its gaffe by devising a special award for the Duke. The year: 1999. Ellington had been dead for twenty-five years. One is reminded of Johnson's letter to Lord Chesterfield, on the value of patrons.

Q is for *The Queen's Suite*

Composed for an actual queen, Her Majesty Elizabeth II, in the days after a (for the Duke, at least) thrillingly chummy encounter at the Leeds Festival in 1958. Ellington had hobnobbed with the British royal family on previous visits to Britain, and was able to tell the young monarch stories about playing four-hand piano with the Duke of Kent, and attending parties with her uncle Prince Edward, who once sat in with the Ellington band on drums. The Duke promised the Queen that he would write her a special piece, as he had already done for Princess Margaret; in response, she invited him and Billy Strayhorn to Buckingham Palace that weekend, where the two Americans played piano solos for their hosts. *The Queen's Suite* was recorded in February 1959, but only one copy was pressed, for presentation to Her Majesty, and the work did not become available to the public until well after its composer's death in 1974. Ellington was rather touchingly star-struck by encounters with the great and the good, and one of his musicians noted that he devoted far more care to *The Queen's Suite* than was usual for him. He also continued to wear the same pair of shoes he had worn when presented to the Queen until they began to fall to pieces.

Q is also for his comic opera *Queenie Pie*, commissioned by a TV station and all but complete at the time of his death, though not staged until some twelve years later, in 1986.

R is for Race

As these things go, Ellington passed almost his entire life without feeling the full sting of racial hatred. The friend of kings and queens, the darling of white intellectuals, the idol of millions in many countries, Ellington was handsomely paid, ceaselessly praised and, for most of his adult life, could go where he wanted and do as he pleased.

The same may not be said of his band. As late as the Second World War (and beyond) Ellington's key musicians had to endure humiliations that today seem so extreme as to border on the surreal. Where Ellington could almost always register in the most expensive hotels, his entourage would have to head straight for the black neighbourhoods... and usually by foot, as taxi drivers would not take them. Nor could they usually eat in restaurants; they would resort to sending a local white man out to buy sandwiches – and if the storekeeper found out that they were to be eaten by black musicians, he would often refuse to sell them even to the white stooge. It was not Ellington's way to protest about such idiocies. His exceptionally calm demeanour, always a source of amusement and comment, could in this regard border on the saintly. When a redneck policeman told him – genuinely meaning a compliment! – that he could have been a great musician if only he had been born white, the Duke simply murmured, urbanely, that a great deal of his life would have been different had he been born white.

R is also for President Roosevelt. When FDR died on 12 April 1945, the airwaves of the United States were filled with sombre classical music. With one exception: the Ellington band played a programme of blues, spirituals and their own numbers, including 'Mood Indigo', 'Come Sunday', 'Creole Love Call' and 'Moon Mist'. *Variety* raved, saying that no other dance band could possibly have filled the spot without causing scandal, and that it was a vastly more moving tribute than any of the symphonic works broadcast that day. There are many anecdotes to corroborate the *Variety* line: even one rival musican was heard to murmur, as the final chords of 'Moon Mist' faded to radio hiss, 'Nobody but Duke could have pulled that off.'

S is for Strayhorn

Not precisely an unsung genius, for the *cognoscenti* have always recognised his contribution, but still, perhaps, an under-sung genius, Billy 'Swee' Pea' Strayhorn (1915–67) first met Ellington in 1938, and joined him full-time as a composer and arranger in 1939. (His nickname came from the baby in the *Popeye* cartoons; and he does indeed look very young in the group portraits.) Quincy Jones, no less an authority, once said that Strayhorn was 'the boss of the arrangers', the unequalled head of his field. In addition to the gift of his invaluable formal skills, he enriched the Duke's life by becoming one of his few real intimates. On Strayhorn's death – 31 May 1967 – Ellington, deeply affected, wrote a short but eloquent piece entitled 'Eulogy for Swee' Pea' for *Down Beat* magazine, in which he sketched out the 'four freedoms' Strayhorn had enjoyed. A few years later, when President Nixon awarded Ellington ('the greatest Duke of them all') the Presidential Medal of Freedom on the occasion of his seventieth birthday, Ellington gave a swift verbal summary of the Strayhorn credo:

> ...I use those four moral freedoms by which Strayhorn lived as a measure of what we ourselves should live up to. Freedom from Hate. Unconditionally. Freedom from self-pity. Freedom from the fear of possibly doing something that would benefit someone else. And freedom from the fear of being better than one's brother.

In the autumn of 1967, the Ellington Orchestra recorded an album entitled *And His Mother Called Him Bill*, consisting entirely of Strayhorn pieces. At the end of the final session, Ellington played a piano solo of 'Lotus Blossom'; intensely moving.

S is also for the three Sacred Concerts, which dominated so much of Ellington's creative energy in his last years; and for **Shakespeare**, whose characters inspired the sequence of witty musical vignettes known as *Such Sweet Thunder*; and for that eminent Ellingtonian Igor **Stravinsky**, whose admiration for the American composer is well known. Less well known is Ellington's more measured liking for Stravinsky's work: 'he has a terrific conception and he sure knows how to handle his material, but I really can't feel his music with my heart. I'm wild about some of it though. What's that bird… "Firebird", that's it. Great stuff!' Elsewhere, he remarked that he had detected the presence of 'hot jazz in Stravinsky and other long-haired composers'.

A final Ellingtonism on some of the more extravagant prose inspired in classically trained intellectuals by his music: 'I don't know. May be something to it. But it seems to me such talk stinks up the place.'

T is for Television

On 8 May 1957, CBS television broadcast the first-ever jazz 'spectacular', Ellington's *A Drum is a Woman*, which sketched the history of jazz from Africa to New York and, fancifully, the Moon. It had its origins in an abandoned collaboration with Orson Welles (see W, below); Ellington was very proud of it, and considered it one of his finest hours.

T is also for Tempo music, Ellington's publishing firm, founded in 1941; and for **'Take the A-Train'**, Billy Strayhorn's most deathless hit, the first piece Tempo published. It became the Ellington band's radio signature theme in the same year, and remained so for the rest of his life.

U is for Barry Ulanov

The music critic (born 1918) and sometime editor of *Metronome* magazine, who was the earliest of the would-be collaborators on an Ellington biography; the Duke withdrew his support after a few chapters, saying that his story was far from finished and shouldn't be written down. Ulanov proceeded solo; his pioneering biography was published in 1946 and republished in 1972.

V is for Victor Records

At the time Ellington signed to Victor in 1927 with his (then) ten-piece band, it was the leading record label in the world, with the best technicians and the most advanced recording equipment. Its other stars included Leopold Stokowski, director of the Philadelphia Orchestra. (There is an amusing story of Stokowski's dropping by the Cotton Club to see Ellington perform. When asked by a customer who this striking figure might be, a waiter replied 'That's the white man's Duke Ellington'.) One of the things that must be remembered in favour of Irving Mills is that he demanded that Ellington's music be treated with the same deference and professionalism as Stokowski's. Thanks to this insistence, the Victor recordings for the eight years Ellington remained under contract are vastly superior to those he cut for competing labels from time to time.

W is for Ben Webster

Or 'Rooster Ben', the tenor saxophonist (1909–73) from Kansas City. Webster spent relatively little time with the Ellington Orchestra: a few early stints in the mid-1930s, followed by two full-time engagements from 1940–3 and 1948–9. Despite this fairly brief tenure, Webster's formidable, charismatic presence looms as large as that of, say, Johnny Hodges in the band's history, and his genius for improvisation was hugely influential both within Ellington's outfit and beyond. Webster's playing inspired some outstanding pieces of jazz criticism, including a minutely detailed and richly evocative analysis by Stanley Crouch first published in 1986. (Sample: 'Sculpting his emblematic passion through ballads and blues or serving as heavy artillery on stomping, swinging numbers, Webster's roar of triumph, terror and rage celebrated existence, revealed the shocks of life, and declaimed a bubbling disgust for all limitations…')

And for **Orson Welles**, an enthusiastic fan of Ellington's work. The two men first met when Welles, fresh from his director's chair on *Citzen Kane*, watched an early performance of *Jump for Joy*, found it wanting, and fired off a long impromptu list of all the stage directions that would be needed to bring it up to speed. Ellington later said that this was the single most impressive display of mental power he had ever witnessed. A few weeks later, Welles persuaded his studio bosses at RKO to commission a score from Ellington which would be used in his next film, *Saga of Jazz*. Like so many other Welles projects, the film never materialised, but Ellington still pocketed $12,500 for his work, and some fifteen years later recycled some of the *Saga of Jazz* material into *A Drum is a Woman*.

is for Malcolm X

In the *Autobiography* (1964), Malcolm X (*né* Little) reminisces about his salad days as a shoe-shine boy at the Roseland State Ballroom in Boston, and the proud relish with which he would shine for the likes of Ellington, Cootie Williams and other members of the Orchestra when, at about 8 o'clock, they would come up to the men's room just before going on stage. Johnny Hodges, he recalls, was once so caught up in a heated argument with Sonny Greer that he forgot to pay for his shine: 'I wouldn't have dared to bother the man who could do what he did with 'Daydream' by asking him for fifteen cents…' Later, the young Malcolm became quite friendly with several Ellington musicians – Greer, Cootie Williams and Ray Nance.

is for 'Yellow Dog Blues'

Written by 'the Father of the Blues' W.C. Handy, and recorded in 1928 during the sessions which introduced Johnny Hodges to the record-buying public. Hodges took a soprano sax solo, audibly influenced by his mentor Sidney Bechet, which meshed pefectly with the growling of Nanton and 'Bubber' Miley. There are purists who say that no Ellington band was ever greater than the line-up which produced this recording, and that 'Yellow Dog Blues' stands beside 'East St. Louis Toodle-Oo' and the various versions of 'Black and Tan Fantasy'.

Z is for 'Zweet Zurzday'

The third of the four parts which make up *Suite Thursday*, inspired by John Steinbeck's novel *Sweet Thursday* (1954) and first performed at the 1960 Monterey Jazz Festival – Monteray being, of course, Steinbeck country. The brilliant Stanley Crouch, among others, considers it a perfect example of the variety and power of which the Ellington–Strayhorn team had become capable: noting how it all grew from permutations of a minor sixth interval, Crouch proposed it as a clear indication of Ellington's extreme musical sophistication. Let the last words of this alphabet belong to Mr Crouch, summarising Ellington's career as a performer:

Those many nights and matinees provided Ellington with inspiration, and made his orchestra so accurate at wedding human meaning and musical technique that its powers of expression came to seem infinite.

A
FREUD
ALPHABET

A is for the Analysis of Art and Artists

Two quotations:

To interpret the unconscious as Freud did, one would have to be, as he was, an encyclopaedia of the arts and muses…
(Jacques Lacan, 'The Instance of the Letter in the Unconscious', 1957)

Before the problem of the creative artist analysis must, alas, lay down its arms.
(Sigmund Freud, 'Dostoevsky and Parricide', 1927–8)

Freud was a revolutionary thinker – even more revolutionary than we generally admit, said Lacan – but he was also a conservative in many aspects of his life, including his tastes in literature and art. For pleasure and inspiration, he read Goethe, Shakespeare and Milton, and could not stand any kind of avant-gardism, least of all the wild productions of his noisy fan club, the Surrealists. When he spoke of psychoanalysis 'laying down its arms' before Dostoevsky and other artists, Freud meant that that he could only account for the *content* of art, its subjects and themes and symbols, or for the neuroses of particular artists, and not for their formal, aesthetic dimensions – the qualities which earned them enduring recognition as 'great'. Like many people with a powerful aesthetic sense, one suspects, the great solver of the Sphinx's riddle actually preferred to leave some mysteries mysterious. Even so, Freud's humble concession did not prevent him from writing copiously on the likes of Leonardo da Vinci, Michelangelo's 'Moses', Jensen's *Gradiva*, Shakespeare's *Richard III*, Ibsen and many other artists and works.

Like other wings of the vast, rambling, utterly splendid Victorian mansion which is his written *oeuvre*, these once-admired essays have, in recent decades, become the objects of criticism, refutation, derision and abuse. Still, if the letter of Freud's teachings has come under heavy fire from both scientists and human-ists, no one could reasonably dispute the pervasive influence of his work in the realm of culture throughout the century or so since *The Interpretation of Dreams* (1900; year of Nietzsche's death) was first published. Whether in pure, vulgarised, scholastically hyper-elaborated or grossly caricatured forms – from

Derridean deconstruction to shrink jokes, from subtle, psychoanalytically informed biographies to the most debased verbal currency of 'repression', 'neurosis' and the like among the lumpen-intelligentsia – the long shadow cast by his genius has been all but ubiquitous in the educated West.

One consequence of this unpredictable triumph is that – though the development would surely have dismayed him – it has long been acceptable in literate circles to speak of Freud not as a (reputedly discredited) figure in the history of scientific psychology, but as a major artist in his right: not simply, as is widely admitted, a fine craftsman of the German language, but a kind of novelist or short-story writer in his case histories, a dramatist in his view of the forces contending within and between psyches, a poet in his epic conception of the developmental history of individuals and cultures. In short, Freud can fairly be regarded as an imaginative writer, the value of whose work can no more be obliterated by ignorant cracks about his cocaine abuse or anxious allegations about his fudging of clinical evidence than could the writings of, say, Milton or Goethe by comparable slurs.

This is why Freudian terms continued to echo – often to silly or even ludicrous ends – in departments of literature and Cultural Studies long after they started to be phased out from psychology courses; and it is also why the following twenty-five entries have taken as their major bias the various ways in which Freud's work has told in the sphere of the arts. For example, in the case of the letter B, we will first turn not to such obvious contenders as his early collaborator Bruer, nor the extraordinary Bruno Bettelheim (author, among other works, of *The Uses of Enchantment*) nor Wilfred Bion (the fascinating British analyst who once treated Samuel Beckett) nor Bowlby nor Binswanger, nor even André Breton (who can wait for the Alphabet of Surrealism) – but to the rather less self-evident, perhaps quixotic choice:

B is for Burgess

Anthony Burgess (1917–93), like other writers of his generation, admired Freud deeply: as a heroic liberator, as a thrillingly original student of literature, as the eminent scientist who had corroborated or vindicated the insights of the poetic imagination, and as a fascinating enquirer into the basic substance of literature itself: language. Burgess, who took James Joyce as his mentor in the radically ambitious yet playful re-invention of literary forms, noted with relish the trans-linguistic pun which made Freud and Joyce symbolic cousins, *Freude* being the German for 'joy'. (In *Finnegans Wake*, Joyce had made a slightly more edgy pun about children who were 'jung and easily freudened'.) Burgess died too soon to complete the Wagnerian opera he had in mind about the career of Freud, but the master is respectfully evoked in his triple-layered novel *The End of the World News*, which concentrates on Freud's visit to the United States in 1909. According to one legend, Freud turned to Jung as they sailed past the Statue of Liberty into harbour, and said: 'They don't realise we're bringing the plague.' (Did he think of himself as a rat?)

C is for Clift (and Cinema)

Montgomery Clift was the unconventional choice of John Huston to play the title role in *Freud: The Secret Passion* (1962) – not one of that robust director's most successful products, but not as poorly done as to warrant its present-day neglect. (Jean-Paul Sartre, incidentally, worked on early versions of the screenplay.) Freud's influence both on film-makers and on film criticism and theory has been vast beyond summary; for slightly more, see below, H is for Hitchcock.

D is for Dostoevsky

Freud's fascinating late paper on Dostoevsky (1928) begins by suggesting that the Russian novelist was four souls in one – the creative artist, the neurotic, the moralist and the sinner. Admitting that he has no way of explaining how such a shattered psyche could have issued works of such singular authority and power, Freud goes on to give a compelling account of the psychological crises from which Dostoevsky built his fiction. As usual, Freud insists that this is not done in a spirit of disparagement. He declares uncompromisingly that *The Brothers Karamazov* is 'the most magnificent novel ever written'; and goes on to propose that it was hardly a coincidence that three of the greatest literary masterpieces of all time – *Karamazov*, *Hamlet* and the *Oedipus* plays – should all have parricide at their heart. (Later readers, who have taken in Freud with, so to speak, their mother's milk, might wish to ask whether Freud's attitude to literary giants does not itself exhibit the war between reverence and hate that he regards as central to the Oedipal struggle: whether, that is 'Dostoevsky and Parricide' is not a kind of parricidal attempt on Dostoevsky. The same sceptical souls may also wonder whether the intermittent quiet flippancies in an otherwise reverential exposition in this Freud Alphabet do not bear witness to similar unconscious tangles in the present author. Just a thought.)

Those who have browsed the essay in the past will probably recall its long disgression on Dostoevsky's compulsive gambling (which Freud links, as usual, with masturbation), and its suggestion that Dostoevsky's epilepsy had a neurotic rather than a physical origin. They may not recall the bleak yet sublime manner in which Freud, freely admitting all of Dostoevsky's gifts, goes on to pass sombre verdict: 'Dostoevsky threw away the chance of becoming a teacher and liberator of mankind and made himself one with their gaolers.'

D is also, and alas, for Salvador Dali: see F is for Freud in the Alphabet of Surrealism; and for **'Dora'**, one of his most controversial case histories, the basis for a rather tedious avant-garde film in the late 1970s.

E is for Empson

Probably the greatest English literary critic of the twentieth century, as well as a richly gifted poet and philosopher, Sir William Empson was among the earliest British intellectuals to absorb and apply the lessons of psychoanalysis as they applied to culture; and to apply them with a shrewdness and quicksilver subtlety that makes most 'Freudian' criticism seem club-footed. The most widely read of his overtly Freudian scrutinies is the rich and strange discussion of *Alice in Wonderland*, 'The Child as Swain', in the collection *Some Versions of Pastoral*, but all of Empson's work is saturated with psychoanalytic wisdom, including the formal linguistic studies of *The Structure of Complex Words*.

F is for 'Freudian'

In popular chat, and the less refined modes of critical discourse, an adjective routinely yoked either to the noun 'symbol', and meaning 'sexual' (i.e., anything longer than wide, like an umbrella; or concave, like a cup; or reminiscent of a piston and cylinder in motion) or to the noun 'slip', and meaning, as Cliff the Postman in *Cheers* once explained, those moments when you say one thing and mean a mother. (Cliff, it should be explained to those who did not follow that agreeable show, was something of a mummy's boy.)

F is also for Peter Fuller, the prolific English art critic whose bumpy intellectual trajectory from Marx to Ruskin encompassed a lengthy spell as a Freudian, and who left a harrowingly frank account of his own spell on the analytic couch in *Marches Past*.

G is for Goethe

On 28 August 1930, Freud was awarded the Goethe Prize of 10,000 Deutschmarks. His graceful acceptance speech, delivered by Anna Freud since Freud was in poor health, expressed the hopeful view that Goethe 'would not have rejected psychoanalysis', and indeed that, like other poets, he had often antipated its findings himself. Freud cites a short verse as evidence that Goethe's view of dream-life and the unconscious was in profound sympathy with his own:

> Was, von Menschen nicht gewusst
> Oder nicht bedacht,

Durch das Labyrinth der Brust
Wandelt in der Nacht.

(Approximately: 'That which, unknown by mankind/or not heeded/through the labyrinth of the heart/wanders in the night.') He also mentions a little-known episode in which Goethe carried out a spectacularly successful Talking Cure of a certain Frau Herder, who was in a state of hypochondriacal distress until the poet made her confess all and then declared her absolved. Freud made the conventional comparison of Goethe with Leonardo da Vinci (see V, below) as two great Universal Men, but declared that Goethe must be seen as the greater of the two because he always respected the power of Eros, while Leonardo had banished everything erotic – including human psychology *in toto* – from his sphere of interests.

If Freud had a single lifelong culture-hero, it was Goethe (though that has been the case with many outstanding German-speakers), and it was hearing Goethe's essay on Nature read out loud while he was still a schoolboy that determined him to study medicine. He gave his full asssent to Goethe's maxim that 'the first and last thing required of genius is a love of truth'. He became uncomfortable, though, when his disciple Ferenczi pointed out a series of similarities between the two men. When Ferenczi persisted in the over-flattering comparision, Freud pointed out a series of dramatic unlikenesses, including their respective attitudes towards 'tobacco, which Goethe simply loathed, whereas for my part it is the only excuse I know for Columbus's misdeed'.

G is also for Jensen's *Gradiva*, the not particularly distinguished novel which provided Freud with the subject of his first extended literary essay, 'Delusions and Dreams in Jensen's *Gradiva*'. Freud's dissection has helped keep awareness of the book alive long after it would otherwise have fallen into the oblivion reserved for most minor books.

H is for Hitchcock

As even the least theoretically inclined film fan will be obliged to admit, Alfred Hitchcock's themes are a treasure trove of 'Freudian' themes and motifs, and had a considerable influence in conveying at least a pop version of psychoanalysis to the masses. Consider just a few of the more notorious cases: James Stewart's voyeurism (or scopophilia) in *Rear Window*, his necrophilia in *Vertigo*, Anthony Perkins's Oedipal anguish in *Psycho*, Tippi Hedren's kleptomania, repressed memory and frigidity in *Marnie*, the institution of psychoanalysis itself in *Spellbound* (which includes dream sequences designed by Salvador Dali and an elementary course in dream analysis as central to the Talking Cure)... the list would fill a book, and probably has. Hitchock himself, as he revealed in the course of his interviews with François Truffaut, was a naughty and highly self-conscious deployer of 'Freudian' images, such as the train entering the tunnel for the final shot of *North by Northwest*.

H is also for *Hysteria*, Terry Johnson's fantasia-farce on Freudian (and Dalinian) motifs.

I is for Ibsen

Freud appears to have considered the Norwegian dramatist a genius comparable to Shakespeare and the Greeks. His longest discussion of Ibsen's work comes in the context of analysing those neurotics who are, as he puts it, 'wrecked by success' – that is, who discover on attaining some long-desired goal that they are not merely incapable of relishing their triumph, but are more miserable than they were in their years of striving. He takes for his case study the character of Rebecca West in *Rosmersholm*; his reading of the play is founded on the premise that Rebecca is far from completely conscious of her own motives, and that Ibsen subtly punctuates his drama with all the clues that a sharp-eyed audience member would need to be able to grasp, or at any rate intuit, those buried motives. Briefly, *Rosmersholm* is the story of a free-thinking young woman who enters a rather sterile, pious household and, conceiving a wild passion for the man of the house, Johannes Rosmer, resolves to get rid of his childless wife Beata. Rebecca's plan is so successful that Beata is driven to suicide; but when, after a respectable passage of time, Johannes asks Rebecca to be his second wife, Rebecca insists that she has to refuse him because of her 'past'. What this 'past' truly means, Freud suggests, is not just any old bohemian indiscretion of her youth but a full-blown Oedipal affair with the man she once thought was only her adopted father, but has subsequently proved to be her true, biological father. Crippled by the (unconscious) repetition of the Oedipal role in the Rosmer household, she is obliged to reject the consummation she once devoutly wished. On Freud's reckoning, this makes *Rosmersholm* the greatest literary treatment of a fantasy encountered again and again among young female patients, who have dreamed of taking the place of the woman of the house, whether she be the mother or the employer.

At which point, it almost goes without saying that **I is also for Incest** (see O is for Oedipus); and for *The Interpretation of Dreams*.

J is for Jokes

Freud's classic work *Jokes and their Relation to the Unconscious* is, notoriously, only fractionally more entertaining than Bergson's utterly glum *Laughter*. But, as fans of Woody Allen and subscribers to the *New Yorker* can attest, psychoanalysis itself has given rise to an immeasurably vast number of jokes and witticisms. Thus:

Q. How many psychoanalysts does it take to change a lightbulb?
A. Only one, but it takes seven years, and the lightbulb really has to want to change.

Or:

Q. What's the difference between a psychotherapist and a psychoanalyst?
A. The analyst has a house in the Hamptons.

J is also for Jung, the Freudian heir-apparent turned major heretic whose breakaway movement of 'Analytical Pyschology' is often found more congenial than psychoanalysis by those who – rightly or not – consider it more generously disposed to creativity, spiritual values and the like. And for **Ernest Jones**, who wrote the first full-scale English biography of Freud – much read, bitterly criticised.

is for Kraus

Karl Kraus, the bitter and brilliant Viennese satirist, editor of a spiky periodical called *Die Fackel*, was a sworn foe of all things Freudian; his most-cited jibe was that psychoanalysis was the sickness of which it believed itself the cure. One of the reasons for his hostility was that he had got wind of a paper by Fritz Wittels, delivered to the Vienna Society in 1910, which offered a clever reading of Kraus's writings in psychoanalytic terms.

K is also for Melanie Klein, among the most influential of British psychoanalysts, some of whose teachings were translated into the realm of aesthetics by the extraordinary art critic Adrian Stokes; and, more recently, for **Julia Kristeva**: semiotician, psychoanalyst, literary theorist and *grande dame*. Her work on melancholy, *Black Sun*, is worth reading.

is for Lecter

Stand-up comedians have derided Thomas Harris's choice of Christian name for his nightmarish shrink; as they point out, it looks very much as if Harris simply plumped for the one plausible (if exotic) name that rhymes neatly with cannibal. But is there perhaps a second layer of meaning or association here? Readers of Ernest Jones's standard biography will be aware of Freud's 'ancient and passionate identification of himself with the semitic Hannibal' – a fantasy which seems to have had its roots in an occasion when his father was humiliated by an anti-Semite, and the young Sigmund dreamed of a Hannibalic revenge. The Hannibal fantasy had some strange issues: for example, though he greatly desired to visit Rome, his earliest attempts to vist the city brought him no nearer than Trasimeno (in 1897) – the very place where Hannibal had stopped two thousand years earlier. It was only after his period of self-analysis that Freud was finally able to enter 'the Mother of all Cities'.

L is also for Jacques Lacan (1901–81), by far the most powerful figure in the history of French psychoanalysis, and in the eyes of (mainly) anglophone non-believers – see, for an extreme case, the raucous attack by Camille Paglia in *Sex, Art and American Culture* – a figure every bit as sinister as Dr Lecter. More sinister, in that he actually existed... and trailed a hefty list of suicides among his former patients. Despite the wilful impenetrability of some of his work, and the occasional dubiousness of his therapeutic methods (he shrank the length of the standard psychoanalytic session down from almost an hour to, in some cases, barely a couple of minutes; Lacan was very fond of money, and the luxuries it will procure), Lacan has – for much of the last three decades and more – been the object of widespread adulation among intellectuals and cod-intellectuals alike, and the Lacanian influence permeates the fields of Film Studies, Cultural Studies, Gender Studies, Literary Studies and, indeed, just about every academic department currently blazoned with the word 'Studies'. Even his enemies will have to concede the fact that in the wake of 1968 Lacan became a giant of French culture, one of the thinkers it was compulsory to have read if one wished to be in tune with the most advanced modes of thought. In observance of the British principle of Fair Play, it should also be said (1) that not all of Lacan's writing is rebarbative gibberish – some of the *Ecrits* are fairly easy reading even for the uninitiated, and at times amusing, and (2) that at least some of the Lacan ramblings which *do* appear to be gibberish, or simply silly (it's usually a bad sign when he starts going on about mathematics, which he appears not to understand – or not as mathematicians understand it) are offered as... well, as a unique kind of dramatic performance, 'actings-out' of the unconscious; or maybe as slabs of unadulterated paranoia; or as some form of shamanism; or as an initiation ceremony, a put-on, a joke... The story of Lacan's extraordinary career is lucidly told in Sherry Turkle's *Psychoanalytic Politics* (2nd edition, 1992) and – in greater detail, and with a far deeper account of Lacan's intellectual formation – Elisabeth Rodinesco's *Jacques Lacan & Co.* (1990). When it comes to the sacred texts themselves, *caveat lector*.

is for Metaphor

It has become a commonplace, though still quite an interesting one, that Freud sees the human mind as a machine for producing metaphors. (And also that, as in that last sentence, the metaphors that Freud uses when he comes to describe mental processes are themselves often rather mechanistic; born in an age innocent of all but the most rudimentary modes of information technology, Freud thought in terms of steam engines, furnaces and plumbing rather than computers.) One could go further, and say that the democratic promise of the Freudian model is that each of us is a kind of poet: in our dreams, as the saying goes. Lionel Trilling put it more elegantly: '[Freud] showed us that poetry is indigenous to the very constitution of the mind; he saw the mind as being, in the greater part of its tendency, exactly of the poetry-making faculty...'

M is also for *Moses and Monotheism*, one of Freud's bolder ventures into large-scale historical and anthropological speculation; and for **'Mourning and Melancholia',** a short, late essay which has yielded a great deal of critical commentary in recent years; and for **Jeffrey Masson,** the quondam Sanskrit scholar and Director of the Freud Archives, whose best-selling books *The Assault on Truth* and *Final Analysis* have done considerable damage to the intellectual respectability of psychoanalysis in the lay community, if not among the faithful. If so much as a small fraction of what Masson alleges is true, then the profession of psychoanalysis, at any rate in Canada and America, is morally and intellectually bankrupt beyond the most lurid caricatures of its earlier enemies. However, for a sceptical account of Masson himself, see Janet Malcolm, *In the Freud Archives* – a book which resulted in a protracted and bitter legal action.

is for Norman O. Brown

One of the most conjurable names of the 1960s counter-culture, now largely forgotten save by ageing nostalgists and conscientious historians of ideas, the classicist Norman O. Brown attained a freakish measure of fame with the publication of his (re)visionary Freudian tract *Life Against Death*, which became one of the indispensable bibles of the hippy sensibility. Some of those who bought the book even read parts of it: the chapter on Jonathan Swift's 'excremental vision' launched a thousand undergraduate essays. (Including one by the author. *Mea Culpa.*)

And, of course, for **Neurosis**.

O is for Oedipus

Almost everyone who has heard of Freud's notions concerning incest fantasies and patricidal urges is aware that he turned to Sophocles for his tag. (His earliest formulations of the complex may be dated to about 1897, and arose from his self-analysis.) It is less well known that his involvement with the Oedipus plays was career-long. He fantasised about having a portrait-bust commissioned for display in his old university, and adorning it with the Sophoclean boast 'Who solved the Riddle of the Sphinx, and was a man most mighty.'

P is for Adam Phillips

Today, in the early twenty-first century, Adam Phillips has established himself as the most graceful, imaginative and humane English exponent of the psychoanalytic essay. His many books include the likes of *On Kissing, Tickling and Being Bored, Darwin's Worms, Terrors and Experts* and so on. Phillips has also edited a number of literary works, notably by Lamb, Pater and Burke. His first substantial publication was a study of the English psychoanalyst D.W. Winnicott; he is now the series editor for the new Penguin Freud edition.

P is also for Parapraxes: hence:

Q is for Questenberg

A character in Schiller's play *Wallenstein*. In the *Introductory Lectures on Psychoanalysis* – Chapter 2, 'Parapraxes' – Freud quotes an exchange between Questenberg and another minor character, to demonstrate that dramatists and poets had long understood the psychoanalytic insight that an apparently meaningless verbal blunder might point to some unconscious anxiety or desire.

R is for Reading

In 1906, the Viennese publisher Hugo Heller asked a number of eminent public figures to nominate ten good books. Freud's eclectic list will suprise many:

Multatuli, *Letters and Works*
Rudyard Kipling, *The Jungle Book*
Anatole France, *Sur la pierre blanche*
Emile Zola, *Fécondité*
Merezhkovsky, *Leonardo da Vinci*
Gottfried Keller, *Die Leute von Seldwyla*
C.F. Meyer, *Huttens letze Tage*
Macaulay, *Essays*
Gomperz, *Griechische Denker*
Mark Twain, *Sketches*

For a more detailed discussion, see Peter Gay, *Reading Freud* (1990).

R is also for Charles Rycroft, one of the more appealing English psycho-analysts of the mid-twentieth century, and of considerable interest to anyone concerned with issues of creativity.

S is for Shakespeare

One of the minor oddities of Freud's Shakespearean ponderings is that he privately subscribed to what has been called the Looney hypothesis; he thought, in other words, that the author of the poems and plays was not the Stratford man, but 'the nobly-born and highly cultivated, passionately wayward, to some extent *déclassé* aristocrat, Edward de Vere, seventeenth Earl of Oxford, hereditary Lord Great Chamberlain of England'. Charitable commentators have assumed that Freud's English was not quite fluent enough to alert him to the unfortunate implications of Looney's name in the ears of Shakespeare's countrymen (or perhaps it was: some authorities maintain that Looney's name is pronounced lone-y.) However...

Freud first wrote on Shakespeare in *The Interpretation of Dreams*, introducing the world to the Oedipal reading of *Hamlet* with which all subsequent generations have had to contend, eagerly or otherwise. He went on to write at some length on other plays: in 'The Theme of the Three Caskets' (1913) on *The Merchant of Venice* and *King Lear*, and in subsequent essays on the characters of Richard III and Lady Macbeth. In the first essay, Freud unmasks Bassanio's choice of the lead casket in preference to the flashier gold and silver containers as a wise choice between three women, and thus a variant of King Lear's unwise choice of the voluble Goneril and Regan over the true but taciturn Cordelia. (A further unmasking of this pattern might include the detail that Freud himself had three daughters.) This apparently trifling observation leads Freud, by paths that wind backwards through the murk to the Norns and the Valkyries, to one of his most sombrely elegant phrases: 'Eternal wisdom, clothed in the primaeval myth, bids the old man renounce love, choose death and make friends with the necessity of dying.'

His essay on *Richard III* expresses admiration for the subtle way in which Shakespeare evokes our partial or grudging sympathy for his hero-villain, noting that a less gifted artist would have been more explicit about Richard's infantile rage against the world, and thus leave himself 'confronted by our cool, untrammelled intelligence': the latent identification, the dramatic illusion would pop like a bubble. Lady Macbeth he regards as another of those characters, like Ibsen's Rebecca, who is wrecked by success; but though he regards the play as steeped in the theme of childlessness, and expresses several sharp insights about that theme, he finally admits that there are perplexities here which he is unable to resolve. (A cheering and even touching instance of Freud's intellectual humility. Would that some of his epigones had learned that lesson.) Freud's emphasis on character criticism, albeit a mode of character criticism which embraces the unconscious, now makes him seem very much a man of his time, and it has sometimes been objected that his willingness to treat the imaginary characters on a stage as if they were three-dimensional patients on a couch is somewhat naive. The counter-objection is that Freud's motives were themselves multiple: not a professional literary critic, he was concerned on the one hand to resolve some of the excitment and unease he had felt in his experience of the dramatic arts, on the other to clarify the findings of psychoanalysis by turning to sharply defined and easily available fictional characters. A further motive still might be the quest for a particular type of respectability: the implication, once more (see Q, above), being that Freud was doing no more than bring to the light of prosaic consciousness truths which had always been intuitively available to poets. A last word on this topic from Lionel Trilling, our next entry: 'If we look for an analogue to Freud's vision of life, we find it, I think, in certain great literary minds. Say what we will about Freud's dealings with Shakespeare, his is the Shakespearean vision.'

(**S is also for Surrealism**; again, see the Alphabet of Surrealism.)

T is for Trilling

The American critic and novelist Lionel Trilling, now deeply unfashionable in self-consciously advanced literary circles (especially those where Lacan's name is spoken in reverent terms), was not merely a profound reader of literature but one of the most astute anglophone commentators on Freud's work from a perspective outside the therapeutic world. More: Bruno Bettelheim credits Trilling with having kept alive an accurate image of Freud and his teachings at a time (the 1950s) and in a place (the USA) where he was being grossly misunderstood – for example, by the disciples of Karen Horney, who had diluted and prettified Freud into a facile, optimistic preacher of self-improvement. Elaborated in a series of essays from *The Liberal Imagination* via *The Opposing Self* to *Sincerity and Authenticity*, Trilling painted Freud after his own image: as a moralist in the classic Western tradition. 'Like any tragic poet, like any true moralist, Freud took it as one of his tasks to define the border of necessity in order to establish the realm of freedom': 'Freud's Last Book', in *A Gathering of Fugitives*.

Also for **Totem and Taboo**, one of Freud's imaginative ventures into anthropological speculation.

U is for the Uncanny

A Freudian term which has earned such universal popularity as to be usable in its original form even by those with little or no grasp of German: *Das Unheimliche* – the 'un-homely', the 'un-cosy', the 'un-familiar'... Freud's classic exposition was first published in 1919, and its thirty-odd pages cover a good deal of ground, some of it apparently quite distant from his avowed subject. He begins with an enquiry into the etymology of the word *Unheimliche* and its cognates in other languages, and uncovers the interesting fact that there are many instances where its antonym, *Heimliche*, becomes a synonym. This oddity is of great consequence for Freud's later discussions, for he wishes to establish that an important mode of the uncanny is the recovery in a later stage of life of what was known, or believed, in an earlier condition. He proceeds to dissect E.T.A. Hoffman's story 'The Sand Man', seeing it as a classic metaphor of castration anxiety; discusses such assorted oddities as the Double, experiences of recurrence and coincidence ('...whatever reminds us of [an] inner "compulsion to repeat" is perceived as uncanny...') and the evil eye. Broadly speaking, he concludes by suggesting that the experience of the uncanny in everyday life is most likely to occur whenever a previously buried infantile urge is in some way revived by outside circumstances, or when primitive, animistic beliefs which the adult self has officially repudiated suddenly appear to be corroborated: 'So the dead really can re-appear in the form of ghosts!' Freud terms these two areas the Repressed and the Surmounted; he goes on to add that the experience of the uncanny in art and literature is rather more complicated. This essay has spawned a legion of imitators, and is almost invariably cited whenever theorists turn their attention to horror films and the like; which is why our next entry, V, could easily be made to stand for 'Vampires'. Instead, let us suggest that:

V is for Leonardo Da Vinci (and Vultures)

'Leonardo Da Vinci and a Memory of his Childhood' (1910) was Freud's first full-length attempt at psychoanalytic biography, and also his last, possibly because – despite some pre-emptive rhetorical manoeuverings in its opening and closing sections, disavowing any intention of besmirching genius – it was met with widespread hostility. Freud's detractors like to recall it as an essay which is founded, and thus founders, on a simple blunder. Freud quotes from an autobiographical passage in which Leonardo recalled an event from his infancy, when a vulture flew down and batted its tail against his mouth. Freud uses this memory, fantasy or fantasy-memory for a wonderfully digressive series of observations on the vulture as a mother-symbol in Ancient Egypt and elsewhere, which culminates in the 'discovery' of a vulture form concealed in the blue robes of the Virgin Mary. (Freud credited this find to Oskar Pfister.) Lovely stuff, but, alas, wholly fanciful. The Italian word *nibio* (modern form: *nibbio*) in Leonardo's memoir translates as 'kite', the bird of prey, and not 'vulture' (in Freud's original German: *Geier*). An embarrassment, then; but hardly a catastrophe, since many of Freud's other observations on Da Vinci – all interesting, many entirely plausible – rely on sources which are not comparably disputed. Following contemporary accounts and rumours which identified the Renaissance Man as a chaste homosexual of the passive type, Freud is able to provide a delicate and sympathetic account of the directions which Leonardo's genius took, from his interest in flight to the legendarily enigmatic Giaconda smile. Freud understands the adult Da Vinci's polymathic tendencies as an elaboration of his infantile sexual researches, duly refined and sublimated; if this sounds reductive in an all-too-familiar manner, it should not, since Freud's admiration for his subject is evident on every page, and prompts him to an uncommon degree of plangency: 'From that time onward, madonnas and aristocratic ladies were depicted in Italian painting humbly bowing their heads and smiling the strange, blissful smile of Caterina, the poor peasant girl who had brought into the world the splendid son who was destined to paint, to search and to suffer.'

V is also for Vienna, where Freud's family moved when he was a young child, where he studied, qualified as a doctor, married, became a father, set up in private practice, wrote papers and changed the world. He was driven out of the city in 1938, after Hitler's armies invaded Austria, and died the following year, on 23 September, in his newly adopted home, London.

W is for W.R. – *Mysteries of the Organism*

The Freudian heretic Wilhelm Reich, previously something of a minority interest, became popular with a much wider audience thanks to the cult success of this knockabout film – part drama, part documentary, part prank – by the Yugoslavian director Dusan Makavejev (whose subsequent work has failed to set the art-house circuits alight in any comparable degree). Reich, who still has his defenders, and is commemorated by a museum in Maine, developed his heretical tendencies early on, with a paper (1932) proposing an amalgamation of Freudian and Marxist theories, and maintaining that Freud's *thanatos*, or death instinct, was a product of capitalism rather than biology. Reich resigned from the psychoanalytic movement, moved to America, and came to hold increasingly bizarre views about the nature of the cosmos, which he held to be suffused with something called orgone energy. His followers – including the Beat novelist William Burroughs – believed that they could boost their levels of this vital substance by squatting in an 'orgone accumulator' – basically, a lead-lined wooden box. Reich's experiments were brought to an end by the intervention of the US government; a few people continue to regard him as a martyr.

is for X-Certificate

As older readers will recall, this was the British category of film exhibition which prevented the showing of erotic images, such as those in *W.R. – Mysteries of the Organism* to young cinema-goers, originally identified as those under twenty-one. (It has long since been replaced by the 18 certificate.) The pertinence of this phenomemon to a discussion of Freud is not so much a matter of the taboos we continue to place – if less stringently – on sexually explicit pictures and language, as to the analogy between this mode of censorship and that which, in Freud's view, the mind performs each night in dreams. Just as cunning screenwriters and directors once had to convey their erotic themes through witty indirections, so the endlessly inventive mechanisms of repression dress up desires in all manner of apparently non-erotic forms. (Modern readers often ask, not without justice, why it is that Freud has so little to say about overtly erotic dreams: did the Viennese bourgeoisie not experience them as we do? Or did they simply not report them?)

 is for *Young Man Luther*

A typical, and in its day celebrated, biography in the psychoanalytic mode; though, as the twentieth century progressed, the term 'psychoanalytic biography' came to seem almost a pleonasm, since biographers of all but the most doggedly old-fashioned stripe were finding Freudian concepts at once so rich and so revealing as to be all but indispensable to their art. It is hard to think of a a single major biography of the post-Freudian period which has not in some measure been swayed by Freudian assumptions about the underlying dramas, conflicts and drives of (particularly) exceptional people: for a thoughtful discussion, see Richard Ellmann's 'Freud and Literary Biography' (in Peregrine Hordern, *Freud and the Humanities*, 1985).

Z is for Stefan Zweig

The younger writer was a good friend of the Master, as well as one of his patients; a certain measure of equality was established between them on the basis that each admired the other's talents as a prose stylist. Freud once praised Zweig's work in terms that it is tempting to apply to his own writing: 'The perfection of empathy combined with the mastery of linguistic expression left me with a feeling of rare satisfaction.' Zweig's most public opportunity to return that compliment came when Freud was – assuming that his sturdy atheism proved well-founded – in no position to hear it. It was Zweig who delivered the German-language oration for Freud's funeral at the Golders Green crematorium. Zweig's speech showed, according to Ernest Jones, a degree of eloquence more than worthy of a major writer.

A
GOETHE
ALPHABET

 **is for Auden**

W.H. Auden not only admired Johann Wolfgang von Goethe (1749–1832), the writer he sometimes chummily called 'Mr G', but felt a deep affection for him: hence his fond, mildly camp exclamation '*Dear* Mr G!' It saddened Auden to think that in the mid-twentieth century the British and American literary worlds, whose grandparents had once worshipped Goethe, now had little time for him. At most, anglophone intellectuals were willing to acquiesce, somewhat passively, in the conventional bracketing of Goethe with Dante and Shakespeare as the Three Great Europeans. But they seldom troubled to read him, even in translation. (Remember Joyce's knockabout trio of 'Daunty, Gouty and Shopkeeper' in *Finnegans Wake*; and see T.S. Eliot's 1955 essay 'Goethe as the Sage'. Elsewhere, Joyce referred to Goethe as 'a boring civil-servant'.) Auden tried hard to over-come this inertia, and the three short, decidedly un-Gouty essays he wrote on Goethe provide an excellent introduction: they can be found in *Forewords and Afterwords*. In his late-ish poem 'The Cave Of Making' (1964), Auden expressed his modest-ish ambition to become 'a minor atlantic Goethe'.

is for Biology

Crucial consideration: by the educated standards of his day, Goethe was as much a scientist (or, let us more appropriately say, Natural Philosopher) as an artist, and devoted a good deal of his life to researches in evolutionary botany, geology, physics, psychology… even meteor-ology. By the more exacting standards of later scientists, Goethe must often be found sadly wanting; even by such a harsh assessment, though, his scientific achievements remain both varied and remarkable. He was among the earliest supporters of the theory that the earth had experienced an Ice Age; he coined the still-extant German term which translates as 'morphology'; he carried out valuable investigations into the growth of plants; he established major collec-tions devoted to geology, botany and zoology; he was among the founders of comparative anatomy. At least one historian (Rudolf Magnus, in *Goethe as a Scientist*, 1949) has also credited him with having provided the essential groundwork for modern weather forecasting, since he was an active participant in the earliest co-ordinated system of meteorological observation posts; moreover, he corresponded eagerly with Luke Howard, the Englishman who first classified cloud formations, and gave us the terms stratus, cumulus, cirrus, nimbus…

The poet-scientist's most substantial single discovery, the one which would have earned the name 'Goethe' a small place in the reference books had he never published another word, was his decisive refutation, in 1784, of the then-orthodox view that the inter-maxillary (vulgarly: snout) bone, common to the jaws of other mammals, did not occur in humans. This apparently humble discovery was of considerable moment in the later development of evolutionary theory. Still, despite this anatomical coup, Goethe the Scientist is usually remembered for his rather more controversial work in optics, which is why:

C is for Colour

Primarily an attack on Newton (or what he understood Newton to have been saying in his *Opticks*), Goethe's *Theory of Colours* is a fascinating if ultimately fanciful work which cost him many years of effort. 'I do not repent it at all,' he told a friend shortly before his death, 'though I have expended half a life upon it. Perhaps I might have written half a dozen tragedies more; that is all, and people enough will come after me to do that.' Wrong-headed as it may be, the work has inspired artists (Kandinsky), philosophers (Wittgenstein) and film-makers (Jarman). It has been the subject of a fair amount of critical commentary in the last few decades.

C is also for many other things, including Christine Vulpius, Goethe's lover, whom he finally married in 1806, at the age of fifty-seven, though they had been living together in Weimar for the better part of twenty years, and she had borne him several children, only one of whom survived infancy; and for **Thomas Carlyle**, who translated *Wilhelm Meister* and was the most important early broker of Goethe's reputation in Britain with his encomia in *Sartor Resartus*, *On Heroes* and elsewhere; and, inevitably, for **Classicism** (*Klassik*): that is, 'Weimar Classicism' – the term generally applied to that robustly anti-Romantic phase of Goethe's career which begins shortly after his move to Weimar and lasts until about 1805, the year in which his friend and co-worker Friedrich Schiller died. Since the origins of German Romanticism are generally ascribed to around 1797 or so, one could say that Goethe had outgrown Romanticism before it had even been born.

 is for *Dichtung und Wahrheit*

Or *Poetry and Truth*, Goethe's minutely detailed autobiographical account of his youth. Why so detailed? 'The most important part of an individual's life is that of development... Afterwards begins the conflict with the world, and that is interesting only in its results.' That, at least, is the explanation he gave the man who has uncharitably been described as 'Goethe's photocopier': see E is for Eckermann.

And also for **Demons**, or **Daemons**: "'The higher a man is," said Goethe, "the more he is under the influence of daemons, and he must take heed lest his guiding will counsel him to a wrong path. There was something altogether daemonic in my acquaintance with Schiller..."' (Eckermann, *Conversations of Goethe*, 24 March 1829).

 is for Eckermann

As Boswell to Johnson, as Plato to Socrates, so Eckermann to Goethe. Nietzsche surprisingly called Eckermann's *Conversations of [or with] Goethe* (1836; third volume 1848) 'the best German book there is', thus ranking Goethe's impromptu, imperfectly recalled performances as an elderly conversationalist above any of his written works – and, implicitly, Eckermann as a great verbal artist. (At the other extreme, Heine had dismissed Eckermann as a 'parrot'.) The warmly affectionate image of Goethe which has survived into the twenty-first century is largely the creation of Eckermann – which is not to say that it is a dishonest or unduly idealised portrait – and the *Conversations* can be read with pleasure by those for whom *Faust* and *Wilhelm Meister* spell unmitigated tedium.

Johann Peter Eckermann was born in 1792, near Hamburg. From a poor background – his father was a sometime shopkeeper turned itinerant sock pedlar – and considered too sickly to earn an honest living as a craftsman or labourer, the boy was largely self-educated, and scraped by in a number of very minor clerical posts. He tried his hand at both poetry and drawing, showing real if not incandescent talent at both, and, in the course of his autodidactic researches, discovered and developed a passionate admiration for the writings of Goethe. They first met on 10 June 1823. Goethe was seventy-four; Eckermann thirty-one. Though still healthy and active, Goethe recognised (1) that his vitality was gradually waning, (2) that he urgently needed to put his collected works into the definitive shape he wished to hand on to posterity, and (3) that the assistance of an ardent young disciple would be of great help in this mission. So, Eckermann was hired – for a pitifully low salary, which he had to eke out by giving German lessons to English students. Apart from some minor romantic complications, which were resolved in 1831 when Peter finally married his long-suffering (and Goethe-sceptical) fiancée Johanna 'Hanchen' Bertram, he spent almost every day from 1823 to 1832 (as Havelock Ellis put it) 'in the temple where he was high priest'.

After Goethe's death in 1832, Eckermann stayed on in Weimar, editing the master's *Nachlass*. He was happy enough in his work, but wretched in his life: Hanchen died giving birth to their first child, Peter himself suffered from persistent ill health, and there was never enough money. On the publication of their first two volumes in 1836, the *Conversations* made no great public stir but were well received by the *cognoscenti*, who appreciated the balance and accuracy of Eckermann's portrait. The third volume, issued in 1848, was greeted with almost universal indifference, and by the time of Eckermann's sudden death from a stroke in 1854, he was all but forgotten, even in Weimar. Nietzsche's accolade, in *Human, All Too Human*, was a turning point, and by the centenary of Goethe's death, the *Conversations* had gained the classic status they continue to enjoy.

E is also for T.S. Eliot, who, having moved (at least for public consumption) beyond his earlier antipathy, kept a drawing of Goethe on his mantelpiece throughout the Second World War; and for **Egmont**, a historical prose drama which preoccupied Goethe in fits and starts for several years. He had written quite a bit of it as early as 1775; six years later, in 1781, it seemed to him all but complete save for a hopelessly tangled fourth act, which he vowed to rewrite immediately, but in the event left untouched for another six years, until 1787. Briefly, the play concerns the heroism of an exceptional military hero, Count Egmont; the place of love in his life; and his cruel but liberating death. The play is set in the Netherlands in the mid-sixteenth century, at the point when the country is on the verge of revolt against Philip II of Spain. Egmont, a spokesman for the cause of the people, is betrayed, arrested, imprisoned and – after a brief respite in which he appears to be on the brink of escape – is executed, though not before experiencing an allegorical dream which leaves him confident, as he steps to the gallows, that his martyrdom will unleash a revolt that will eventually do away with Spanish rule.

F is for *Faust*

The one work which every English-speaking person with modest literary equipment can confidently assign to Goethe, this epic, metaphysical, verse drama was the (intermittent) work of a lifetime. Its composition falls into three main phases: he started on it in his twenties, eventually completing a version of the so-called *Urfaust* in 1790 (see U, below); returned to the work between 1797 and 1806, publishing *Faust*, Part One, in 1808; then proceeded slowly with the remainder in the final years of his life, putting the intended finishing touches to his manuscript on 22 July 1831. He seems to have had second thoughts and fiddled with it a little the following January, and died on 22 March 1832. The complete *Faust*, some 12,000 lines long, was published posthumously.

Its fortunes in the English-speaking world have been mixed, partly because of the shadow cast by Marlowe's much briefer and far more thrilling treatment of the Faust legend, partly because there has been no classic English version of the play. Coleridge once planned a translation, but – characteristically – never got around to it; Shelley left off after a few fragments. Many of the better-known English translations, including those by Louis MacNeice, Randall Jarrell and – lately – Howard Brenton have been fairly loose; David Luke's faithful and well-annotated version for Oxford World's Classics is probably the best starting point for the reader without any German.

G is for the German Language

While it is not altogether true to say that Goethe invented modern German, it is not altogether preposterous, either. In the cautious summary of T.J. Reed, author of *The Classical Centre: Goethe and Weimar 1775–1832*, 'He was the first to explore fully (which means that he virtually created) the expressive registers of modern German.'

G is also for *die Goethezeit*, 'the age of Goethe', a term which designates the sixty-odd years between Goethe's first mature work and his death in 1832, and which bears witness to his cultural pre-eminence during that great national flowering; and for **Götz von Berlichingen**; see below, J is for Jaxthausen.

H is for *Hermann und Dorothea*

Not much read now except by Goethe specialists, and noted in reference books mainly as an instance of that comparatively rare form, the verse novel, *Hermann und Dorothea* (1796) was a considerable hit with the reading public. 'Almost the only one of my larger poems that still satisfies me', was Goethe's verdict in old age.

And for **Johann Gottfried Herder** (1744–1803), an early and important mentor figure. Goethe met Herder, a clergyman and prolific writer, during his law studies in Strasbourg, which began in April 1770. Herder, whose theoretical and critical polemics were to have a considerable influence on the direction of German culture, encouraged Goethe to collect, study and translate folk poems and songs, previously ignored by literary intellectuals. The impact of these studies was salutary and long-lasting. Goethe shook off the trifling, prissy mode of his juvenilia and began to write the kind of haunted, haunting verses which reached their high point in the likes of *The Erl King* (*Erlkönig*, 1782) – Germany's equivalent of, say, *The Ancient Mariner* or *La Belle Dame Sans Merci*.

I is for Italy

On 2 September 1786, aged thirty-seven and suffering from what we would now call a mid-life crisis, Goethe adapted the pseudonym of 'Herr Möller' and made a bolt for Italy. The two years he spent in and around Rome changed him utterly: he gorged his eyes on the art and architecture, he learned to draw… and, it seems, he enjoyed his first fully consummated love affair. Auden, contrasting portraits painted before and after the stay in Rome, baldly asserted that the latter showed 'a man who has known sexual satisfaction'. The book which immortalised at least some of these experiences, the *Italian Journey* (*Italienische Reise*), was co-translated by Auden in the hope that it was the text most likely to wean anglophone readers from the widespread prejudice that Goethe is a frightful bore.

I is also for *Iphigenia in Tauris*, Goethe's classical drama.

J is for Jaxthausen

The main setting of *Götz von Berlichingen*, Goethe's earliest play, written at white heat in six weeks in November and December 1771, then rewritten at the start of 1773. Heavily influenced by Shakespeare's history plays, *Götz* is a sprawling, episodic and often violent work, set in the early years of the sixteenth century. It was his first great success, critical if not financial (everyone agreed that it was virtually unstageable), winning him national fame and establishing him as a leading figure in what became known as the *Sturm und Drang* movement (see S, below).

Goethe initially wrote the play for submission to his mentor Herder, and intended the play to do for German audiences what Shakespeare – or so he pictured the case – had done for the English: to provide a new national drama by returning to episodes from national history. *Götz* is hard to summarise neatly, not least because it reads like two distinct plays forcibly crammed into one. The first story is that of Götz himself, a warlord who rules over his (fairly limited) territory of Jaxthausen during the period just before and just after Luther's rebellion against the church in 1517. (Many commentators believe that Luther himself puts in a cameo appearance as a minor character, Brother Martin.)

Götz's assorted battles with other small territories and with the armies of the Emperor, which manage to include a period of embroilment in the Peasant's Revolt, eventually issue in defeat and a long period of imprisonment in his own castle. The second main plot concerns Götz's lifelong friend Adelbert von Weislingen, a somewhat Hamlet-like figure who is torn between his loyalty to Götz, his political ambition and a passionate infatuation with a *femme fatale*, Adelheid; he, too, comes to a sorry end. Critics have made the not too implausible suggestion that Götz and Weislingen are at some level meant to represent two aspects of one soul; in fact, two possible versions of the man Goethe might go on to be, the one a bold and forceful champion of his national culture, the other a sensitive plant, too irresolute to be anything other than a traitor to all he holds dear. Sir Walter Scott produced an English translation in 1799, and, closer to the present, in 1961, the radical English playwright John Arden used Scott as a crib towards his own free but powerful adaptation of the play, naming it *Ironhand*; refuting the 'unstageable' verdict of Goethe's contemporary critics, it was successfully staged in Bristol.

 is for Knowledge

Who was the last true polymath of European culture? Dante? (See the Dante Alphabet.) Leonardo da Vinci? (Freud had his doubts; see the Freud Alphabet.) Pico della Mirandola? Athanasius Kircher? Some more recent figure, such as Joseph Needham? There are many contenders, but few would contest that Goethe is among the most plausible. Of all the disciplines of knowledge available to his time, only astronomy seems somehow to have failed to catch his interest; and in addition to his literary and scientific work, one must remember his skill as a draughtsman, his practical efforts as a statesman, theatre administrator, inspector of mines...

L is for *Lehrjahre*

In full: *Wilhelm Meisters Lehrjahre* (*Wilhelm Meister's Apprenticeship*), Goethe's exceedingly long novel about a young man's coming of age. Schegel thought its publication an event as momentous as the French Revolution, and though this verdict now seems a trifle over-enthusiastic, the book has lasted surprisingly well, and found its way into some unexpected corners. Jean-Luc Godard quoted from it extensively in his film about a later generation of French revolutionaries, *La Chinoise*, and Wim Wenders took it as the basis for his glum road movie *Wrong Movement*.

M is for Music

The roll-call is sonorous: Beethoven (the *Egmont* overture), Schubert ('Wer nie sein Brot'), Schumann ('Der Sanger'), Liszt (the *Faust* symphony), Wolf ('Kennst du das Land...?')... outside the German-speaking world, Goethe is sometimes better known as the poet who inspired composers rather than an artist in his own right. A music lover himself, he might not have been too disgruntled at this development. Incidentally, he seems to have anticipated Schelling's famous definition of architecture as 'frozen music', though his own formulation is happier still: 'petrified music'.

N is for Nature

At the age of seven, Goethe recalled in *Dichtung und Wahrheit*, he had set up an altar to Nature on his father's ornate music stand. It was an ingenious contrivance, in which aromatic pastilles were to be ignited by the rays of the sun, focused through a magnifying glass – slightly more powerfully than little Johann had intended, since the pastilles burned down into the stand's delicate red lacquer. This charming episode speaks volumes. Nature, conceived as a manifestation of the divine, remained his preoccupation as both artist and scientist. On the other hand, as he insisted to Eckermann, 'I have never observed Nature with a view to poetic production', a declaration which makes life slightly more awkward for those who like to compare early Goethe with early Wordsworth. That there are certain points of resemblance is beyond dispute, but still more indisputable is Wordsworth's violent hostility to Goethe's work in his later years, a hostility in no way tempered by the English poet's confessed ignorance of the larger part of that edifice:

> ...there is a proflicacy, an inhuman sensuality, in his works which is utterly revolting. I am not intimately acquainted with them generally. But I take up my ground on the first canto of *Wilhem Meister*; and, as the attorney-general of human nature, I there indict him for wantonly outraging the sympathies of humanity.

Wordsworth's reaction, though extreme, was far from unique among his generation of writers. In 1824, Thomas De Quincey published a review of Carlyle's *Wilhelm Meister* translation which fulminated about its immorality in comparable terms. It was left to the next generation of English Romantics, Byron and Shelley, to enthuse over *Faust* – and, in Shelley's case, to translate some of it.

N is also for Neologism: one of Goethe's many contributions to the refinement of German as a literary language was the plethora of invented words he sprinkled liberally throughout the verses he wrote in Frankfurt and during his early Weimar years.

is for Orientalism

At the age of sixty-five, Goethe re-invented himself for the nth time by writing a series of poems, the *West-östlicher Divan*, in imitation of the Persian lyricist Shams-ud-din Muhammad, better known to the occidental world as Hafiz. Many of these poems are erotic, and a few, the so-called *Shenke* (Cupbearer) group, are nonchalantly homo-erotic. Alas for gay scholars, there is not much else in Goethe's *oeuvre* to earn him a justified place in the pantheon of homosexual genius.

O is also for the Occult; for a brief period in his youth, in 1769, Goethe became obsessed with magic, Neo-Platonic cosmology, the Western Hermetic tradition and suchlike arcana. He built himself an alchemical laboratory, and drew endless diagrams of the angelic hierarchies; it may have been at this time that he first toyed with the notion of writing a drama about Faust – a figure already, in 1759, described by Lessing as an ideal hero for some putative German Shakespeare. (Incidentally, Lessing had a try at such a drama himself; though only fragments remain, one thing is clear: Lessing's was the first of the many German *Faust* plays in which the magician does not end up in Hell. The way to Goethe's grand finale had been opened.)

 ## is for Poetry

'Goethe is above all else a poet': T.J. Reed. And, like all poets, stubbornly hard to render into other languages. Here's one valiant and fairly well known attempt, by Longfellow:

Über allen Gipfeln	O'er all the hill-tops
Ist Ruh',	Is quiet now
In allen Wipfeln	In all the tree-tops
Spürest du	Hearest thou
Kaum einen Hauch;	Hardly a breath;
Die Vögelein schweigen im Walde.	The birds are asleep in the trees.
Warte nur, balde	Wait; soon like these
Ruhest du auch.	Thou, too, shalt rest.

And here is Coleridge's version of 'Kennst du das Land':

Know'st thou the land where the pale citrons grow
The golden fruits in darkest foliage glow?
Soft blows the wind that blows from that blue sky!
Still stands the myrtle and the laurel high!
Know'st thou it well, that land, beloved friend?
Thither with thee, O, thither would I wend!

is for Qualitative Knowledge

Goethe's scientific writings place so much emphasis on the importance of qualitative knowledge (as opposed to the quantitative kind; mainly mathematics) that his contemporaries sometimes assumed that he was a philistine when it came to maths. Not so, he replied, mathematics is 'the most sublime and useful science', but only in its proper place, which in many instances was a subordinate one: '…it would be foolish for a man not to believe in his mistress's love because she cannot prove it mathematically'.

 is for the *Roman Elegies*

Or *Römische Elegien* (c. 1778–90), usually described as Goethe's first fully Classical work, composed after his Italian journey in emulation of the Roman love poets Catullus, Propertius and Tibullus. Ebulliently sexy in a manner quite at odds with Goethe's pompous image as 'Gouty', the collection is full of lifted skirts, discarded corsets and creaking beds; Auden's guess about what went on during Goethe's Italian journeys seems to be more than acute.

 is for *Sturm und Drang*

Literally 'Storm and Stress' – a tag evolved by nineteenth-century German critics to designate a previously nameless group of 'wild' young German writers who flourished in the 1770s – a circle of which Goethe was unquestionably the star, from the publication day of *Götz von Berlichingen* onwards. The name has proved durable, and is now a standard literary-historical term.

S is also for Friedrich Schiller, the young poet and philosopher who was the most significant of all Goethe's creative and intellectual partners, especially in the years after 1799 when Schiller moved to Weimar.

T is for *Torquato Tasso*

A verse drama (1790), loosely based on the life of the Italian poet of that name (1554–95). It is conventional to observe that this work says rather more about the youthful Goethe than the actual Tasso; rather less so to note, in the words of the distinguished Goethe scholar and translator David Luke, that it may well be the world's earliest drama of 'the romantic dilemma between the demands of the aesthetic and of the practical life'.

U is for *Urphanomen*

or 'primal phenomenon': in Goethe's natural philosophy, a kind of archetype, template or essential form which the trained or visionary eye may detect in all its various and particular manifestations, such as the 'primal plant' (*Urpflanze*), that ideal structure which unites all actually existing plants. Most literary historians say that the idea of of *Urpflanze* burst upon him during a stay in Palermo. The keepers of the Botanical Gardens in Padua, where visitors can see the 'Goethe Tree' to this day, dispute this point.

It is only fitting to point out that **U may also stand for the *Urfaust***, the earliest known version of Goethe's lifelong project – more exactly, of what is now known as *Faust*, Part One. This substantial fragment of verse and prose was discovered in 1887, and was written in about 1774–5. Goethe stays fairly close to the storyline of the *Faust* puppet plays, with one major exception: he invents an original plot about Faust's tragic love affir with a simple girl, Margarethe (or Gretchen), which results in an illegitimate child, infanticide and her execution.

V is for the Victorians

'Minds like Goethe's are the common property of all nations,' Carlyle insisted in the Preface to his 1824 translation of *Wilhelm Meister's Apprenticeship*. The succeeding generations of British intellectuals heartily agreed: for the likes of George Eliot, G.H. Lewes – who published his biography of Goethe in 1855 – and Matthew Arnold, Goethe was unquestionably one of the formative spirits of the modern world; perhaps the indispensable one. Thanks to Carlyle's advocacy, Goethe was an indispensable presence in British intellectual life, studied and in some cases revered by almost every major figure of the age, from John Stuart Mill to Walter Pater. Matthew Arnold wrote that '... no persons [are] so thoroughly modern, as those who have felt Goethe's influence most deeply'. The key point for most of these intellectuals was Goethe's apparently triumphant negotiation of the problem – an urgent one for earnest and high-minded freethinkers and agnostics – of how Christianity might be transcended. A touching vignette from the twilight of the Victorian age: Oscar Wilde, imprisoned in Reading, set himself to the study of German and asked to be sent a copy of *Faust*.

 **is for Weimar**

Goethe's base for almost the whole of his productive life, from 1775 onwards; a cultural backwater which, thanks to him, became a whirlpool that drew in both the idle curious and the most prominent men in Europe. He was invited there by the ruler of Saxe-Weimar-Eisenach, Carl August, initially as a guest, but soon became a hard-working member of the privy council.

W is also for Goethe's cryptic Last Word. As he lay dying, bereft of the power of speech, he raised his right hand and traced a word, or words, in the air. All of these airy letters were indecipherable, save one: W. What does it stand for? There have been many suggestions, of which the most pleasing is *Weltliteratur*: world literature, Goethe's term for the books which transcended national boundaries and forged invisible bonds between cultures.

 is for *Xenian*

The title of a collection of sarcastic squibs co-written by Goethe and Schiller. Goethe was surprisingly proud of them: 'The good effects which the *Xenian* had upon the German literature of their time are beyond calculation,' he told Eckermann.

Y is for *Young Werther*

Or *Die Leiden des jungen Werthers* (*The Sorrows of Young Werther*), the short novel about an excessively sensitive lad who affects a blue frock-coat and kills himself after an unhappy love-affair. Written 'almost unconsciously, like a somnambulist' (*Dichtung und Wahrheit*) in just four weeks, and published in 1774, when he was twenty-five, this was the book which soon made Goethe famous throughout Europe – 'an early exemplar of the rock star', as one American critic recently gushed. It remained the one book that every pilgrim to Weimar was all but guaranteed to have read, even if they knew nothing else of his work at first-hand. In 1808, Napoleon told Goethe that he had read *Werther* seven times. As one would expect of such a work, *Werther* contains fairly substantial slices of (only partly disguised) autobiography, and had its origins in a summer idyll passed in the small town of Wetzlar, about forty miles from Goethe's native town, Frankfurt.

The original of the novella's heroine was the nineteen-year-old Charlotte Buff, usually known as Lotte, who was informally betrothed to Goethe's new friend Christian Kestner. Goethe was immediately smitten by the attractive young woman, and for a few months the three of them managed to enjoy an entirely chaste but emotionally exalted friendship, which began to crack up slightly when Christian grew jealous of 'Dr' Goethe's closeness to his intended. Lotte finally told Johann that she could not return his affection; he withdrew into gloom and was gone within four weeks. The couple eventually married in the spring of 1773; Goethe began his book about a year later. Its suicidal finale is not merely melodrama or self-commiserating hyperbole, but inspired by the actual suicide of another young member of the Kestner circle, Karl Wilhelm Jerusalem, at the end of October 1772. Like Werther, or so the rumours went, Jerusalem had been spurned by the woman he loved, in this case a married lady, Frau Herd.

Today, most (killjoy) historians say that the traditional stories about the book's freakish success prompting a wave of copycat juvenile suicides throughout Europe are apocryphal, but it does seem to have done wonders for the sale of blue frock-coats and buff waistcoats, as well as for the international tourist trade: Jerusalem's grave became one of the unmissable sights of a German holiday. *Werther* mania gripped Europe for a good fifteen years, inspiring all manner of imitations, homages, souvenirs and quick-cash-ins, including *Werther*-themed jewellery, perfumes, clothes, china, paintings and geegaws – a disgustingly precise anticipation of present-day Hollywood merchandising tactics, which might otherwise seem uniquely modern in their tastelessness, opportunism and idiocy. Like modern-day crazes, too, if a little more slowly, the *Werther* fad burned itself out, leaving a residue of indifference or even distaste, particularly in Britain, where German writers were now identified with the worst excesses of the French Revolution. But the book remained popular in other parts of Europe, as well as in America and beyond – a Japanese translation appeared in 1894. The legend of this precocious triumph made it something a stone around the neck of its venerable and greatly changed author; and yet:

Z is for Zelter

On 3 December 1812, at the age of sixty-three, Goethe told his good friend Karl Friedrich Zelter (for whom he designed a charming coat of arms, including a winged horse) that he felt quite capable of writing a second *Werther*, which would make people's hair stand on end. For all his hard-won, 'Olympian' serenity – to put it more crudely, his popular reputation as a tediously wise old man – Goethe plainly felt that his work was far from finished. In some senses (a Nietzschean sense, for instance) it remains unfinished. As Nietzsche wrote in *Human, All Too Human*: '... one can claim that Goethe's effect has not yet been fully realised, and that his time has yet to come'.

Perhaps so: but, for us at least, Nietzsche's soon will. Please read on.

A
HARLEM
RENAISSANCE
ALPHABET

is for African-American

'African-American': not just an appropriately polite (if, at times, slightly stiff) way of avoiding the use of 'black', 'coloured', 'Negro' or some even more charged and demeaning term, but, like other such hyphenations, an appropriately exact term for designating a culture, an identity, a challenge, a fate, a promise. As W.E.B. Du Bois (see D, below) wrote in 1903, 'One ever feels his two-ness – an American, a Negro...' Many of the stories that can be told about that two-ness are tragic, violent, shameful. Some, though, are triumphant. The Harlem Renaissance, though not without its flaws and failures, may justly be classed among those tales of triumph.

What was it? The term itself was not often heard at the time, though in 1920 Du Bois had famously predicted an imminent 'renaissance of American Negro literature'; the phrase 'New Negro' was a more common journalistic tag. Cultural historians insist that the Renaissance was a literary and intellectual movement, for the most part, even though music (wonderful music) and parties and painting and booze and love affairs and slumming and inter-racial friendships or vendettas were an indispensable part of the brief, glorious, unpredictable outburst. Still, there is no doubt that the movement's leading lights were all writers: Langston Hughes, Zora Neale Hurston, Claude McKay, Jean Toomer, Countee Cullen, Wallace Thurman and the rest. To be sure, countless African-Americans had written and published in earlier centuries – we are still recovering their lost writings, thanks to the labours of such scholars as Henry Louis Gates, Jr – but there had never before in the United States been such a ferocious concentration of ardent young black talent, never such a self-conscious sense of mission and moment, never such exhilarating cross-fertilisations of personalities and ideas... and never such attention from the rich white world.

Like most avant-garde flowerings, the Harlem Renaissance was as short-lived as it was intense: in its purest form, barely a decade. The most generous assessment might just about stretch towards two decades, from the performance in 1917 of three short plays with all-black casts at the Provincetown Playhouse, to the publication of the final Renaissance novel *Black Thunder* in 1936 (though the Harlem Riot of 1935 makes a more definitive end-point). But a better starting point would be the return from Europe in 1919 of the all-black 369th Infantry Regiment (New York's 15th): the 'Hellfighters', who marched proudly up Fifth Avenue, then turned west at 110th Street towards Lenox Avenue: home. As they hit 130th Street, the band gave up its martial thump and took off with 'Here Comes My Daddy': the troops behind them broke step and began to swagger and strut. The crowds were in ecstacy. Harlem had come of age.

In the ten years between that delicious moment and the Wall Street Crash of 1929, Harlem blossomed and blazed in a way that earlier generations could not have foreseen, and later generations – for whom the term 'Harlem' signifies an urban hell of crime, poverty and drug addition – sometimes find hard to credit. If the 1920s was the 'roaring' decade, then nowhere was the roaring louder, angrier, more seductive or more mellifluous than in the blocks from Manhattan's 130th to 145th streets. Fuelled by post-war exuberance and bootleg gin, swelled by the flood of rural blacks into the big city, and payrolled, often, by rich white hedonists, the formerly drab, German-influenced neighbourhood became New York's Montmartre and Montparnasse rolled into one. More: it became the acknowledged capital of the black world.

Nostalgia should not soften the picture too much: Harlem still had its woes. Rents were often criminally high, unemployment was a chronic condition (after the Crash, almost 50 per cent of Harlem's families were unemployed), rates of typhoid and pneumonia were twice those of white Manhattan, tuberculosis five times higher and syphilis nine times higher; the only public hospital to deal with 200,000 black citizens contained just 273 beds. If this was Paradise, it was a Paradise teeming with venomous serpents. But even the poorest blacks could sometimes share in the fun (rent parties, thrown whenever the landlord needed to be paid, were a regular entertainment), and, even if they were not always able to read them, then at least notice the new papers and magazines and books, and maybe hear gossip about the 'New Negro' names, and realise that something entirely fresh and different was suddenly happening in the streets of north-eastern New York City.

B is for Blues

With the honourable exception of Langston Hughes – in *The Weary Blues* and subsequent books – the new Harlem writers paid rather less attention than one might have assumed (in print, anyway; life was another matter) to the intoxicating music that was flooding through their neighbourhood; music performed by the legendary likes of Bessie Smith (1894–1937) or Duke Ellington (see E, below). In fact, it was left to a (now much condemned) white man, Carl Van Vechten, to propose that blues songs should be recorded in large numbers lest they be forgotten, and to use the pages of *Vanity Fair* to bang the drum for blues music as a vital and valuable art form. Why the baffling neglect? For one wing of the Renaissance, at least, the answer is an excess of gentility: more austere intellectuals felt that blues and jazz were undignified. Elsewhere, the cause was a justifiable suspicion bred of watching white folks, especially well-heeled white folks, pick up on the new 'jungle music' craze. Which brings us to:

C is for the Cotton Club

The most famous Harlem landmark of the Renaissance years. Opened at 644 Lenox Avenue in the autumn of 1923 by a mobster, Owney Madden, it operated a notoriously racist admissions policy – which greatly boosted its popularity among the more timid white explorers of the unknown lands across 100th Street. Even the name was meant to evoke the ante-bellum South of plantations, and (perhaps) the whiteness of its clientele.

C is also for Countee Cullen (1903–46), one of the Renaissance's leading poets. Originally from Lexington, Kentucky – or possibly Baltimore, or Louisville, or New York (he deliberately shrouded his origins in mystery, and never revealed the identity of his parents) – the adolescent Countee was adopted by a Harlem minister, Rev. Frederick Asbury Cullen, at the age of fifteen. He showed a flair for writing at an early age, and was appointed editor of his high school newspaper. In 1925 – the year of his graduation from New York University – he was elected to Phi Beta Kappa, won the Witter Bynner prize for poetry, and published his first collection of verses: *Color* (1925). His path to such rewards was considerably smoothed by his impeccable manners, equally impeccable dress, conspicuously cheerful disposition and mellifluous speaking voice: the very image of an Adonis from what Du Bois called 'the Talented Tenth'. More honours came in quick succession, including an MA from Harvard (1926), prizes from *Opportunity* magazine, a Harmon Foundation gold medal and, in 1928, one of the first Guggenheim Fellowships to be awarded to an African-American. Crowning these triumphs, in a move that would have been immediately understood by the young ladies of Jane Austen's fiction, he married into the local aristocracy: on 9 April 1928, he took Yolande Du Bois as his wife, and thus became son-in-law to Harlem's intellectual patriarch. The marriage proved short-lived, and the couple divorced in 1930 – largely, it seems, because Cullen had powerful homosexual feelings, and took off for Paris shortly after the wedding with his high-school beau, Harold Jackman. (Cullen also cultivated a romantic friendship with Langston Hughes, among others.) Surprisingly, W.E.B. Du Bois sided with Cullen, and blamed the divorce on his daughter's flightiness. Meanwhile, Cullen had published further collections, including *Copper Sun* (1927) and *The Black Christ* (1929), as well as an anthology, *Caroling Dusk*. He favoured demanding traditional verse forms such as the villanelle, and was strongly, no doubt too strongly, influenced by the English Romantics. His single most famous couplet now reads awkwardly:

> Yet do I marvel at this curious thing:
> To make a poet black, and bid him sing!

Sadly, Cullen's career began to fall apart at the same time as his marriage, and the decline of his reputation was as rapid as his earlier ascent. His first novel *One Way to Heaven* was almost entirely ignored on its publication in 1932, and by 1934 he was forced to go back to his old high school as a French teacher. He remained in that job for the rest of his life, and his only further publications were books for small children about the adventures of his cat, Christopher. He died on 9 January 1946, of uremic poisoning. Harlem did him proud in death: his two-hour funeral was attended by the likes of Alain Locke, Paul Robeson and Carl Van Vechten, and W.E.B. Du Bois delivered a moving speech of elegy and eulogy.

C is also for Nancy Cunard, the aristocratic Harlemaniac and editor of the anthology *Negro*; and for one of the movement's leading magazines, ***The Crisis***, an organ of the NAACP, the National Association for the Advancement of Colored People. Which brings us to:

D is for W.E.B. Du Bois

Unquestionably the most respected and influential African-American intellectual of his day – and one of the most formidable of any era – Du Bois (who worked on into his nineties: he lived from 1868 to 1963) was the great Father to the Renaissance – a stern and haughty father, not always fully respected by his wayward and rebellious children, but a father none the less. A native of Great Barrington, Massachusetts, Du Bois blazed his way through schools and universities from Boston to Germany, and became the first black student ever to be awarded an Ivy League Ph.D. His subject: the slave trade. His college: Harvard. In 1899 he was appointed Professor of Sociology at Atlanta University, and, four years later, published his classic study *The Souls of Black Folk*. In 1910 he founded *The Crisis*, and became involved (and identified) with the fledgling NAACP. Then, in addition to all his other activities, he turned to writing fiction – militant fiction: 'I do not care a damn', he said, ' for any art that is not used for propaganda.'

  The Souls of Black Folk electrified its younger readers; 'The book shook me like an earthquake,' said Claude McKay; *The Crisis* was the catalyst for the Renaissance. Du Bois had correctly identified the sphere of culture as a weak point in white defences. Among Du Bois' more hotly debated ideas was a kind of cultural trickle-down theory: the way forward for African-Americans was for the most energetic, disciplined, educated and mature members of 'the race' to forge ahead in their own careers, and thus create an élite force which would then drag a few of the less advantaged up to (almost) its own level. His term for that élite was 'the Talented Tenth'. (There were many more abusive terms for such people on the streets of Harlem, *dicty* or *dickty* – 'snobbish', 'stuck-up' – being the most common.) 'The Talented Tenth rises and pulls all those who are worthy of saving [*sic*] up to their vantage ground.' Not unreasonably, Du

Bois' opponents felt that this policy smacked of snobbery, though it took a brave soul to argue with Du Bois face to face.

D is also for Aaron Douglas, one of the most successful visual artists of the period; influenced by African and cod-Egyptian forms, his work for magazines, book covers and the like did much to give the key Renaissance publications their distinctive graphic style. His cover for *Nigger Heaven*, for example, indicated something of his characteristic approach: crisply silhouetted and stylised forms – a ladder to the left, a balletically arranged male figure to the right – arranged with dramatically blank space at the centre.

 is for Duke Ellington
The Joseph Haydn of the Cotton Club, and the most prodigiously talented and enduring of all the performer-composers who provided the Renaissance with its incomparable music. He is discussed at more adequate length above, in the Ellington Alphabet.

 is for Jessie Redmon Fauset
A woman of, for the day, almost unprecedentedly advanced education, Jessie Fauset served the Renaissance in a number of capacities. Born c. 1882 near Philadelphia, she was educated at Cornell, and became the first black woman there to be elected to Phi Beta Kappa (1905). She went on to do graduate work both in Phildelphia and at the Sorbonne, then returned to Washington DC, where she taught Latin and French. At the same time, she began to correspond with Du Bois, who became her mentor. After publishing a number of pieces in *The Crisis*, she became its literary editor from 1919 to 1926, and helped foster the careers of Jean Toomer, Langston Hughes and others. In 1924 she published *There is Confusion*, generally regarded as the first of the Renaissance's novels – it went on sale several months before Walter White's *The Fire in the Flint*, another plausible contender. Her subsequent works, which were many, included the novels *Plum Bun* (1929) and *Comedy: American Style*. More radical voices decried her excessive gentility, but few have disputed

her gifts as a novelist (she has been compared to Edith Wharton) or as a talent scout.

F is also for *Fire!!* – with two exclamation marks – a beautifully produced and almost comically short-lived magazine (one issue only: November 1926), conceived and executed by Langston Hughes, Wallace Thurman and others. It was such a costly failure that Thurman spent the next four years paying off the printer's bill.

G is for Marcus Garvey

Not, strictly speaking, a figure in the Harlem Renaissance itself, but a giant presence in the African-American culture of that time who should not be ignored. Marcus Mosiah Garvey (1887–1940) was a largely self-educated Jamaican who began his professional life as an apprentice printer, before travelling in Central America and to England. In 1914, or so he later claimed, Garvey had a vision: he would lead the African race to freedom. In 1918 he began his own newspaper, *The Negro World*, which soon found a wide readership among the dispossessed, and began to solicit funds from black supporters on lecture tours through the United States. By 1920 he was rich and famous enough to stage mass rallies, buy a freighter and a passenger-ship for his projected fleet, the Black Star Line, and persuade many thousands of the practicality of the (frankly, crackpot) Back-To-Africa scheme, designed to populate territories in Liberia with his followers. Garvey's management skills did not match his talents as an orator, and the scheme soon fell apart. Convicted of mail fraud in 1923, Garvey was eventually deported back to Jamaica. Many years later, his exploits and vision were celebrated in songs by another prominent son of Jamaica, the reggae star Bob Marley.

G is also for Gay: (reasonably) safe from persecution and prosecution, homosexual and bisexual liaisons flourished in Harlem, and many of its leading figures, from Cullen to Van Vechten, were either discreetly or openly gay.

H is for Zora Neale Hurston

For a period of some three decades, until the publication of Alice Walker's influential essay 'In Search of Zora Neale Hurston' in 1975, the quondam 'dominant black woman writer in the United States' (the words of Henry Louis Gates Jr) was virtually forgotten, even during the explosion of African-American cultural awareness in the 1960s. Today, she is probably the most famous and widely read of all the Harlem Renaissance writers, not excluding Hughes, and any decent bookshop in the United States will stock, at the very least, an edition of her classic novel *Their Eyes Were Watching God* (1937), and probably a couple of her other six main books, too. Professor Gates estimates that 'more people have read Hurston's works since 1975 than did between that date and the publication of her first novel, in 1934'.

She was born, she told everyone, in 1901 (but was she? At least one reputable account is definite that her date of birth was a full decade earlier than she claimed: 7 January 1891), in the exclusively black town of Eatonville, Florida. Her mother, a former schoolteacher, died while she was still a child, and her father, though she persisted in adoring him, soon abandoned her. She attended Morgan Academy in Baltimore, then Howard University (associate degree, 1920), where she published her first short story in the college literary magazine, and – finally, crucially – Barnard College in New York. Here, she became a pupil and disciple of that giant of American anthropology, Franz Boas. Under his influence, and with the financial support of her sponsor Charlotte Mason (see M, below) she travelled the Southern states gathering black folklore; eventually, in 1936 and 1937, she did more ambitious anthropological fieldwork, financed by two Guggenheim Fellowships, researching voodoo practices in Jamaica and Haiti. The fruits of these researches appeared in *Tell My Horse* (1938).

Meanwhile, her literary career flourished. (Her marital career did not; she separated from and then divorced her two husbands quite rapidly.) She made her Manhattan debut with the short story 'Drenched in Light', published in *Opportunity*, December 1924; co-edited the single issue of *Fire!!* (November 1926), with Wallace Thurman and Langston Hughes; was satirically portrayed as 'Sweetie Mae Carr' in Thurman's novel *Infants of the Spring* (1928); collaborated with Hughes on *Mule-Bone* (see below, L is for Langston); contributed six essays to Nancy Cunard's *Negro*; and, in May 1934, published her first novel, *Jonah's Gourd Vine*, partly based on the experiences of her own family. It became a Book of the Month Club selection; she was well and truly launched.

But her personal breakthrough came as the Renaissance was already close to finished, so that the bulk of her work might best be classified as post-Renaissance. Among the high points of her published work: *Men and Mules* (1935), a study in folklore; *Their Eyes Were Watching God* (1937); *Moses, Man of the Mountain* (1939), a novel inspired by the Book of Exodus; and *Dust Tracks on a Road* (1942) a not entirely accurate autobiography. By 1943 she was at her zenith, famous even among readers of white publications: in the course of that single year she published several major articles, received a couple of major awards, and was featured on the cover of the popular *Saturday Review*. And then came the decline, slow at first, then precipitous. She moved to Florida, and scraped a living as a librarian, a substitute teacher, a housemaid – poorly paid work, broken by spells of unemployment. By the time she suffered a stroke at the end of the 1950s, she was so poor that she had to enter a welfare hospital, where in due course she died, on 28 January 1960. Her mortal remains were buried in a – segregated – cemetery in Fort Pierce.

 is for 'If We Must Die'
The most famous of all Claude McKay's verses, first published in 1919. Though inspired by racial militancy, the poem found great favour in circles which did not suspect its author's race or politics; in later years, McKay was moved to hear of the white GI, found dead on the Russian front in the Second World War, who had a copy in his pocket:

> Like men we'll face the murderous, cowardly pack,
> Pressed to the wall, dying, but fighting back!

J is for Johnson

Two Johnsons in fact: Charles S. (for Spurgeon) Johnson and James Weldon Johnson.

The latter, already in his fifties when the Renaissance took fire, was very much an elder statesman for its ambitions and energies. Johnson was a man of many parts and considerable distinction – indeed, of such exceptional distinction in an age of entrenched racial antipathy that he often looks like a man a century ahead of his time. Among his more conspicous accomplishments, Johnson could boast of having been the founder and headmaster of a high school, the editor of America's first, albeit short-lived, daily paper (the *Daily American*, 1895–6), and a prominent lawyer – the first black man to be admitted to the Florida bar. More impressive still, he was United States consul in Venezuela and Nicaragua from 1906 to 1912 – a recognition of his substantial talents, but also a personal reward from Teddy Roosevelt, for whom he had written the campaign song 'You're All Right, Teddy'. Nor were his talents purely those of the public man. Besides his work as a songwriter – he wrote or co-wrote over 200 songs, including the unofficial 'national anthem' for African-Americans of the day, 'Lift Every Voice and Sing' – he was also a gifted writer of fiction. His novel of 1912, *The Autobiography of an Ex-Colored Man*, has often been regarded as the most sophisticated work of its kind prior to the Renaissance. Throughout the Renaissance years, from 1920 to 1931 (when he left to teach at Fisk University), he served as CEO of the NAACP. His most important literary contributions during this period consisted of two anthologies: *The Book of American Negro Poetry* (1922) and *The Book of American Negro Spirituals* (1925).

Two decades younger than James Welson, Charles S. Johnson was the editor of one of the key journals of the Harlem Renaissance, *Opportunity: A Journal of Negro Life*. Like Du Bois, the younger Johnson shrewdly peceived that the weakest link in white America's chain fence against black advancement was the sphere of art and culture. Part patron of rising talent, part strategist for racial advancement, part diplomat between the worlds of black and open-minded white, he was an essential player. His most spectacular coup was a banquet held on 21 March 1924 – in effect, a large-scale and highly successful courtship dance between aspiring black writers and powerful white publishers and editors. Within months of this enchanted evening, word of the Renaissance had spread across America and beyond.

K is for John Keats

Not a name usually associated with Harlem, but none the less a powerful, in fact the single most powerful, influence on Countee Cullen, who not only strove to imitate the Englishman, but visted his grave in Rome and wrote him a new epitaph, 'For John Keats, Apostle of Beauty':

> Not writ in water, nor in mist,
> > Sweet lyric throat, thy name;
> Thy singing lips that cold death kissed
> Have seared his own with flame.

K is also for Knopf, the publishing house which brought many Harlem works to light: among them Langston Hughes' poetry collections *The Weary Blues*, *Fine Clothes to the Jew*, his novel *Not Without Laughter* and his short stories *The Ways of White Folks*; Carl Van Vechten's *Nigger Heaven*; Walter White's *Flight*; Rudolph Fisher's *The Walls of Jericho*; Nella Larsen's *Quicksand* and *Passing*; James Weldon Johnson's celebratory history *Black Manhattan* and his autobiography *Along This Way*.

L is for Langston Hughes

The Poet Laureate of the Harlem Renaissance, Hughes left a large and various body of work, the importance of which has grown more widely recognised with the passage of time – to the extent that his reputation has often eclipsed those of Claude McKay, Countee Cullen and the other poets of the Renaissance. Born 1 February 1902 in Joplin, Missouri, Hughes had a difficult, itinerant childhood; he never forgave his father, an

American businessman based in Mexico, for separating from his mother. Hughes showed literary promise at an early age, but could not settle to the glittering academic career that was all too evidently shaping up for him, and dropped out of Columbia University in his freshman year, to travel and write in Africa and Europe. He was 'discovered' by Vachel Lindsay while working as a bus-boy in a Washington DC hotel (see V, below), and he returned to studies in 1926, the same year that Knopf, on the urging of Carl Van Vechten, published his first collection of poems. One should note that Hughes was slim, graceful and exceptionally handsome – a magnet for would-be patrons and would-be lovers of both – all? – sexes. This was the start of an intense prolific period for Hughes, who in brisk succession produced further collections of verse, a novel (*Not Without Laughter*, 1931) and the drafts of a folkloric dramatic comedy, *Mule-Bone*, co-written with Zora Neale Hurston under the patronage of Charlotte Mason. (The collaboration ended in tears.) With the help of a grant from the Rosenwald Fund, Hughes took his poetry on the road, touring the deep South and West for seven months in a Model A sedan, reciting poetry, selling cheap copies of his works, and engaging in political debate.

Royalties from his novel allowed Hughes to quit Harlem in favour of Cuba, and then, in 1932, to the Soviet Union (see below, U is for USSR), to participate in the abortive film project *Black and White*. Increasingly radical in his views, he spent more time and energy in the 1930s addressing political rallies and lecturing than on creative writing, though he kept himself afloat financially by writing a successful Broadway melodrama, *Mulatto*, an undistinguished film script, *Way Down South*, some commercial magazine fiction and the like. He returned to Harlem for good in the early 1940s, gradually eased away from his more extreme views, and settled down to producing an unceasing stream of articles, poems, libretti, anthologies and song lyrics. Briefly hounded by the McCarthy mob, he was so meek under cross-examination that McCarthy himself declared Hughes a 'friendly witness'. Like Auden, Hughes supressed his earlier, radical verses when the time came for a *Selected Poems* in 1959; like Auden, he became something of a Grand Old Man; as in the case of Auden, there are those who maintain that all of Hughes's best poetry was written while he was still young. He died on 22 May 1967.

L is also for Alain LeRoy Locke (1885–1954), the dandyish philosopher and editor of *The New Negro* (1926). He was a crucial promoter of almost all the major Renaissance figures, and courted Charlotte Mason (see M, below) to telling effect. There is a rather touching account of his earlier years in Louis Menard's *The Metaphysical Club*: Locke was the first African-American Rhodes Scholar, horribly snubbed by his fellow Americans in Oxford.

And also for **Nella Larsen** (1891–1963), some time librarian at the 135th Street branch of the New York Public Library. Her literary career was as short as it was highly publicised: she remains best known for her two novels, *Quicksand* (1928, see below) and *Passing* (1929, see P, below), which won her the Harmon Foundation's bronze medal; she also won a Guggenheim Fellowship, the first ever awarded to an African-American woman. She moved to Spain to begin work on a third novel, which was never completed, suffered from a painful divorce and a humiliating plagiarism charge, and withdrew from the public arena for the rest of her life. She spent her later years working as a nurse at New York's Gouverneur Hospital, where she was much admired by colleagues and patients alike.

 is for Claude McKay

Born in Jamaica, 15 September 1889, the youngest of eleven children, McKay began writing at a very early age and in an unusual form: poems of peasant life, written in patois. At seventeen, he met a gay English expatraite, Walter Jekyll, who encouraged his efforts and introduced him to the likes of Schopenhauer, Goethe, Whitman. He published his first two books in 1912, then, with the help of scholarships, emigrated to the United States in 1912 to study agronomy. But the course bored him, so he dropped out and spent much of the next two years simply wandering and doing casual work as a fireman, a waiter for the Pennsylvania Railroad, a porter and many other menial jobs. His experiences in the United States came as a blinding, bitter revelation: suddenly, he was the target for racial hatred and contempt; suddenly, he saw the reality of the Jim Crow laws. 'It was the first time I had ever come face to face with such manifest, implacable hate of my race, and my feelings were indescribable…'

So, when he finally arrived in Harlem in 1914, he felt as if he had passed through Purgatory and entered Paradise – 'a paradise of my own people'. He played hard, and sampled the illicit delights of opium, cocaine and sexual adventure; he also worked hard, developing his literary style and his increasingly radical political views. Once again, a white patron played a crucial role in his development: McKay was taken up by the urbane socialist Max Eastman, editor of the left-wing journals *Masses* and *The Liberator*. In 1919, horrified by the epidemic of lynchings which had followed the end of the war, McKay wrote and published his first politically engaged poems, seven of which were published by Eastman. One of these poems, 'If We Must Die' (see I, above) became his single most famous work.

In 1921, Eastman invited McKay to be an associate editor of *The Liberator*, to which the young writer contributed some forty-odd poems as well as several essays. In 1922 – *annus mirabilis* of high Modernism – McKay published his most substantial collection to date, *Harlem Shadows*. It was reviewed rapturously, and is now seen as the first fully mature publication of the Renaissance years. Yet McKay was too troubled, both personally and politically, to be content to bask in local admiration. With the help of a whip-round from the NAACP and others, he set off to the USSR (again, see U, below) to attend the Third International. He stayed there for twelve years.

M is also for Charlotte van der Veer Quick Mason: a wealthy, mildly dotty white dowager with a self-appointed mission to protect and develop the spiritual qualities she attributed to 'primitives' – that is, Native Americans and Negroes. Initially courted by Alain Locke, Mrs Mason became a significant patron both to Langston Hughes and to Zora Neale Hurston, and is estimated to have given away the then considerable sum of $75,000 to assorted Harlem artists and writers. Her generosity often proved a mixed blessing, not least because she demanded almost preposterous degrees of emotional loyalty from her pets – they were encouraged to call her 'Godmother' – in return for her cash and treats. In the case of Hurston, where the bond of patron and client came to border on the telepathic as well as the pathetic, Mrs Mason's behaviour was openly exploitative – she insisted on keeping the rights to all the folkloric material Hurston was gathering during her Chevrolet trips through the South, and she told Hurston that she could not publish anything, not even fiction, without direct permission. When Hughes and Hurston began to collaborate on *Mule-Bone*, and then fell out, the end was in sight. Mason cut off Hurston's finances for the last time in 1932, expelled Hughes from her salon and ultimately withdrew from matters Negro back to her beloved Native Americans.

N is for 'Niggerati Manor'

Zora Neale Hurston's tart and wilfully abrasive nickname for a celebrated rooming house at 267 West 136th Street, home and HQ for some of the most avant-garde and louche members of the Renaissance. One of the great attractions of the 'Manor' was that its owner, Iolanthe Sydney, would let rooms for free to those she regarded as bona fide artists and intellectuals. Zora Neale Hurston and Langston Hughes both stayed there in 1926; Wallace Thurman and his white lover 'Bunny' Stephanson also stayed for a time, as did the artist Aaron Douglas. 'Niggerati Manor' quickly became a legendary centre for bohemian debauchery of all kinds: 'gin flowed from the water taps', as one amused witness exaggerated. Hurston, who had a distinct knack for irreverent neologisms, also coined the wittily apt term 'Negrotarian' for the rich white supporters of the Renaissance.

N is also for Alain Locke's influential anthology *The New Negro*, 1926; and for **Nordic** – a contemporary term for 'white'. Hence:

O is for Ofay

Derisive Harlem slang for a white person (still in currency for many years after the Renaissance, and scarcely unknown today). The non-black dimension of the Renaissance is a rich subject in its own right, though few of the white artists who participated or served as fellow travellers are of much intrinsic interest (**Eugene O'Neill** – another 'O' – would be one of the exceptions, and the first performance of his all-black play *The Emperor Jones* in 1920 is a major event in early Renaissance chronologies). But there can be little doubt that white patrons and publishers and party-goers helped make the phenomenon possible, and – for good and ill – brought something of their own tastes and preoccupations to the movement: see C for Cunard, K for Knopf, M for Charlotte Mason, V for Carl Van Vechten...

And for *Opportunity* magazine, a key organ of the Renaissance, and sponsor of an influential series of awards dinners, first held in 1925.

P is for Passing

Any person with sufficiently light skin colouration and vaguely European features to be accepted as (or mistaken assumed to be) white was said to be 'passing': the term could be neutral, derisive, sometimes even affectionate, depending on context. Hence the title of *Passing*, the second novel by Nella Larsen, who was herself part-Danish and thus a candidate for 'passing' status; hence, too, another work about those who could infiltrate the white world:

Q is for *Quicksand*

Nella Larsen's (partly autobiographical) first novel, published in 1928. Its heroine, Helga Crane, travels from a Southern negro college, to Chicago, on to Harlem, and then to relatives in Copenhagen, where a successful painter proposes to her. Sensing that he – and the Danes in general – regard her not as one of their own, but as a kind of sensual, exotic primitive, she flees back to Harlem, which initially seems like a great relief, but which then gradually wears her down with its narrowness. Properly at home neither in black nor white America, Helga ends up in a wretched marriage, worn out with too many pregnancies.

is for Paul Robeson

The world-famous actor and singer (and athlete, lawyer, political activist) was from Princeton, not Harlem, but it was Harlem
which lured him away from the law and on to the stage, decisive
moments in that progress being his part in Eugene O'Neill's play about miscen-
genation *All God's Chillun Got Wings*, and his lead role in the 1925 revival of
O'Neill's *The Emperor Jones*, soon followed by performances in *Porgy* and
Showboat.

 is for the Scottsboro Boys

A notorious miscarriage of justice, in which nine black Alabama
youths, aged between thirteen and nineteen, were sentenced to death
for the alleged rape of two white prostitutes. In a gesture of solidarity,
Langston Hughes went to read to them during one of his poetical tours of the
South (see L, above), but they were more comforted by his cigarettes than by
his verses.

And for **the Savoy Ballroom** – the large, wildly popular venue on Lenox
Avenue (140 to 141st Streets), opened in 1926, which became the birthplace
of the 'Lindy Hop' and other athletic dances.

 is for Jean Toomer

A troubled and fascinating man, best remembered today for his one-
off masterpiece *Cane* (1923), one of the earliest and by far the most
formally innovative of all the novels produced during the
Renaissance – a genre-resisting work which combines techniques derived from
poetry, drama and reportage. Dazzlingly handsome in a racially ambiguous way
(see above, P is for Passing), Toomer suffered throughout his life from the
torments of uncertain identity. He was born on 26 December 1894, and grew
up in an affluent, indeed grand, white neighbourhood of Washington DC. Like
McKay, his years before coming to New York were impoverished, peripatetic
and often miserable. He worked as a salesman for Ford Motors, a professional

body-builder and PE teacher, a welder and in other marginal jobs; when not working, he lapsed into tramping. After seven years of this rootless existence, he found salvation in a chance meeting with the novelist Waldo Frank, who introduced Toomer to a crowd of writers who lived and loafed in Greenwich Village: the most famous figures eventually to emerge from this idealistic milieu were Malcolm Cowley and Hart Crane. He began to write, to publish, and to be praised by major critics. *Cane*, though it sold dismally, was enthusiastically reviewed and inspired many of the younger Renaissance writers. But Toomer had already peaked as a writer, and though he continued to churn out endless fragments of further strange works, he had no more literary career. Instead, he became first a disciple, then an employee of the strange Armenian mystic Gurdjieff, and for a time managed to rope in some other notable Harlemites to the Gurdjieffian cause. On the rare occasions when editors sought the rights to his earlier work for anthologies of African-American writing, he would refuse to admit that he was black. By the time of his death in 1967, he was all but forgotten; he did not survive to see the republication and warm revaluation of *Cane*.

T is also for 'the Talented Tenth' – see above, D is for W.E.B. Du Bois.

And for **Wallace Thurman**, the short-lived (1902–34) playwright and novelist, originally from Utah. He made his first Harlem splash by editing *Fire!!* (which lasted for one issue; see F, above), then its successor *Harlem* (two issues), then went on to write a hit Broadway play, also called *Harlem*, and three novels. Disillusioned with the movement, he went to Hollywood for a couple of years, then returned ill, alcoholic and broken. He died in City Hospital after ignoring his doctor's warnings about drink.

U is for the USSR

On 14 June 1932, Langston Hughes climbed the gangplank of the *Europa*, the last New York passenger to board the Europe-bound vessel. His ultimate destination: Russia, which he regarded as the great hope of oppressed humanity. Twenty-two black comrades, male and female, shared his third-class deck (co-incidentally, Alain Locke was up in first, travelling on Charlotte Mason's business) – a delegation which would present the realities of life in the American South in a projected Soviet film, *Black and White*. (The title comes from Mayakovsky.) The film was never completed, but Hughes spent many months in the USSR, travelling, lecturing, participating in conferences. Nor was he the only Harlem intellectual to seek Paradise among the Soviets – Claude McKay (see M, above) recalled being greeted as a kind of good luck charm on the streets of Moscow, and one one occasion was hoisted up by a huge cheering crowd of soldiers, sailors and civilians: 'Never in my life did I feel prouder of being an African, a black, and make no mistake about it, I was like a black Ikon.'

V is for Carl Van Vechten

With the possible exception of Nancy Cunard, Van Vechten was far and away the most colourful, as it were, of all the white fellow-travellers of the Harlem Renaissance, and of very great importance as an energetic publicist, go-between, host, sponsor, critic, and general gadfly. Already well into his forties when the Renaissance gathered momentum (he was born in Cedar Rapids, Iowa in 1880), this dandyish, gay music critic, collector and photographer was initially lured up to Harlem in about 1924 by the jazz and the blues. Before long, he was a regular fixture on the scene, usually acompanied by some white celebrity (Somerset Maugham, Edmund Wilson, William Faulkner) to whom he would show off his intimacy with the black scene. The next move was to host a series of lavish parties at his apartment (150 West 55 Street) explicitly designed to break down the barriers of colour. Everyone who was anyone attended: from Uptown, the likes of Countee Cullen, Bill 'Bojangles' Robinson, Paul Robeson and Bessie Smith; from Downtown, George Gershwin, Theodore Dreiser, Helena Rubinstein and the Astors.

Realising what rich subject matter was passing right before him, Van Vechten set himself to writing the novel *Nigger Heaven* (1926) – a title received about as warmly then as it might be today, though he appears to have been naive rather than calculatedly offensive, and was genuinely baffled by the work's frosty reception among the very circles he thought he was doing a favour.

W.E.B. Du Bois wrote that 'it is an affront to the hospitality of black folk and to the intelligence of white… It is a caricature. It is worse than untruth because it is a mass of half-truths.' Despite these more than justified strictures, the novel became a best-seller – 100,000 copies sold within weeks of publication – and served as a *vade mecum* for those whites who felt like 'Van Vechtening' around Harlem. In fact, it launched what became known as 'Harlemania'.

Sometimes treated harshly by those historians who consider him a parasite or a predator, Van Vechten is an interesting figure, and not only for his invaluable, if occasionally self-serving, Harlem activities: he was an immensely perceptive critic of many arts – a pioneering appreciator of, among others, Stravinsky and Isadora Duncan – a champion of Gertrude Stein and Wallace Stevens, an elegant satirist in the Firbankian vein, a somewhat better novelist than *Nigger Heaven* suggests, and a pretty good portrait photographer. (Among his more unpredictable productions was a much admired book about cats.) He may well be ripe for a thorough upwards revaluation.

V is also for Vachel Lindsay, in the 1920s one of America's most popular poets, who was partly responsible for launching Langston Hughes's career. In November 1925, Lindsay was about to give a reading at a fashionable Washington hotel. Hughes, who was working as a bus-boy (see above, L is for Langston Hughes), shyly dropped three of his poems on Lindsay's dinner table. Later in the evening, Lindsay boomed that he had just encountered a poet, and read all three verses to the audience.

W is for A'Leilia Walker

Parties were the loudly beating heart of the Harlem Renaissance, and there was no doubt in anyone's mind as to who threw the most lavish parties. A'Leilia Walker was the Empress of Harlem socialising, its greatest hostess and one of its most flamboyant presences. Heiress to a fortune built up by her mother, C.J. Walker, on the back of a successful hair-straightening product (her mother's life story would make a juicy rags-to-riches novel or mini-series), she dressed in lavish style – ermines, sables, silks and a silver turban. Untouched either by frugality or a sense of civic responsiblity, she set about spending her fortune with uncompromising single-mindedness. Her most ostentatious parties were usually held outside Harlem, in the Hudson Valley mansion she had inherited – Villa Lewaro, designed by New York's first licensed black architect and dripping with expensive fittings, including a gold-plated piano and Hepplewhite furniture. Her domestic staff wore white wigs, doublet and hose.

In 1928, suddenly catching the culture bug, she decided to become hostess to an artistic salon, and redesigned her Harlem townhouse at 108–110 West 136th Street for the purpose, calling it the 'Dark Tower', after a column written by Countee Cullen in *Opportunity*. Legend, possibly ill-founded, claims that she liked to play games with racial stereotypes, and would serve her white guests soul food (pig's feet and chitterlings) while her black guests dined on caviar and pheasant. The Dark Tower was furnished with Aubusson carpeting, Louis XIV furniture, Sèvres china and similar expensive knick-knacks, and its guests generally vied to outdo each other in the item of furs and jewels and silks. Her guest list, it was said, read like a 'Blue book of the seven arts'. It is doubtful whether A'Leilia herself read very widely in the works of her pet writers (or in anything else), and many high-minded Harlem intellectuals distrusted her profoundly, but there is no question that she added hugely to the gaiety of the times.

A'Leilia's spree was short-lived; barely a decade, from shortly after her mother's death in 1919 to the Wall Street Crash in 1929. Walker Hair Products was no more immune to the Great Depression than any other company, and by the end of 1930 A'Leilia was facing financial ruin. The Villa Lewaro was auctioned off at silly prices – strip-mined, as the Harlem press (correctly) saw it, by opportunistic white buyers. She died on 17 August 1931, after a midnight snack of lobster and chocolate cake washed down with champagne. Fifteen thousand people filed by her body as it rested in state, and her funeral was like a state occasion. Looking back on it, Langston Hughes saw the funeral as symbolic of another kind of death: 'That was really the end of the gay times of the New Negro era in Harlem…'

W is also for another Walker: Alice Walker, the novelist, who launched the Zora Neale Hurston revival in 1975 with an article in *Ms* magazine.

X is for 'Xylophonic Footsteps'

The trademark move of Bill 'Bojangles' Robinson (1876–1949; a.k.a. Luther Robinson), described by newspapers of the day as the greatest of all tap-dancers. He was certainly the best-known, and even before the First World War (in which he served; it was Robinson who, as drum major, led the military band ahead of the triumphant 369th infantry regiment as they made their historic march up Fifth Avenue) he was able to earn the astonishing sum of $2,000 a week on the Keith vaudeville circuit, where he was billed as 'the Dark Cloud of Joy'. 'Discovered' by the mainstream press in 1928, he soon became nationally famous, boosted his salary more than threefold to $6,500 a week, and went on to star in the movies with Shirley Temple. Robinson was one of the defining presences of the Renaissance, whether entertaining on stage or being entained in salons. Like many another sometime showbusiness millionaire, he died in poverty.

Y is for 'Yet Do I Marvel'

The most frequently cited poem by Countee Cullen: a rather self-conscious and academic sonnet on the ways of God ('I doubt not God is good, well-meaning, kind…'). The sestet, which ends with a notorious final couplet (see C, above), and suggests that he may have been reading Blake, runs, in full:

> Inscrutable His ways are, and immune
> To catechism by a mind too strewn
> With petty cares to slightly understand
> What awful brain compels His awful hand.
> Yet I do marvel at this curious thing:
> To make a poet black, and bid him sing!

Z is for Ziegfeld

Florenz Ziegfeld, the show-biz impresario, was also a notable 'Negrotarian' who frequently hired black performers for his revues – Bert Williams, for example, who from 1910 to 1920 became the first African-American star of the *Ziegfeld Follies*.

Z is also for the fortunately antiquated term 'Zip Coon' – a stock figure from the old 'Nigger Minstrel' entertainments. The Harlem Renaissance may not have been an unqualified success, but it played more than a minor part in consigning such images to the dustbin of history.

A
HILDEGARD
OF BINGEN
ALPHABET

is for Abbess

All but unknown to the world at large for the first four, secluded decades of her life, the visionary woman we now call Hildegard of Bingen (1098–1179) rapidly became one of the most prominent figures of the twelfth century – a magnet for pilgrims and a religious authority to whom even kings and emperors felt obliged to defer. Though she was often neglected or all but wholly forgotten throughout the eight centuries after her death, Hildegard's enthusiastic and multi-faceted rediscovery in our own time – a cultural revelation and revaluation which is still very much in progress – has gone a considerable way towards making her former eminence comprehensible. To a secular age, it is less her unquestioned piety than the sheer range of her accomplishments which is most immediately impressive. As a writer and scholar, her studies embraced not only the expected areas of theology and philosophy, but – albeit in forms appropriate to her pre-scientific age – the disciplines we would now class as anatomy, anthropology, botany, cosmology, geology, medicine and zoology. Her acknowledged genius in poetry and music (see below, C is for Composer) is still more overwhelming. (And her obvious appeal to feminist historians – she has been admiringly described as 'one tough sister' – needs no labouring.)

And yet, despite her great eminence in later life, Hildegard was granted only one major public honour. She was named Abbess of Rupertsberg on 18 April 1163, in a decree of Frederick I. (This is the sole contemporary document of her official standing.) It was a late honour: Hildegard was already sixty-five.

is for Barbarossa

Frederich Barbarossa, also known as Kaiser Frederick I. On his coronation – 9 March 1152, in Aachen – she sent him a letter paying her respects. A couple of years later, in 1154 or thereabouts, she met him at the royal palatinate in Ingelheim; we do not know what they discussed. When a schism opened up between Frederick and the papacy in 1159 with the crowning of the first 'Imperial Pope' or anti-pope, Victor IV (the schism was to continue for eighteen years), Hildegard initially maintained neutrality. Later, though, with the coming of the second anti-pope, Pascal III, in 1164, she adopted a more militant tone towards Frederick and declared her allegiance to the true Pope, Alexander III; a stand she renewed in an even more stongly worded letter written in response to the installation of the third anti-pope, Callistus III, in 1168. The schism lasted until 1177, just two years before her death, when Kaiser Frederick and Pope Alexander held a meeting of reconcilation in Frieden von Venedig.

B is also for Bernard of Clairvaux; see below, L is for Letters.

C is for Composer

Though her songs and compositions were widely known as early as her fiftieth year (a letter from Odo of Paris dated 1148 confirms this), it would have perplexed her contemporaries greatly had some prophet foreseen that she would be known to distant posterity first and foremost as a composer, rather than a woman of God. Her musical works are contained in the book called the *Symphonia*; the complete title may have been the *Symphony of the Harmony of Celestial Relations*. Hildegard wrote more than seventy liturgical songs, both for her own establishments and, later in life, for others: antiphons, hymns, sequences, responsories, and versicles. Some editions of the *Symphonia* also include the musical *Ordo virtutum* or *Play of the Virtues* (an abbreviated, non-musical version of which also appears as the final vision of the *Scivias* – see S, below). It depicts a wandering soul, torn between the tempations of Satan and the urgings of a choir of embodied Virtues. According to some accounts, this work was performed by nuns at Rupertsberg in 1152.

D is for Disibodenberg

At the age of eight, in 1106, Hildegard was sent by her parents to the Benedictine monastery of Disibodenberg, at the confluence of the Glan and Nahe rivers. Here, she was put in the care of Jutta of Spanheim (see J, below), whose father, Count Stephen of Spanheim, had founded a hermitage on the site. She lived here in humble retreat until 1136, when Jutta died, and Hildegard was unanimously chosen as the mother of the community. In 1141 came the first of the great visions which led to the *Scivias* and changed her life; in 1148 another form of vision instructed her to deal with the increasingly cramped conditions at the cloister by building a new foundation at Rupertsberg, across from Bingen. The monks of Disibodenberg were ferociously opposed to this plan, but Hildegard put up a spirited and ultimately successful resistance, and led her sisters – about twenty in number – to Rupertsberg in 1150. According to a slightly later source, the new foundation could house fifty nuns, two priests, seven poor women, and assorted domestic servants and guests. Legal wranglings with the monks of Disibodenberg dragged on for many years, but Rupertsberg remained her home and headquarters until her death on 17 September 1179.

In 1170, Hildegard compiled a *Life of St Disibod* at the behest of Abbot Helenger of Disibodenberg. This text is the principal source for almost everything we know of the saint, represented as a wandering Irish bishop, exiled from his native country, who eventually built a hermitage at the site which henceforth became known as Disibodenberg. Hildegard also wrote a Responsory and a Sequence for the saint.

In the decades after her death, armed battles were fought on the site, and the monastery was transformed into a fortress before its final ruin in the middle of the thirteenth century.

E is for Eugenius III

It was Pope Eugenius who brought Hildegard to the attention of the powerful and the learned. He sent a commission to Disibodenberg to report on the authenticity of her visions, and in 1147–8, at the Synod of Trier, Eugenius proclaimed *ex cathedra* that her work (by which he meant the portions of the *Scivias* he had read aloud to an assembly of theologians) was indeed divinely inspired. He went on to give her permission to continue recording her visions – a happy task she went on to perform in her three major theological works: see below, T is for Trilogy. Her known correspondence includes four letters to Eugenius and two of the Pope's replies.

is for Fish

Connoisseurs of the *Physica*, Hildegard's vast compendium of medical folklore, are often particularly impressed by its accounts of fish – evidently drawn from close personal observation of the Glan and Nahe (Disibodenberg stands at their confluence) and of the Rhine near Rupertsberg. Among the thirty-five indigenous species she describes are eels, herring, perch, pike, salmon, sturgeon, trout; lacking the Latin names for these fish, she often coined German names, some of which are still in use. Her piscine lore is an interesting compound of the proto-scientific and the merely folkloric. One the one hand, for example, she appears to have had a biologically accurate account of the process of spawning; on the other, she recommends, for the cure of dropsy (*Physica*, Fish, 2) extracting the bladder of a sturgeon, immersing it in water until the liquid tastes fishy, and then taking frequent draughts.

 is for Gottfried

Which is to say, the monk Gottfried of Disibodenberg, her first biographer. He became her secretary in 1174–5, after the death of Volmar (see V, below), having been dispatched by Abbot Helenger to be the prior at Rupertsberg. Soon, he began work on the *Hildegard-Vita* or *Vita Santae Hildegardis*, of which he managed to complete only Book I before his death in the early months of 1176. His task was taken over, and Books II and III of the *Hildegard-Vita* completed, by a team of monks under the direction of Theodoric of Echternach, in the period between 1180 and 1190.

 **is for Healing (and *Heilkunde*)**

The theme of healing enters Hildegard's life in both sacred and secular forms. As a holy virgin, Book III of the *Vita* explains, a healing force shone from her so fiercely that almost any sick person who came near her was immediately and completely cured. (For further details, see below, M is for Miracles) Hildegard was also greatly preoccupied with more prosaic forms of healing (again, see below, N is for *Naturkunde*). It was a natural topic of fascination for a woman whose entire life could fairly be described, to echo Alexander Pope, as a long disease:

I is for Illnesses

Serious illnesses afflicted Hildegard at various periods of her life. The gravest of these occurred in 1155; from the three years of 1158 to 1161; and for another three years between 1167 to 1170, including an exceptionally severe forty-day period which brought her very close to death. Hildegard describes her symptoms at this time as including sluggishness of the blood, weakness of the limbs, and an exhaustion which she compares to brown winter grass.

Some twentieth- and twenty-first-century commentators – notably the historian of science Charles Singer – have been sceptical as to the view that her principal affliction must have been caused by demons, and have proposed instead, with some plausibility, that she may have been a martyr to migraine. Singer's theories, outlined as early as 1917 in his essay 'The Scientific Views and Visions of Saint Hildegard' (*Studies in the History and Method of Science*) have been taken up and endorsed by, among others, the neurologist and popular-science writer Oliver Sacks in *Migraine: Understanding a Common Disorder* (1985).

Migraine was certainly a complaint identified, if not quite comprehended, by Hildegard herself, who held that migraines – like that other malady of monks, melancholy – were the product of an excess of black bile.

J is for Jutta of Spanheim

An anchoress of noble birth, and Hildegard's spiritual mother from 1106 until her death thirty years later, in 1136. (See above, D is for Disibodenberg.)

J is also for the American feminist artist Judy Chicago, who in 1979 included Hildegard as one of the great women of history celebrated in her famous ceramic-cum-conceptual piece *The Dinner Party*, a trans-historical banquet table in which each place-setting alludes both to the female genitalia and to some aspect of the particular woman of accomplishment assigned to that place.

is for *Kyrium*

Or, in full, *Kyrium Presbyter Derisit, Ascendat Paenitens Homo*: 'The priest ridiculed the Lord; let him rise again as a penitent.' This phrase is the fulcrum of a story found in the *Vita*, Book III, Chapter 16. It appears that a young priest of Schwabia, whose conduct was not always as pious as it should have been, entered his church one evening to light the sanctuary lamp, and discovered – to the holy terror of other witnesses – that some non-human agency had lit the altar candles and spread the altar cloth. At the centre of the cloth, in the shape of a cross, were five cryptic letters (P being pressed into double service):

K

A P H

D

This occult message remained intact on the cloth for seven days, then disappeared on the eighth. For the next sixteen years, the troubled priest consulted every learned cleric he could find, but none could interpret the letters, until finally he consulted Hildegard. Like Daniel – as her biographer underlines – Hildegard saw the meaning at once: 'The priest ridiculed the Lord; let him rise again as a penitent.' Overcome with remorse and dread, the priest resolved to mend his ways, became a monk, and spent the rest of his days in atonement.

is for Letters

In her later life, Hildegard became a remarkably prolific, not to say unstoppable writer of letters: about 400 of these have survived, and her correspondents range from the humblest to the most elevated. Few of them strike any kind of personal note. Her major correspondence with public figures begins after her vindication by Pope Eugenius at the Synod of Trier in 1147–8: she writes, among others, to the Pope himself, on the matter of Abbess Richardis of Stade (he replied); to Frederick I (including a note of respect shortly after his election in 1152, and a thank-you for his granting a deed of security to Rupertsberg in 1163); to Archbishop Eberhard of Salzburg; Henry II of England and his wife Eleanor; and to Archbishop Christian of Rome

Even before this outpouring, however, she had already corresponded with Abbot Bernard of Clairvaux in about 1146–7. A Cistercian, Bernard (1090–1153) was one of the most influential religious thinkers in Christendom: Pope Eugenius III, in earlier life Bernardo Pignatelli, had been one of his pupils. It was Bernard who first urged Eugenius to read the *Scivias*.

Her letter to one Wibert of Gembloux , written when she was seventy-seven and near death, became famous for its eloquent account of her visions, and her explanation that she saw them by daylight, and in waking hours – saw them not with her bodily organs, but inwardly, so that she never lost consciousness. (Wibert later – 1177 – took on the short-lived task of being her final secretary.) She also wrote to the likes of Tengswich of Anderbach, Richardis of Stade, Hartwig of Bremen, Elizabeth of Schonau, and many, many others, including her brother Hugo.

There are many editions of her letters, notably the German *Briefweschsel*.

is for Miracles

Many of the short chapters in the third book of the *Vita* consist of anecdotes – sometimes only a paragraph or so in length – telling of her miraculous powers to heal the sick and banish evil spirits. The chapter headings announce their own stories: 'Healing of a Young Girl with Three Days of Fever'; 'Healing of a Monk with Similar Suffering'; 'Curing of a Lady with a Tumor of the Neck'; 'Healing of a Throat Ailment' and so on. She was particularly gifted in ending cases of possesssion. Nor did she always have to be physically present to make her merciful interventions. It appears, for instance, that women suffering the agonies of childbirth were often greatly relieved by having just one or two hairs from Hildegard's person laid against their bare skin; that Hildegard could make appearances in dreams (and so warn pious people of imminent danger), or in feverish visions of the desperately ill, who would at once regain their health. Notwithstanding this facility for effecting supernatural cures, Hildegard devoted much of her non-mystical life to the study of orthodox medicine, or what amounted to scientific medicine in her day. Thus:

 is for *Naturkunde*

The German name for the *Physica* or *Natural History*, written in the period 1151–8. Also known as the *Book of Simple Medicine* – and thus the companion volume to her other major work, the *Causes and Cures*, which is also known as the *Book of Compound Medicine*. It is a large work: nine books and 513 chapters, of which over half – 293 chapters – are devoted to botanical lore. She also applies herself to geology (precious stones and metals), and, though some of her observations on the creatures of land, sea and air now seem less than rigorous (she discourses at some length on the unicorn), the range of her learning is none the less impressive and her powers of observation frequently acute. And even when she falls short as a naturalist, her accounts are often charming and memorable. For example:

 is for Owls

In the *Naturkunde*, she writes that 'the owl is warm and has the habits of a thief, who knows the day but avoids it, and loves the night'. Among the folkloric beliefs to which she cleaved were that the owl hates all other birds; can sense when a person is about to die; is attracted to sites of imminent sorrow, but always flees before misery erupts.

P is for Page

Dr Christopher Page, the emiment scholar of medieval poetry and music, and director of the Early Music vocal ensemble Gothic Voices, whose CD *A Feather on the Breath of God* – the title is taken from the *Scivias* – introduced many thousands of listeners to the delights of Hildegard's sequences and hymns. To the surprise of almost everyone concerned, the CD, released in 1983, won a *Gramophone* award, went to the top of the classical music charts and inspired many, many subsequent recordings by other ensembles. Dr Page informs me that the record has sold well in excess of 300,000 copies… and emphasises that his contract did not, alas, include a royalties agreement. Dr Page's next contribution to Hildegard studies will be found in his epic two-volume work *The Rise of Western Europe and Its Music*.

P is also for the **Physica**; and for **Preaching Tours**; and for the **Private Language** which, *pace* the wisdom of the later Wittgenstein (who explained that no such thing could exist), Hildegard outlined in two minor works, the *Lingua ignota* and the *Litterae ignota*, between 1150 and 1160. Hildegard's invented language includes some 900 words, most of which appear to be of use in medical or biological studies. Its fundamental purpose remains, to date, cryptic.

Q is for Queen Eleanor of Aquitaine

To whom Hildegard wrote in about 1154, instructing the wife of Henry II that her mind was like a wall covered with clouds, that she should calm herself and seek stability in her relations with both God and man.

R is for Rupertsberg

As noted: Hildegard moved her convent here in 1150, in the face of opposition from the monks of Disibodenberg. It was in the monastery of Rupertsberg that she died on 17 September 1179. According to her earliest biographers, a marvellous perfume arose from her grave.

R is also for Richardis of Stade; in 1151, Hildegard opposed her dismissal as abbess of a convent in Bassum, Saxony. Richardis died within a year.

S is for *Scivias*

Hildegard's earliest major literary work. It began with a vision she had experienced in 1141; she felt compelled to make a record of what she had seen. The title may be translated as 'Know the Way' or 'Know the Ways'. The work is divided into three books, each book being subdivided into six, seven and thirteen accounts of visions – visions which enlightened her as to the deepest realities of creation, redemption and sanctification. Book I tells, among other things, of the rebel angels and their fall, Adam and his fall, the nature of the universe, the soul, and the angelic orders. Book II tells of the struggle against Satan and the coming of Christ. Book III treats the conditions of salvation and the Last Judgement. She completed the text in 1151.

In 1999, the novelist and critic Marina Warner named *Scivias* her Book of the Millennium.

And, of course, for **the *Symphonia***: see above, C is for Composer.

T is for Tours

Despite her often invalid condition, Hildegard undertook several major preaching tours. The first, which coincided with the early months of her first three-year illness (1158–61), included stops in Mainz, Wertheim, Wurzburg, Kitzingen, Ebrach and Bamburg. The second, in 1160, was the so-called Rhine–Lothringen journey, took in Trier, Metz and Krauftal bei Zabern. The third, known as the Rhine trip, saw her in Boppard,

Andernach, Sieburg and Cologne, among other stops. For her fourth and final tour, see Z.

T is also for her theological Trilogy. After the *Scivias*, she wrote the *Liber vitae meritorum* – *Book of Life's Merits*; and then the *Liber divinorum operum* – *Book of Divine Works*, begun in 1163 and concluded in 1173–4.

U is for Ulrich

Ingeborg Ulrich (1929–89), author of *Hildegard von Bingen: Mystikerin, Heilerin, Gefahrtin der Engel* (1990; *Mystic, Healer, Companion of the Angels*; translated into English by Linda M. Maloney, 1993). This is an idiosyncratic work, part biography, part novel, part miniature anthology of Hildegard's own words. Hildegard has inspired at least two other recent works of fiction: *The Journal of Hildegard of Bingen* (1993) by Barbara Lachman, and *Scarlet Music: Hildegard of Bingen. A Novel* (1997) by Joan Ohanneson.

V is for Volmar of Disibodenberg

Hildegard's teacher, a monk, who served as her secretary until his death in 1173. He warmly supported her composition of the *Scivias*, and is sometimes suspected of having had at least some part in it, though Hildegard insisted that the only role he played when it came to transcribing her visions was in correcting her grammar.

V is also for Visions, and for the *Vita*.

W is for Writing

To recapitulate, then: Hildegard is the author of three large visionary works of theology (the *Scivias*, the *Liber vitae meritorum* and the *Liber divinorum operum*), two major works of natural history, medicine and related topics (the *Physica*, the *Causae et curae*), a cycle of divine poems set to her own music (the *Symphonia*), a musical play (the *Ordo virtutum*), two hagiographies (*Vita S. Ruperti* and *Vita S. Disibodi*) and hundreds of letters. It is far from impossible that further works may be uncovered.

W is also for the Hildegard Websites: of which dozens have been set up in the last two decades or so, most of them fairly New Agey, Green or feminist in tone and general tendency.

X is for Christ

In the third book of the *Vita*, Chapter 24, Theodoric quotes at length from Hildegard's account of her personal vision of Christ, who appeared to her at the very end of her agonising forty-day illness. Hildegard reports that on His arrival, she experienced an intense flood of joy, and her body was suffused with the delightful smell of balsam. Christ commanded her tormenting spirits to quit her – 'Away with you; I do not wish her to be punished any longer!', and the demons fled in a chorus of shame-ridden howls. Her illness ended at once. Hildegard's euphemism for Christ is 'the most beautiful and intimately beloved Person'.

Y is for Youth

Born in Bermersheim, near Alzey, in the diocese of Mainz, some time in 1098, Hildegard was the tenth and last child of a nobleman, Hildebert of Bermersheim and his wife Mechtild. We know the names of seven siblings: Drutwin, Hugo (precentor of Mainz Cathedral and, for a brief period after the death of Volmar, Hildegard's secretary), Roricus (a canon), Irmengard, Odilia, Jutta (not to be confused with Jutta of Spanheim), and Clementia (a nun at Rupertsberg). That so many of their offspring went into holy orders lends some weight to the claim that, though themselves both rich and wordly, they were of a pious disposition and happy to let their youngest daughter die to the world. (It is even possible that, as a tenth child, Hildegard might have been regarded as a kind of biological 'tithe'.) Her parents seem to have regarded her as uniquely gifted from her earliest days, and not without justice: as soon as she was capable of the most rudimentary forms of speech, Hildegard told her family of her visions, which had begun with the terrifying visitation of a brilliant light when she was only three. Later, she grew more discreet and confided these visions only to Jutta and Volmar.

The painful illnesses which plagued her mature years also began early, preventing her from going into the open air save on rare occasions, and, as Gottfried observes, making her life into 'a picture of precious death'. She was just eight when she entered the cloister at Disibodenberg and, it seems, somewhere between fourteen and seventeen when she made her vows and was given her veil by Bishop Otto of Bamberg. Her education had its limits; according to her earliest biographers, Jutta taught her nothing save the Rule of St Benedict, humility, chastity, and singing the Psalms of David. In later life, Hildegard habitually referred to herself as *indocta*, untutored, though in reality Volmar (see above) must have taught her a great deal. She claims to have owed her power to read and interpret the Bible to a blinding shaft of light from the sky which struck her when she was twenty-four; on the other hand, she could read and write Latin, and had closely studied both the Church Fathers and assorted medieval authors (at least in extracts).

 is for Zorn

Zorn, the German word for 'Wrath', is a personified Vice in the *Liber vitae meritorum*. He has a mainly human face, but the mouth of a scorpion, and terrifying eyes which show more white than pupil. His arms end in claws, his torso is like a crab and his limbs are serpentine. His head is hairless, and he vomits fire.

Z is also for Zoology; and, finally, for **Zweifalten**, the final stop on her last preaching tour in 1170–71.

Here ends the Alphabet of the Blessed Hildegard.

A
PAUL KLEE
ALPHABET

is for Abstraction

'The more fearful the world becomes, the more art becomes abstract': Paul Klee, 1915. Few would wish to deny that the world of 1915 was an exceptionally fearful place, and Klee had as sound reasons as any European to be in state of deep terror. His close friend and colleague August Macke had died in the first few weeks of the war; Klee himself was just a few months short of being drafted and, so he feared, meeting a similar fate. (In the event, Klee was lucky: his period of war service was spent away from the front. His other colleague, Franz Marc, died in March 1916.) But was Klee right in implying that abstract art is a response to the peculiar terrors of the modern world – a necessary zone of retreat, a place of separate peace? Even if it was so for him, it was not always regarded in the same way by his contemporaries. Artists had moved towards non-representational art for all manner of avowed reasons – a (quasi-) scientific quest to bring painting into line with the revised conceptions of reality introduced by modern physics; a (quasi-) philosophical exploration of the Platonic forms underlying palpable reality; a social-revolutionary wish to strip art of its bourgeois reassurances; an urge to Make It New; a craze for quests into the so-called Fourth Dimension; a spiritual hunger for the Absolute...

At the time Klee wrote, abstract art was still a very new thing under the sun, barely more than a noisy toddler. Historians have achieved no reliable consensus as to the identity of the first abstract painting, but one can reason-ably trace the origins of modern abstraction to experiments which began barely five years earlier, in several different European locations, around the years 1910–11. One clear point of departure was Paris, home to the increasingly radical Cubist work of Picasso and Braque, who were soon to be followed on the path to abstraction by the varied likes of Picabia and Marcel Duchamp; home, as well, to the so-called Orphism of Robert Delaunay (1885–1941) – a major influence on Klee – and his wife Sonia Delaunay (1885–1979).

Meanwhile, in Italy, some of the machine-happy and proto-fascist Futurists, notably Severini and Balla, were dabbling in their own modes of abstraction; in Germany, the Munich-based Russian Wassily Kandinsky (1866–1944), deeply influenced by Goethe's theories of colour, was not merely creating his own mode of painterly abstraction but providing it with a widely read theoretical manifesto, *On the Spiritual in Art* (1912); from Holland, Piet Mondrian (1872–1944), like Kandinsky, was making his own ventures into the abstract as part of a larger spiritual mission, and was specifically a disciple of Madame Blavatsky's briefly modish ersatz-faith Theosophy; and in Russia, which was on the brink of becoming the Soviet Union, Kasimir Malevich (1878–1935) was working on such unadorned geometrical patterns as *Eight Red Rectangles* (1915) and *Dynamic Suprematism* (also 1915). Add to this simultaneous, continent-wide eruption of abstract art the work of, among others, Kurt Schwitters, Hans (a.k.a. Jean) Arp, Naum Gabo, Vladimir Tatlin, El Lissitsky and dozens of similar contemporaries or near-contemporaries, and one can see that Klee's engagement with abstraction made him very much a man of his times. Like many of the others, he tended to see his work as a spiritual enterprise; like a lot (though not all) of the others, and like their forebears in the Romantic movement, he was haunted by images of lost Paradise.

What, then, was the distinctive nature of Klee's contribution to this new movement? One answer – not a complete one, yet not too misleading – is that he was of all the abstract tribe the most keenly alive to what might be called the 'musical' qualities of non-representational art. (Recall Pater's dictum that all art aspires to the condition of music.) The son of a music teacher, and himself highly trained as a performer, Klee's rapturous admiration for – above all other musical forms – the polyphony of the late eighteenth-century composers told deeply in his work, where he sought to find visual equivalents for those otherwise unequalled miracles of formal organisation. He thought of shape as, among other things, rhythm, and of colour as harmony. By 1917, he was confident enough of his achievements that he could proudly claim that 'polyphonic painting is superior to music in that here, the time element becomes a spatial element. The notion of simultaneity stands out even more richly.'

And, of course, Klee was more than just an abstract artist. Considerably more.

B is for Bern

Bern – or, strictly speaking, one of its suburbs, Münchenbuchsee – was Paul Klee's place of birth, on 28 December 1879. Most reference books call him a Swiss artist, but since his father, Hans Klee (1849–1940), was German, Paul retained German citizenship throughout his life. (His mother, *née* Ida Marie Frick (1855–1921) was of unambiguously Swiss descent.) Though he was to travel quite widely in Europe, America and North Africa, Bern remained Klee's home throughout the years of his education, early career and final illness (1936–40). He attended the Bern Gymnasium from 1886 to 1898, where he cultivated a lifelong interest in, among other subjects, French literature and the classical world. (See below, X is for Xenophon.) Uncertain for a long time as to whether he should concentrate on music or art, he finally settled for the latter and set off for Munich in October 1898. Here, he studied art at the Academy under Franz von Stuck – Kandinsky was a fellow student, but they did not cross paths – and met his future wife Lily, to whom he became secretly engaged in 1901. After a tour of Italy (see I, below), he returned to Bern from 1902 to 1906, and continued to visit or reside there at various intervals over the next three decades. He married Lily in 1906, and the newlyweds moved back to Munich for several years. His first solo exhibition was held at the Kunstmuseum Bern in August 1910, and the town is now home to the Paul Klee Foundation.

B is also for the Bauhaus (see G, below), and **the *blaue Reiter*** (see K, below), and for **Walter Benjamin** (see S, below).

C is for the 'Creative Credo'

The familiar English name for a celebrated essay by Klee which appeared in an anthology of artists' writings, *Schöpferische Konfession*, in November 1918. It begins with one of his most famous maxims:

> Art does not reproduce the visible; rather, it makes visible.

C is also for Cézanne, who bowled him over at first sight ('In my eyes he is the teacher *par excellence*, much more of a teacher than Van Gogh': Klee, 1909); and for Voltaire's **Candide**, which Klee adored and, from 1911–12 onwards, illustrated with rather elongated, spectral figures (the results were not published until 1922); and for **Children's Art**, of which Klee was among the earliest admirers (though not the very earliest: for instance, the English novelist Samuel Butler was a notable collector of child art in the late nineteenth century); and for **Colour**: as he told his Bauhaus students:

To paint well is simply this: to put the right colour in the right place.

is for Diaries

Between the years 1898 and 1918, Klee filled four private notebooks with observations on literature, music and art, reflections on the creative process, memories of his childhood, comments on his (later famous) friends, including Franz Marc and Wassily Kandinsky, accounts of his military service and so on. Edited by his son Felix in 1957 and translated into English in 1964, the *Diaries* soon became acknowledged as a classic of their kind, worthy of a place on the shelf next to the *Letters* of Van Gogh – of whom Klee writes in the *Diaries*: 'His pathos is alien to me… but he is certainly a genius… Here is a brain consumed by the fire of a star. It frees itself in its work just before the catastrophe… Permit me to be terrified!' (Or, again: 'Too bad that the early Van Gogh was so fine a human being, but not so good as a painter, and that the later, wonderful artist is such a marked man.')

D is also for Robert Delauney – see A, above – whose influence on Klee's ideas of pictorial space was immense. They first met in 1912, when Klee visited Delauney's Parisian studio (it was during this visit that Klee first saw the work of Picasso, Braque, Matisse and Derain); the following year, *Der Sturm* magazine published 'Über Das Licht', Klee's loose translation of Delaunay's essay 'La Lumière'.

And for **Don Quijote de la mancia** (Klee's preferred spelling): his favourite book.

E **is for *Entartete Kunst***

Or 'Degenerate Art', the title of the notorious Nazi exhibition of bolshy, weird and brilliant modern work held in Munich in 1937: they paid Klee – by this time an exile in Switzerland – the far-reaching compliment of including seventeen of his paintings.

F **is for Felix Klee**

Paul's only child, born in 1907, and later to become the editor of a number of his literary works, including the diaries (*Paul Klee: Tagebucher 1898–1918*; see D, above) and his letters (*Paul Klee: Briefe an die Familie 1893–1940*).

G **is for Walter Gropius**

The visionary young architect (1883–1969) who, in 1919, set up the most influential (and frequently derided) academy of pure and applied arts of the twentieth century – the Bauhaus, in Weimar. When the school-cum-think tank-cum-commune was barely a year old, at the end of 1920, Gropius sent Klee a telegram, inviting him to join the staff as a 'Master'. Klee taught at the Bauhaus from 1921 onwards, first in Weimar and then, from 1926 to 1931, at its new base in Dessau. (After leaving the Bauhaus, he joined the faculty of Düsseldorf Academy as Professor of Painting.) These were intensely productive years, in which Klee not only produced hundreds of drawings and paintings but also composed a vast body – more than 4,000 pages – of theoretical writings: the largest such enterprise of any twentieth-century painter. This prodigious written output included papers gathered posthumously as *The Thinking Eye* (1961), one of the most ambitious manuals of design ever published, which outlined his theories on the visual equivalents of spiritual states. And, of course, he taught: everything from bookbinding and stained glass manufacture to textile design and sculpture.

G is also for Glyphs: Klee's art is full of bits and pieces of alphabetical and analphabetical writing, or conventional signs and symbols like arrows, or commas, or musical clefs; and also for **Goethe**: 'Klee's spiritual development followed a course which was in the main absolutely parallel with that of Goethe' (Werner Haftmann, 1967). 'As a matter of fact,' Klee confided to his diary in 1902, 'Goethe is the only bearable German. (I myself would like perhaps to be German in his way.)'

H is for Hammamet

'The city is magnificent, right by the sea, full of bends and sharp corners... Superb gardens in the vicinity... At the cafe in the evening, the blind singer and his boy beating the drum. A rhythm that will stay with me forever!' (Klee, *Diaries*, Easter 1914). It has often been said that there were three great turning points of Klee's creative life: the horrors of the First World War (initially rather militaristic, he changed his views dramatically when his friend August Macke was killed in action); his recruitment to the Bauhaus; and, earliest of the epiphanic trio, a short trip to Tunisia shortly before the war broke out, in the company of Macke and Louis Moilliet. Though the journey lasted only seventeen days, the experience of North African landscapes, architecture, light and sound ravished Klee and – as he correctly predicted – changed him for good: 'Colour has taken hold of me; no longer do I have to chase after it,' he wrote a few days after the visit to Hammamet. 'That is the significance of this blessed moment. Colour and I are one. I am a painter.' He exhibited eight of the watercolours he made at this time in the New Munich Secession. For direct visual evidence of this metamorphosis, see, for example, *Abstraction of a Motif from Hammamet*.

I is for Innocence

'I want to be as though newborn, knowing absolutely nothing about Europe; ignoring facts and fashions, to be almost primitive.' (A deeply European ambition, as Robert Hughes has rightly observed.) Sceptics accused – still accuse – Klee of being infantile, and the hoary mantra of the robust philistine, 'A child of three could do it!', might have been custom-coined for smearing his *oeuvre*. He would not necessarily have dissented: 'Do not laugh, reader! Children also have artistic ability, and there is wisdom in their having it!'

And for Italy. Klee travelled there for six months in 1901–2, at the end of his formal studies. He visited Milan, Genoa, Pisa, Rome, Naples and Florence. For the young Klee, the experience of a first-hand encounter with the fruits of antiquity and the Renaissance was almost devastating: he began to dread that he was living in a radically diminished age, where only small and derivative works were possible.

J is for Jugendstil

An offshoot of the Art Nouveau movement which flourished in Munich during the years when Klee was a student; one of the fashions he was obliged to spurn en route to maturity.

J is also for Japan. Like the Impressionists before him, Klee was fascinated both by Japanese visual arts and by many other aspects of Japanese culture: see below, Y is for Sada Yaco.

K is for Kandinsky

Despite the difference in their ages – the Russian artist was thirteen years older than the German – Wassily Kandinsky (1866–1944) became one of Klee's closest friends. Unknown to each other at the time, they both studied at the Munich Academy at the turn of the century; their first known meeting was in 1911, and in 1912 Klee joined Kandinsky and Marc in the so-called *blaue Reiter* or 'Blue Rider' group, exhibiting a number of paintings at their second Munich show. But the war put paid to this phase of their collaboration, and their friendship only ripened from 1922 onwards when Gropius invited Kandinsky, too, to join the Bauhaus. When the Bauhus moved to Dessau in 1926, the Klees and the Kandinskys became next-door neighbours, maintaining a charming balance between old-world formality and affectionate warmth.

K is also for **Alfred Kubin**, painter, novelist and lifelong friend. They first met in Bern in 1911.

L is for Lily Klee

Paul's wife, *née* Lily Stumpf (1876–1946): as outlined above, they met as early as 1899, in Munich, and were secretly engaged in 1901, but did not marry until September 1906. Lily was a professional pianist, and in the early years of their marriage, Klee kept house while she helped support them by giving piano lessons. His early letters to her are not simply declarations of love and sweet nothings, but are generally regarded as among the more revealing of his writings on art.

M is for Music

Had Klee not finally made the decision to devote himself to art, he could easily have made a distinguished name for himself as a musician. (See above, A is for Abstraction.) His father, Hans Klee, was a music teacher; Paul showed precocious skill as a violinist and soon won a place in the local orchestra; he continued to play the violin throughout his life, and his love and knowledge of music permeated both his theoretical writings (he was, incidentally, a semi-professional music critic at one time) and his art – see, for example, *Alter Klang* (*Ancient Harmony*; 1925). His *Diaries* – which seldom fail to record what he has been playing or hearing or contemplating of the great and not-so-great composers – are punctuated with swift annotations of themes that struck him in the concerts he attended – he seems to have been able to jot them down as effortlessly as a writer with a good memory might record speech. Musicians have often returned the compliment of admiring attention: the conductor and composer Pierre Boulez wrote a major critical study of Klee, *Le Pays fertile* (1989).

M is also for for the French philosopher Maurice Merleau-Ponty, who specialised in phenomenology (roughly: the analysis of the conditions under which certain experiences – including experiences of the visual – are possible). After Cézanne, Klee was his favourite painter.

 is for Nazis

Besides the 'Degenerate Art' incident of 1937, the tale of the Nazi hostility to Klee has three notable dates: March 1933, when his Dessau house is searched in his absence; 6 April 1933, when he is expelled from his faculty post at the Düsseldorf Academy – 'Prof Klee as Jew [*sic*] and teacher impossible and dispensable'; and December 1933, when he and his family go into their final Swiss exile.

 is for Oscar Wilde

One of Klee's most unexpected enthusiasms: he loved 'The Soul of Man Under Socialism', 'The Ballad of Reading Gaol' and even – though he was slightly alarmed by it – *Dorian Gray*. 'I copied the foreword to *Dorian Gray*. Did the same for other thoughts of Oscar Wilde. In a way because it was foreign to me, but perhaps true after all. Terrible this: all art is useless…'

 is for the *Pedagogical Sketchbook*

The *Pädagogisches Skizzenbuch* (1925; English translation by Sibyl Moholy-Nagy, 1953) was the second of the analytical textbooks produced by the Bauhaus under the editorship of Gropius and Lászlo Moholy-Nagy: still in print and easily found, it is one of the most widely read and influential of artistic manuals.

P is also for Photography: 'Photography was invented at the right moment as a warning against materialistic vision' (*Diaries*, entry 677).

is for *Die Quadratbilder*

The German term means 'Painter of Squares', and has been applied to Klee in discussions of (logically enough) his so-called 'square paintings'. It was in the wake of his Tunisian epiphany that Klee began to map out areas of colour in square shapes – see, for example, the *Statische-Dynamische Steigerung* (1923) and others – and to by-pass the 'distraction' of subject matter.

 is for Bridget Riley

The major Klee show at London's Hayward Gallery (2002) was put together at the suggestion of the veteran English Optical artist, who explains that '…Paul Klee was of seminal importance to me because he showed me what abstraction meant'. He is unique, she suggests, because 'he demonstrated more fully [than Picasso, Matisse, Braque, Kandinsky, Mondrian or any other artist of the age] that the elements of painting are not just means to an end but have distinct characteristics of their own'.

 is for Solitude

'Kafka lives in a *complementary* world. (In this he is closely related to Klee, whose work in painting is just as essentially *solitary* as Kafka's work is in literature)': Walter Benjamin, 'Max Brod's Book on Kafka' (1938), in *Illuminations*. Benjamin, the great philosopher of culture, was profoundly moved and no less profoundly influenced by Klee's work. 'I am coming more and more', he wrote, 'to the realization that I can depend sight unseen, as it were, only on the painting of Klee, Macke and maybe Kandinsky…' Benjamin owned at least two paintings by Klee: *Vorführung des Wunders* (*Introducing the Miracle*), which his wife gave him as a birthday present in 1920, and *Angelus Novus*, which he bought in Munich – for 'one thousand marks' – in the spring of 1921. The latter image, a watercolour, was of deep private significance to Benjamin. He adopted *Angelus Novus* as the title of his abortive literary magazine (planned for January 1922), and he used the image of Klee's angel in a haunting and much-discussed paragraph of his 'Theses on the Philosophy of History'. (See *Illuminations*, pp. 259–60.)

And for **Surrealism**: as Robert Hughes has pointed out, Klee has a number of obsessions and hobby-horses in common with that group of apparently very different artists, including an interest in dreams, in mythology, in 'primitive' societies and their arts, and in various kinds of incongruity.

Finally, **S is also for Scleroderma**. Klee was diagnosed with this rare and incurable illness in 1936, and lived for only four more years: years in which his skin progressively hardened, his ability to move became ever more restricted, and he was obliged to develop an entirely new pictorial style – often referred to as 'monumental' – characterised by thick, dark bold lines on relatively plain backgrounds. Klee reacted to the onset of his illness badly, and by his own prodigiously fertile standards almost gave up painting entirely for a year or so. But he soon regained the will to create, and in the year 1939 created an astonishing and unprecedented 1,253 pieces.

is for 'Taking a Line for a Walk'

Perhaps the most famous of all Klee's coinages, this much-quoted definition of the act of drawing is a slight misquotation of the original sentiment, which attributes far more agency to the line itself: 'A line comes into being. It goes out for a walk, so to speak, aimlessly for the sake of the walk…'

T is also for Taoism: in his idiosyncratic study of melancholy, *The Unquiet Grave*, Cyril Connolly identified Klee as a 'modern Taoist'.

is for *Über die moderne Kunst*

In *On Modern Art* (translated 1947), his single most influential lecture, delivered in Jena in 1924, Klee compares the transformation of the visual image as it 'passes through' the artist into his completed work with the passage of sap through a tree: 'Nobody will expect a tree to form its crown in exactly the same way as its root… But it is just the artist who at times is denied these departures from nature which his art demands. He has even been accused of incompetence and deliberate distortion...'

V is for Verses

Not content with his achievements as artist and musician, Klee also wrote a good deal of poetry – generally brief, gnomic, naive or fake-naive, a bit sentimental: the harsh word would be 'precious'. Some of the very simplest sound less like conventional lyrics than inventories of subjects for paintings, real or imaginary:

> Water,
> topped by waves,
> topped by a boat,
> topped by a woman,
> topped by a man.

W is for *Wander-Artist*

One of Klee's very last works, *Wander-Artist (ein Plakat) – Travelling Player (A Poster)* – shows a rudimentary stick-man holding up one hand in saluation or (more plausibly, since his life was rapidly ebbing away) in valediction. Robert Kudielka, the German art historian, finds it optimistic, and suggests that it 'cheerfully celebrates the journey between that which has been and that which is not yet'. Other, more melancholic readings are possible.

X is for Xenophon

Klee's love of the classical world, and particularly of Greece, was the affair of a lifetime. He was particularly taken by the noble image of Socrates, not only as he appears in Plato's dialogues but as he is depicted in the slightly less well known accounts of Xenophon. 'One of the most beautiful aspects of antiquity appears in Xenophon's *Banquet*. The presentation fascinates by its grace, by the refinement of its jesting... Thus I penetrate more and more deeply into the ancient world.'

 is for Sada Yaco

Klee's journey to Italy (October 1901–2) gave him the opportunity to witness a performance by the Japanese actress Sada Yaco and her company – an experience which left him in raptures. 'Sada Yaco herself has the dimensions of a Tangara figurine. Everything about her is as lovely as the way she chatters. Nothing is left to chance!... The way she goes to bed, sheer enchantment. A sprite or a woman? In any case, a *real* sprite. For all style here is directly based on reality...'

 is for Zurich

In 1940, the Zurich Kunsthaus mounted an exhibition in honour of Klee's sixtieth birthday (1939), showing works he had produced from 1933 onwards. It was the last public honour of his lifetime. He died on 29 June 1940, at a hospital in Muralto-Locarno.

Translated into English, his tombstone, in the Schlosshalden cemetery, reads:

I CANNOT BE GRASPED IN THE HERE AND NOW
FOR I LIVE JUST AS WELL WITH THE DEAD
AS WITH THE UNBORN
SOMEWHAT CLOSER TO THE HEART
OF CREATION THAN USUAL
BUT FAR FROM CLOSE ENOUGH

A
NIETZSCHE
ALPHABET

is for Antichrist

Friedrich Nietzsche (1844–1900; but hopelessly insane from 1889), the son and grandson of Lutheran clergymen, tore himself away from his pious origins to become a startlingly vehement and almost pathologically clairvoyant enemy both of the Christian faith itself and of all those cultural tendencies (including modern democracy) that had been nourished and shaped – or, as he saw it, hideously deformed – by Christian values. It is hard to boil down the large, complex and (sometimes calculatedly) self-contradictory body of Nietzsche's teachings into a blunt mission statement, but it would not be too much of a libel to say that his two primary purposes were (1) to document and understand, in minute and searching analyses, the precise nature of the rot which had wormed its way into Western civilisation (a condition of decadence which, he often suggests, was reaching a crisis point in his own period) and (2) to show how at least some free spirits, 'philosophers of the future' might rise above the disaster.

Among the other 'A's one might cite at this point, both of which bear on the complexity and range of Nietzsche's war against Christianity are:

Asceticism – one of the most nightmarishly life-denying consequences of Christian other-worldliness, Nietzsche thought (and it must be said that his fulminations against the 'perversion' that is chastity are not merely forceful but profound), though much of his own life, poverty-striken, nomadic and lonely as it was, strikes most readers as painfully ascetic itself; and:

Art, a subject on which his most famous aphorism (**Aphorism** being another prime A candidate) runs:

> We have art lest we *perish of the truth*.
>
> (*The Will to Power*)

and another, no less pertinently:

> Artists continually *glorify* – they do nothing else: they glorify all those conditions and things which have the reputation of making men feel good or great or intoxicated or merry or happy or wise.
>
> (*The Gay Science*)

Unlike many earlier philosophers of comparable fame (Hume, Descartes, Kant) though in anticipation of some later Continental thinkers (Heidegger, Sartre), Nietzsche devoted a great deal of time and energy to the discussion of art; indeed, a substantial part of his philosophy takes the form of a discourse on art, from Greek tragedy to the operas of Wagner. He conceived of art both as, at best, a manifestation of all that is most world-affirming – and thus, anti-Christian – and, at worst, as either an instructive symptom of disease or a dangerous vector of disease itself: the long, bitter story of his relationship with Wagner embraces both positions.

One of Nietzsche's last completed works, bluntly entitled *The Antichrist*, howls that 'The Christian Church has left nothing untouched by its depravity...' And who, or what, was the Antichrist of Nietzsche's personal theology? The answer can be found in his short autobiography *Ecce Homo* (III, 2):

Ich bin... der Antichrist.

Does this violent rejection of Christianity then commit Nietzsche to the party of the Devil? Many people have thought so, but the textual evidence does not bear out this popular prejudice. Consider the thrust of our first Nietzschean B:

is for *Beyond Good and Evil*

First published in 1886, when Nietzsche was in his early forties, *Beyond Good and Evil* was the last of his collections of aphorisms. Its title proclaims its purpose, but in a way that has been widely misconstrued. To unpick the case a little: Nietzsche is partly concerned with eroding the familiar, not to say universal, assumption that 'good' and 'evil' represent opposed terms. (As he elaborates elsewhere: 'good' actions may be, usually are, sublimated 'evil' ones. Hence, for example, his sly rewriting of Luke 18.14 – 'he that humbleth himself shall be exalted' as 'he that humbleth himself *wishes to be* exalted'.) Good and evil, he proposes, are different not in *kind* but merely in degree. Radical enough; but Nietzsche goes still further, doubting whether there are any opposites at all, and secondly, whether these popular valuations and opposite values on which the metaphysicians put their seal, are not perhaps merely foreground estimates, only provisional perspectives... frog perspectives, as it were...

Nietzsche is trying to pull himself out of the frogpond, and to drag a few disciples with him. According to Nietzsche, 'good' and 'evil' may be, to swap metaphors, just two distorting lenses with which to view reality; and so too – a truly vertiginous move – may those other supposed opposites 'true' and 'false'. As commentators (notably Michael Tanner) have pointed out, what Nietzsche is attempting here is a kind of reverse anthropology. Where the anthropologist immerses himself or herself in an alien culture and, by bracketing away as far as possible all Western prejudices about ethics, cosmology, epistemology and the like, struggles to grasp how an entirely different culture operates (or fails to), Nietzsche, by contrast, is trying to put himself in the position of an anthropologist of his own culture, seeing the familiar and taken-for-granted as weird, baffling and in urgent need of explanation. And high among the takens-for-granted which he has in his sights is binary thinking; it is this tendency in his work which makes him of such importance to Deconstruction. A maxim to ponder:

That which is done out of love always takes place beyond good and evil.

(On which point, B might also be made to stand for another scandalous character in Western philosophy or prophecy: **Georges Bataille**. Composed in the final months of the Second World War, Bataille's book *On Nietzsche* is less a commentary in the usual sense of the term than an intensely personal dialogue with a kindred spirit.)

B is also for *The Birth of Tragedy*, which was Nietzsche's first major publication (1872), much derided by his fellow scholars, who considered it by turns fanciful, irresponsible, unscholarly, irrelevant and mad. The brief flurry of publicity which attended its appearance was the only semblance of fame Nietzsche was to win in his sane lifetime. Though it is dutifully read nowadays by students of Greek drama – and later manifestations of the tragic – most authorities feel that it tells us more about the writer (and, possibly, Richard Wagner) than the Greeks. Yet there is no denying that it can be exhilarating, or that it has prompted many subsequent scholars to fruitful lines of enquiry, or that it did much to correct the dominant cliché of Greek culture as above all things rational and serene. To be sure, it has floated a few clichés of its own, above all the terms 'Apollonian' (or 'Apolline') and 'Dionysian', freely bandied around by thousands who have never consulted the *Birth*. And it is a very partial view of Nietzsche which does not take care to recall that:

C is for Classics

At the age of twenty-four, Nietzsche was appointed to the chair of classical philology at Basel University, and he remained there as professor for the next ten years. His first publication, in 1867, was a textual essay on Theognis, which at first blush is a disappointingly dry overture to a career of intense and radical iconoclasm. The incongruity is more apparent than real: two of the central foundations of his later philosophical work were the the discipline of philology and the example of Greece in the sixth century BC. (Nietzsche, incidentally, took the view that the Greeks were a 'mixed', not a 'pure' race – one of the many perceptions which saved him from the racism of which he is sometimes accused. For Nietzsche, advance is always the result of conflict.) Nietzsche was particularly taken with the Pre-Socratic philosophers Heraclitus, Thales and Empedocles. And one should also note his lifelong fascination with certain Greek gods, which is why:

D is for Dionysus

Nietzsche's obsessive relationship with the deity underwent a number of changes. In *The Birth of Tragedy*, the emotional Dionysian force is set in creative opposition to the form-making Apollonian principle; see B, above. Later, in the middle phase of his career, Dionysus comes to stand for the sublimated 'Will to Power', and is at times synonymous with the *Übermensch* (see U, below): hence the final line of *Ecce Homo*:

Have I been understood? – *Dionysus against the Crucified*.

(Sometimes, he allowed Dionysus a girlfriend: Ariadne.) With the onset of his final madness, Nietzsche absorbs the Greek and Christian godheads into himself and begins to sign his ranting letters 'Dionysus and the Crucified'. (And an early letter of his madness, sent to Cosima Wagner, addresses her as 'Ariadne'.)

D is also for Deconstruction, and for its high priest **Jacques Derrida**, who with the late Michel Foucault (see F, below) is by far the most famous of the modern-day philosophers who have both addressed Nietzsche's work and, in very different ways, pursued it to new ends.

E is for Eternal Recurrence

The mystical doctrine preached in *Thus Spake Zarathustra* and elsewhere, which holds that life (or Time, or Existence, or the Universe…) repeats itself over and over again, without cease. There are some signs that Nietzsche took this doctrine quite literally, and believed that the findings of modern science bore out his intuition about the fundamental nature of the universe. Many of his commentators, though, have made the charitable assumption that the doctrine is to be read figuratively, and expresses a moral injunction: live your life in such a manner that you would be content, indeed joyful, for every moment of it to be repeated in a cycle spiralling away into infinity. It has also been pointed out that, since none of us carries over any consciousness of previous universes from identical cycle to identical cycle, it is hard to see what difference the doctrine makes, save possibly in rather abstruse aesthetic terms.

F is for Forster-Nietzsche

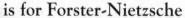

Elizabeth Forster-Nietzsche (born 1846; two years his junior), Friedrich's sister, is very hard to love, let alone tolerate; if there must be a villain in the Nietzsche story, then she is the prime candidate. She was by turns a neurotically protective and vengeful guardian of his sexual purity; a wife, from 1885, to one of the men Nietzsche most heartily despised, a grandiose and swindling bigot by the name of Bernhard Forster, who in 1886 founded a bizarre proto-fascist colony, New Germania, in Paraguay; an attentive nurse of her now-deranged brother in his last few years; and, ultimately, the High Priestess of a Nietzsche cult which sprang up in the last decade of his life and was later taken on board by Hitler and his grimy cohorts. Nietzsche's mental collapse took place just months before Bernhard Forster's suicide in June 1889. She returned from Paraguay and by the summer of 1894 had founded, expanded and declared herself mistress of a Nietzsche archive; by 1895 she had become his legal guardian and owner of his copyrights. (As has been shrewdly put, she had failed to establish one kind of colony, so was now setting about the creation of another.) See below, I is for Insanity. She died in November 1935 at the age of eighty-nine.

F is also for Sigmund Freud, a surprisingly fervent admirer of our Antichrist, who, according to Ernest Jones, once observed that Nietzsche had 'a more penetrating knowledge of himself than any man who ever lived, or was ever likely to live'. (Context: 1908: Freud had just heard Eduard Hitschmann reading extracts from *The Genealogy of Morals*.) At another point, Freud recalled that, when he was a young man, Nietzsche had seemed to represent a degree of nobility beyond emulation. A very substantial part of the psycho-analytic scheme of things is anticipated in Nietzsche's writings, from sublimation to the super-ego.

More recently, the letter F should recall the career of **Michel Foucault**, by many reckonings the single most influential philosopher-historian of the later twentieth century. Many of his projects owe their origins and development to the example of Nietzsche, particularly in Foucault's investigations of capital-P Power in all its polymorphous and often undetected manifestations. See Foucault, 'Nietzsche, Genealogy and History' in *Language, Counter-Memory, Practice* (1977).

G is for *The Gay Science* and *The Genealogy of Morals*

The first being, in German, *Die fröliche Wissenschaft*, Nietzsche's translation of *la gaya scienza* or *gai saber*, meaning the art of the Provencal Troubadours, 'those splendid, inventive men... to whom Europe owes so much and, indeed, almost itself'. Later, in *The Case of Wagner*, he attributed to *la gaya scienza* 'light-footedness; wit, fire, grace... the shimmering light of the South; a *smooth* sea – perfection'.

The second G, *The Genealogy of Morals*, is sometimes considered Nietzsche's masterpiece: his most sustained and brilliant mapping and analysis of the conflict between master and slave ethics through all its paradoxical twists and cunning subterfuges. Its final line: 'lieber will noch der Mensch *das Nichts* wollen, als *nicht* wollen': 'man would rather will *nothingness* than *not* will'. Or, more memorably if less literally: man would sooner have the void for purpose than be void of purpose.

G is also for God. Who is dead. (*The Gay Science*.)

H is for Heine

One of the most interesting pieces of evidence in the case of 'Nietzsche: Antichrist or Anti-Semite?' is his lifelong enthusiasm for the German-Jewish poet Heinrich Heine (1797–1856): 'The highest conception of the lyric poet was given me by Heinrich Heine. I seek in vain in all the realms of the millennia for an equally sweet and passionate music... One day it will be said that Heine and I have been by far the foremost artists of the German language – at an incalculable distance from anything mere Germans have done with it...' The curious background to his snarl at 'mere Germans' is that he had managed to persuade himself, on exceptionally skimpy evidence, that he was descended from a noble Polish family, the Nietzskys. He was not (and 'Nietzsky' is, anyway, not a Polish name); his German ancestry has now been traced back to the sixteenth century, and by the eighteenth century all the Nietzsches were Lutherans (many of them clergymen).

And for **Health**; a major criterion for Nietzsche in judging the soundness of a philosophical view was whether or not it was conducive to good health. His own health was, generally speaking, wretched. A few samples: in 1884–5 he was rendered virtually blind by an intensification of his lifelong eye pains; he always suffered from insomnia, agonising stomach upsets, bouts of uncontrollable vomiting so intense that on one occasion, after three days or so of non-stop regurgitation, he wrote to his doctor (Otto Eisler), that he was longing for death. Add to all this his chronic migraines, periods of collapse, fits of semi-paralysis and the like and it is small wonder that he should feel such warmth and reverence for all things healthy.

And for **Homelessness**: in his later life, from the age of thirty-four until the onset of his madness, Nietzsche became a nomad, apparently incapable in his mature years of settling in any one place for very long, let alone marrying and raising a family. This behaviour is in such marked contrast to the rooted nature of all his forebears that his biographers have found it neurotic, and sought a cause, often finding it in the early death of Friedrich's father, Pastor Nietzsche, in 1849 at the age of thirty-six. Friedrich was still only four years old. The family moved from Roecken to Naumburg, where the boy lived until he was sixteen, entirely surrounded by females after the death of his infant brother Joseph in 1850. His earliest accomplished poem, written in 1859, was entitled 'Ohne Heimat': 'Homeless'.

I is for Insanity

On the morning of 3 January 1889, Nietzsche – who was staying in Turin – left his lodgings, saw a cab-man beating his horse, rushed over to save the poor beast, threw his arms around its neck and passed out. (A plaque in the Piazza Carlo Alberto now commemorates this sad event.) When he revived, he was found to be uncontrollable, and before long was busy firing off megalomaniacal letters to all the crowned heads of Europe, commanding them to do his will. When he quietened down, he withdrew from the world and became first a placid, then an apathetic invalid, quite unaware that his fame was suddenly blossoming so abundantly that by the time of his death in 1900 he had become one of the most famous writers in the world. Students of Ruskin will recall that the sage of Brantwood, who also died in 1900, had suffered a very similar withdrawal from activity and sanity, though the cause of Ruskin's collapse were very different: it has been conjectured that the cause of Nietzsche's insanity was that familiar blight of nineteenth-century Europe, syphilis, contracted from a prostitute in one of the rare and uncharacteristic debauches of his youth.

The eleven years of his living death began in pathos and ended in grotesquerie. For the first seven years of his affliction he was tenderly cared for, night and day, by his doting mother Franziska, who thanked God for returning her son to her, and believed that he had returned to the pure faith of his childhood. In 1897, after her death, Nietzsche was shunted to Elizabeth's 'Nietzsche Archive' in Villa Silberblick, Weimar, where he became the object of mystical veneration. Elizabeth, who had more than a streak of the carnival hustler in her make-up, liked to dress him in white robes and let his moustache flourish. It is to her that we owe most of the familiar images of Nietzsche the Sage. Death put a merciful stop to the mystic side-show on 25 August 1900, six weeks before his fifty-sixth birthday.

J is for Jews

Since the whole world knows that the phrase 'don't get me wrong, some of my best friends are Jewish' is the infallible warning sign that a blast of rancid anti-Semitic drivel is imminent, there is at best a limited value in trying to defend Nietzsche from the routine charge of racial contempt by pointing out that some of his best friends – notably his fellow philosopher, Paul Rée, an important influence on Nietzsche around the time of *Human, All Too Human* – were undeniably Jewish. (And see above, H is for Heine.) Perhaps, then – and especially as Nietzsche was a great hater and despiser – it would bolster his reputation more adequately to point out that some of his worst enemies were anti-Semites. Chief among the bigoted rabble was his brother-in-law Bernhard Forster: Nietzsche was as disgusted by Forster's views ('This accursed anti-Semitism…') as he was by his bodily presence. It's true that

Nietzsche did indeed write some weirdly disparaging things about the Jewish peoples, the sort of thing that can do harm when it falls into the wrong hands, but then he also wrote weirdly disparaging things about almost every other culture, creed and race except the ancient Greeks, with Christians as his most frequent target for abuse. The widespread belief that Nietzsche was an active anti-Semite owes much more to the editorial jiggery-pokery of his sister, and to the sordid fan clubs who took her version of his beliefs as accurate, than it does to his actual writings. A major ground of his late rejection of Wagner was his recognition that the 'ideological' aspect of the composer, the anti-Semite and German nationalist, had come to the fore. (In his flashback to Bayreuth in *Ecce Homo*, Nietzsche recalls that 'Not a single abortion was missing, not even the anti-Semite.') Interesting fact: even in his madness, Nietzsche remained an anti-anti-Semite: as he writes in a letter from Turin on 7 January 1889:

> I have just had all anti-Semites shot…
>
> Dionysus.

J is also for Journalism: many British academic philosophers, and their colleagues elsewhere in the English-speaking world, deny that Nietzsche's project had anything to do with their discipline. As an eminent English Kantian once put it to the author: Nietzsche is not a philosopher, but a brilliant *journalist*.

 is for Kant
Immanuel Kant (1724–1804), generally regarded even by the sceptical British as probably the greatest of all German philosophers, was a particular *bête noire* of Nietzsche's. In his vocabulary, the adjective 'Kantian' (or, more archly, 'Koenigsbergian' – Kant was sometimes called 'the Sage of Koenigsberg') is always pejorative. Like Christianity, Kant was guilty of dividing the world into 'real' and 'apparent' dimensions – a sure dign of *decadence*.

K is also for Walter Kaufmann, the emigré philosopher and translator who, all but single-handedly, restored Nietzsche to the attention and the esteem of the English-speaking world from the early 1950s onwards – a praiseworthy exercise which involved not only the expunging all taint of proto-Nazism from his reputation, but (some say) a more thoroughgoing, and misleading, cleaning-up operation. Hence Michael Tanner's withering aside: '…Kaufmann's ill-organized transformation of Nietzsche into a liberal humanist has its place in the history of Nietzsche reception'. But without Kaufmann's labours, the great rediscovery might never have taken place, or would have come about circuitously, by way of the 'New Nietzsche' movement in Europe.

L is for Lou Andreas-Salomé

One of the most fascinating figures of her own age, and an enduring legend to later ages, Lou Andreas-Salomé was by turns muse to Nietzsche, mistress to Rilke and star disciple to Freud: in other words, a gift to European film-makers, who have not been ungrateful. The daughter of a Russian general, Lou entered Nietzsche's life in 1882, when she was twenty-one. Thoroughly smitten, young Friedrich proposed to her twice and was twice rejected. This disappointment was followed by a short-lived compromise, a *ménage à trois* in which Lou divided her affections between Friedrich and Paul Rée; it seems likely that this arrangement did not include physical consummation, at least not for Nietzsche. One of the most startling relics of this affair is a photograph which Nietzsche stage-managed, showing himself and Rée as bipedal oxen, standing ready to pull a cart by its handles, while Lou eggs them on with a hunter's whip. The image is, however, rather more stagey – and a lot less sexy – than most accounts suggest: the poses are stiff and static, as if everyone is faintly embarassed, and Lou does not seem as if she is going to derive much relish from her flagellatory role. (The following year, in 1883, Nietzsche wrote the most blushful lines in *Zarathustra*, the advice of the old crone: 'You are going to women? Don't forget your whip!') Friedrich's sister Elizabeth was predictably appalled and disgusted by Lou, and did everything possible to prise her out of his life; she was under the almost comic misapprehension that Lou was chasing Friedrich and had ensnared him with her wiles.

When the *ménage* dissolved, Friedrich – who had not suspected that he was about to be jettisoned by the couple – went off in a rage to Italy. He was none too dignified in amorous defeat, and at one point wrote of Miss Salomé as 'a dried-up, dirty, ill-smelling monkey with false breasts'. (The later part of his life was to be as loveless as the earlier.) Then he began to write: *Also Sprach Zarathustra*... Several years later, Lou Andreas-Salomé, too, wrote a book: *Friedrich Nietzsche in seinen Werken* (1894). It says nothing of their difficult time together.

L is also for his celebrated injunction: 'Live dangerously!' (*The Gay Science*).

 is for Maxims

Maxims, aphorisms, apophthegms and dicta are the essence of Nietzsche's literary genius. He is often regarded as one of the very greatest German prose stylists. At least two of his sayings have passed out of philosophical circles and found their way, in one version or another, into popular discourse. 'What does not destroy me, makes me stronger' (*Twilight of the Idols*, aphorism 8) has been used as, *inter alia*, an epigraph to the Arnold Schwarzenegger movie *Conan the Barbarian*, as part of a lyric for the theme song of the blue-collar situation comedy *Roseanne*, and as a tattoo on the finely honed person of a young American actress/*chanteuse*. A close rival for this catch-phrase would be 'Struggle not with monsters lest ye become a monster' (Less snappily translated as 'He who fights with monsters should look to it that he himself does not become a monster'), which continues: 'Stare at the void and the void stares back' (or: 'And when you gaze long into the abyss, the abyss also gazes into you'): *Beyond Good and Evil*, aphorism 148.

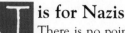 **is for Nazis**

There is no point in attempting to deny the undeniable: the Nazis saw Nietzsche as a precious intellectual powerhouse for their movement, they revered him as a great prophet, and they built him a museum in Weimar. All this has helped poison Nietzsche's reputation right up to the present day, and one can sympathise with those who take it for granted that he was not 'beyond good and evil', but simply evil, or at the very least pernicious.

Yet there is every point in insisting that the Nazi version of Nietzsche's philosophy was an ignorant caricature, based on the rigorous suppression of everything about his work that failed to toe the party line. Examples: he habitually lambasted Germans and Germany; he thought the notion of racial purity was idiotic; and he held the standard racist beliefs of his day in contempt. (And when Nietzsche held something in contempt, he did not do it in half measures.)

N is also for the *Nachlass*, the gigantic body of work written by Nietzsche but not published in his lifetime; these drafts, fragments, personal utterances, juvenilia, letters and suchlike have generated a commensurately large volume of critical commentary. Heidegger, notoriously, chose to ignore the published record and found his highly influential studies of Nietzsche almost wholly on the *Nachlass*.

The name of Heidegger leads us to another aspect of N, the so-called **'New Nietzsche'** – a blanket term for all the radical revisions of his thought which have been put forward in the last few decades by assorted philosophers, psychoanalysts, decontructionists, feminists (a surprising alliance, this one) and pedlars of Cultural Studies.

is for Overcoming

A major term in Nietzsche's later philosophy, which is much concerned with the process of self-overcoming – of an individual, of a people – and the harsh route from the human to the super-human: see below, U is for *Übermensch*.

P is for Power

Un-italicised, the Will to Power is a keystone of Nietzsche's psychology and cosmology, and is at the heart of his mature thought.

Nietzsche believed, or claimed to believe, that the whole universe must be seen as battle of contending wills, and the fight for supremacy visible in every manifestation of life. This may seem to echo, or somewhat garble, the evolutionary theories of Darwin, and there have been a number of studies devoted to Nietzsche as Darwinian – a tricky position to maintain when one notes how often Nietzsche dismisses the biologist as a typical English mediocrity. A more plausible account of this concept's genealogy would look to Nietzsche's thoroughgoing re-reading of Schopenhauer, the first writer to wake him up to a philosophical vocation.

Italicised, *The Will to Power* is the title of a posthumous collection of his *Nachlass* – plans, notes, first drafts and jottings, assembled by Elizabeth Forster-Nietzsche, and variously regarded as (1) the pinnacle of his career as philosopher and moralist; (2) a wholly redundant and, worse, misleading mess of tenuously connected scrap papers, best left in the cupboards where he had abandoned them; (3) neither of the above, exactly, but definitely something to be drawn on with great care, and always bearing in mind the fact that it lacks the imprimatur of Nietzsche as definitely fit for publication. A representative sample:

Q is for Qualities

'Qualities are an idiosyncrasy peculiar to man; to demand that our human interpretations and values should be universal and perhaps constitutive values is one of the hereditary madnesses of human pride' (*The Will to Power*, section 565).

R is for *Ressentiment*

Literally, just 'resentment'; but, as so often, Nietzsche uses the term in a highly personal way. Roughly paraphrased, the French term suggests, first, those feelings of rancour, hatred and envy inevitably experienced by the rabble when they are brought face to face with the true, the noble and the great; second, the system of life-hating, value-decrying ethics created by the herd in revenge. It should come as no surprise to learn that, for Nietzsche, the herd religion of Christianity (and all its mongrel offspring) is the most successful, which is to say the most catastrophic, historical flowering of *ressentiment*.

S is for Socrates

A casual browse through the pages of Nietzsche's *oeuvre* will leave one with the impression that he despised the Greek philosopher: after all, such phrases as 'Socrates was rabble' do not seem to leave much room for manoeuvre. And yet some readers of Nietzsche have suggested that, at a more recondite level, Nietzsche identified strongly with Socrates, and that he modelled at least some of his railing style on the characteristically mocking Socratic method. Thus, the argument runs, when he argues against Socrates he is actually arguing against himself – or, at least, against Socrates-in-himself.

S is also for Schopenhauer: at one time Nietzsche's idol, later his target. Such developments were far from rare in Nietzsche's growth, and it is entirely appropriate that:

T is for *Twilight of the Idols*

The idols including ones that a younger Nietzsche had reverenced. Pithily sub-titled *How to Philosophise with a Hammer*, this is a late work which 'says in ten sentences what everyone else says in a book – what everyone else does *not* say in a book'. A brief and highly readable set of provocations, it is not a bad place for the newcomer to begin a survey of Nietzsche's domain, and certainly a better point of entry than the work most commonly recommended to neophytes, *Thus Spake Zarathustra*, which can be repetitive and, to be frank, dull – at any rate, a great deal less interesting than is usual for this most energetic and confrontational of all philosophical stylists. On the other hand, *Zarathustra* certainly has its quotable moments, as can be seen when we proceed to:

U is for *Übermensch*

'I teach you the Superman. Man is a thing to be surmounted. What have ye done to surmount him?… What is the ape to man? A jest or a thing of shame. So shall man be to Superman – a thing of jest or shame… The Superman is the meaning of the earth. Let your will say: the Superman *shall be* the meaning of the earth…' (*Thus Spake Zarathustra*, Introductory Discourse). The *Übermensch* or Superman is at once Nietzsche's best-known and most variously interpreted creation; its apparent anticipations of some Nazi themes have been regarded as among the most potentially sinister of his conceits.

And for the **Untimely Meditations**: a series of tracts for the times (1873–6), written by Nietzsche shortly after *The Birth of Tragedy*. He planned thirteen, but only completed four, of which the second – 'On the Uses and Disadvantages of History for Life' – has won the most sustained attention and regard.

V is for Values

'One knows my demand of philosophers that they place themselves beyond good and evil – that they have the illusion of moral judgement beneath them. This demand follows from an insight first formulated by me: that there are no moral facts whatever…' (*Twilight of the Idols*). And thus: 'The task of true philosophers is "*to create values…*"' (*Beyond Good and Evil*).

W is for Wagner

In certain respects, the most intense relationship of Nietzsche's life was that which he (first) enjoyed and (later) endured with Richard Wagner. It had its earliest roots in 1861, when Friedrich's friend Gustav Krug introduced him to a piano transcription of *Tristan*; became a passion in 1868 when he first heard the *Meistersinger* prelude; and went through all the classic stages of infatuation, ardent discipleship and proselytising, creeping disenchantment and final repudiation – an emotional spectrum which may be followed in the dramatic narrative implicit in the pages of *The Birth of Tragedy* (1870–71), eventually followed by *Richard Wagner in Bayreuth* (published 1876, to coincide with the first Bayreuth festival), then, following disillusion, *The Case of Wagner* (1888: '*Wagner est une nevrose*') and, finally, *Nietzsche Contra Wagner* (1888–9). The once-revered master becomes the 'artist of *decadence*', just as Schopenhauer had been the 'philosopher of *decadence*'. It is a tale which is at times grimly comic, but not a tale of wasted allegiance: Wagner's contribution to Nietzsche's development is unequalled. As the Nietzsche scholar R.J. Hollingdale points out, close observation of Wagner taught Nietzsche the psychology of genius; and in seeing how Wagner's drive for artistic greatness was founded in his drive to dominate, Nietzsche had the most vivid possible case history of the Will to Power.

W is also for War, and for **Women**: two familiar themes brought together in a single proclamation from *Zarathustra*: 'Man should be trained for war and woman for the recreation of the warrior; all else is folly.' Nietzsche's only military experience was a year of national service in 1867–8, plus a short stint as a nursing orderly in 1870, during the Franco-Prussian war; for his principal experience of women, see above, L is for Lou Andreas-Salomé. It should be noted, however, that when Nietzsche advocates war he is usually, if not always, speaking metaphorically, and often about philosophy and the duties of philosophers. Earlier German thinkers, like Kant, had lived quiet and professorial lives, and kept their noses clean; but a true philosopher should be at war with the established order, and expect ferocious battles.

X is for Xymphora

The Greek word for 'misfortune': in *The Genealogy of Morals* (I, ii), Nietzsche observes that it was a word applied by the sublimely confident noblity to the wretched lower orders. A study of etymology, he asserts, will teach unprejudiced eyes the very same lesson again and again: that our entire store of words meaning 'good' ultimately derive from the qualities of an aristocracy and that all words meaning 'bad' may be traced back to terms originally signifying 'common' or 'plebian'.

Y is for Yea-Saying

If forced at gunpoint to reduce all of Nietzsche's ethical doctrines into a slogan – a verbal hammer, as it were – one could hardly do much better than invert a well-known phrase of the late twentieth century, and proclaim: 'Just Say Yes'.

And for **W.B. Yeats**, whose later verses are saturated with Nietzschean wisdoms.

Z is for Zarathustra

Of course. Nietzsche's single most famous and – for much of the twentieth century – widely read work, written in the immediate aftermath of his rejection by Lou Andreas-Salomé, and acclaimed by its author, if few others, as the most important book in the history of the world. It takes the form of a quasi-Biblical fable, interspersed with (rather feeble) poems, in which the hermit-prophet Zarathustra leaves his mountain home and goes down into the world, not to gather disciples, but to preach his doctrines. Summarily put, these are three- or possibly four-fold. He tells his listeners that they should antipate the coming of the *Übermensch* by (1) being 'faithful to the earth'; (2) embracing the reality of Eternal Recurrence; and (3) grasping the concept of the Will to Power. (The fourth injunction, if it exists, is to doubt everything that Zarathustra says.) One might say that Zarathustra is a kind of John the Baptist figure, preparing the way of the *Übermensch*.

Nietzsche liked to maintain that all of the works he wrote after *Zarathustra* were in the nature of commentaries and elaborations of its themes; it would be closer to the truth to say that those works notably improve on certain Zarathustrian motifs, and quietly drop those which ceased to preoccupy him. Often recommended to the curious as an ideal starting-point (see T, above), it tends to the pompous, the purple and the preposterous, and is certainly nothing like so exhilarating or compelling as his non-narrative works. Yet among its longeurs and repetitions and silliness, it still contains some splendid things. Let the prophet have the last word:

I say unto you: a man must have chaos yet within him to be able to give birth to a dancing star. I say unto you: ye have chaos yet within you...

A
SURREALIST
ALPHABET

is for Automatism

What is Surrealism? Well, in the words of the man who created it – André Breton – and from the document with which he presented it to the world in 1924, *Le Manifeste du surréalisme*: 'SURREALISM, noun, masc., Pure psychic automatism by which it is intended to express, either verbally or in writing, the true function of thought. Thought dictated in the absence of all control exerted by reason, and outside all aesthetic or moral preoccupations.' This rather abstract definition might come as a surprise to those who think of Surrealism mainly in terms of Dali's molten watches and lobster phones or Magritte's apple-faced clerks in bowler hats, but it is precise. Surrealism began as a movement of poets, not of painters, and at its heart were quasi-scientific, quasi-occultist expeditions into the unconscious, conducted though the means of automatic writing – the rapid, uncensored scribbling of whatever comes unbidden into the mind – as well as auto-hypnosis, 'sleeping fits', games of chance and dream records. The earliest literary fruit of these experiments was a collection of poems entitled *Les Champs magnétiques*, written by Breton in a state of collaborative trance with Phillipe Soupault.

A is also for Guillaume Apollinaire, the poet and art critic from whom Breton took the word 'Surrealism', which Apollinaire had coined in 1917, for a programme note handed out at performances of *Parade*, Cocteau's ballet with music by Satie and costumes by Picasso. Apollinaire furnished Surrealism not only with its name but with many of its prevailing themes. However:

 is for André Breton

As noted, André Breton was the founder, chief theoretician and presiding spirit of Surrealism, who became such a ferocious and possessive guardian of its spiritual purity across the decades (and so fond of excommunicating heretics) that he became known by cynics as its 'Pope'. Breton (1896–1966) studied medicine and served – mainly in psychiatric hospitals – with the French army in the First World War before moving to Paris and trying to establish a literary career, initially as co-editor (with

Phillipe Soupault and Louis Aragon; the trio of proto-Surrealists had first met in 1917) of the sarcastically entitled journal *Littérature*. Breton's charisma, energy and integrity were so crucial to the movement that it has sometimes been said that, simply, he *was* Surrealism. A man of many parts – art critic, gallery director, maker and finder of marvellous images and objects, ferocious moralist, pioneering connoisseur in all manner of previously despised, neglected or unseen fields from black humour (of which he assembled a major anthology) to tribal art, amateur philosopher and psychologist, wit, polemicist, propagandist and scholar of the occult – Breton was, above all things, a poet. Today, he is acknowledged as a classic of French literature, and like so many other classics, is more alluded to than read.

B is also for Luis Buñuel, greatest and most enduring of all Surrealist film-makers; which leads us to:

C is for Cinema

Long before any of the Surrealists began to make films, they loved to watch them: crouched eagerly in the front row, they would devour the American slapstick comedies of Mack Sennett, Buster Keaton, Harold Lloyd and – their greatest movie hero – Charlie Chaplin. They also adored adventure serials, and would keenly dispute the relative merits of the Pearl White serials *Perils of Pauline* and *Exploits of Elaine*; or thrill to the local French products, *Judex* and *Les Vampires*, by Louis Feuillade. 'At the time we were developing Surrealism,' Soupault wrote, 'the cinema was an immense revelation to us.' Fantastic, anarchic, vulgar, these silent films were an exhila-rating change from the plodding realism of theatre; and the quasi-hypnotic fascination induced by the silver screen made it all the more seductive. Their enthusiasm for the form waned considerably with the advent of sound, though they made certain exeptions, notably for the movies of Marlene Dietrich and for *King Kong*, hailed in the pages of *Minotaure* – perhaps the most lavish of all Surrealist journals – as a masterpiece of primitive eroticism.

Reference books would say that the first Surrealist film was René Clair's *Entr'acte* (1924), though purists might reply that it smacked more of Dada; other contributions to the form were made by Man Ray, Fernand Leger (*Ballet méchanique*, 1924) and – the twin masterpieces – by Dali and Buñuel with *Un chien andalou* (1928) and *L'Âge d'or* (1930). The earliest screenings of the latter film provoked a highly satisfactory riot, when young thugs from the Patriot's League and the Anti-Jewish League made a mass attack on the cinema – Studio 28 in Rue Tholoze – at which it was being shown. Cyril Connolly includes an evocative memoir of what it was like to witness such spectacles in *The Unquiet Grave*.

D is for Salvador Dali

Still, alas, far and away the best-known of all the Surrealists, thanks largely to his undeniable genius for publicity and knack for giving the public – especially the wealthy American public – exactly what it wanted; a talent which made him dazzlingly rich while many of his contemporaries lived close to the breadline, or died. Breton made an angry near-anagram from his name: 'Avida Dollars'. Dali (1904–89) is an easy figure to dislike, not only for the slick and vulgar mysteries of his later art – that mainstay of the shops which provide cheap posters for student lodgings – but for his grimy politics (he was, for example, an eager supporter of Franco, and claimed to find Hitler profoundly exciting as a sex object), for his tiresome exhibitionism, for the money-grubbing of which Breton justly accused him, and for his all-round meretriciousness. Above all, it was his shameless hijacking of Surrealism from his elders and betters which most appalled those who cared about such things. Dali, incidentally, was also something of a Johnny-come-lately to the movement: he did not make contact with the Surrealists until 1928, and did not paint in that vein until 1929, with *Le Jeu lugubre* (*The Lugubrious Game*). It is appropriate to speak his name with scorn.

And yet, and yet… almost everyone who met Dali in the early years in Paris was swept away by his perspicacity, his intensity, his charm, and his gifts. As one friend of the time wrote, speaking the sentiments of many: 'There is no doubt that he was a genius. He had conceptions of the greatest originality.' That period of youthful promise lasted about five or six years; at any rate, it was in

1934 that Breton, exasperated by Dali's Hitler-fancying and other antics, made an attempt at excommunicating him from the movement. Not long after an inconclusive 'trial', in which Dali succeeded in making Breton look stuffy and priggish, he set off for New York, and first scented the heady tang of high society, universal fame and serious money. A verdict on Dali's whole career, as fair-minded and temperate as it is crushing, comes from the historian Ruth Brandon: 'Dali, who might have achieved greatness, opted instead for popularity.'

D is also for Dada, the anti-art movement which was Surrealism's immediate precursor, provocation, and progenitor; and for the unclassifiable trickster figure of **Marcel Duchamp** – painter, sculptor, chess master, pataphysician, joker and grandfather of conceptualist art – who swam happily for a while with the Surrealist school before heading off into even less well charted waters.

E is for Max Ernst

Perhaps the most abundantly gifted of all the Surrealist painters and image-makers, Max Ernst (1891–1976) was an endlessly resourceful and inventive artist who deserves to enjoy that place in popular consciousness that has long been occupied by Dali and, to a lesser extent, Magritte. In the course of creating his marvellous images, Ernst discovered or adapted a number of novel techniques, including *frottage* – the creation of arresting textures by rubbing charcoal over a piece of paper placed on a rough surface, as in brass rubbing – and *grattage*, a similar technique for producing automatic images using paint. He was a master of the collage form, ransacking old catalogues and science magazines for photographs and engravings which he could combine into witty or macabre multiple compositions, as in his pictorial 'novel' *Une semaine de bonté* (1934).

E is also for the poet Paul Eluard, who some time after the First World War worked out that he must have been firing on the very position occupied by his future friend Ernst. Additionally, E is for **'Exquisite Corpse'**, the Consequences-style game used by the Surrealists to create collective poems and weird hybrid images. A folded piece of paper is passed from hand to hand, and each participant adds a new component to the text or picture without being aware of what his or predecessors have contributed. *Exquisite Corpse*, by the English novelist Robert Irwin, is a splendid fictional evocation of the British Surrealist movement of the 1930s.

F is for Sigmund Freud

Breton and company revered Freud, and regarded his work on the unconscious as one of the essential foundations of their whole enterprise. Freud, to put it mildly, did not return the compliment, and seems to have regarded them as a pack of clowns with no real understanding of the aims and philosophy of psychoanalysis. (See the Freud Alphabet.) Predictably, then, Breton's only meeting with Freud – he made a pilgrimage to Freud's Viennese consulting rooms in 1921 – was something of an anti-climax. Oddly enough, it was Dali who succeeded where the Pope of Surrealism had failed: when he called on Freud in Hampstead, during the psychoanalyst's brief exile there before his death, the patriarch declared himself more impressed than he had anticipated. 'Until now', he wrote to his friend Stefan Zweig, 'I was inclined to regard the Surrealists – who seem to have adopted me for their patron saint – as 100 per cent fools (or let's rather say, as with alcohol, 95 per cent). This young Spaniard, with his ingenuous fanatical eyes, and his undoubtedly technically perfect mastership, has suggested to me a different estimate...' For his part, Dali thought Freud 'adorable' and considered his cranium the Surrealistic equivalent of a snail's shell, demonstrating his point with an on-the-spot sketch.

G is for Great Britain

Surrealism came late to Britain, but when it came, it was with a bang. The International Surrealist Exhibition of 1936 was, beyond dispute, the biggest artistic sensation London had ever seen: thousands of curious spectators defied the soaring temperatures to cram into the Burlington Gallery, traffic was snarled up for hours, and the newspapers had a glorious time filling their columns with (mostly) derisive or outraged commentary. Curiously, one of the very few reviewers to treat the show sympathetically was John Betjeman, later Poet Laureate and national teddy-bear totem.

It's easy to see why Londoners were so amused and perplexed. Quite apart from the sheer novelty and oddness of the art on display, the Surrealists provided all sorts of other enticements. A woman known as the 'Surrealist Phantom' drifted through the proceedings in a long gown, her head encased in a cage of flowers, holding a raw chop in one hand and a wooden leg in another; the poet Dylan Thomas offered visitors cups of boiled string, asking politely whether they preferred it weak or strong; and Salvador Dali lectured inaudibly from inside a deep-sea diving suit, holding a brace of Borzois on a lead and brandishing a ceremonial sword, until the heat overcame him and he had to be rescued. Happy days. There is still only one full-length critical study of British Surrealism, albeit an extremely good one, written by the French academic Michel Remy – a sorry lacuna in British self-awareness, since its early membership included the likes of Henry Moore, Paul Nash and Humphrey Jennings (see J, below). The main British Surrealist group disbanded in 1940, but a number of rival or 'continuity' groups sprang up in its wake, and the roster of post-war British Surrealists includes, among others, the zoologist Desmond Morris and the entertainer and jazz singer George Melly.

is for *The Hidden Woman*

The Hidden Woman – or, in the original, *La Femme cachée* – is a painting by Magritte published in the final issue of *La Révolution surréaliste* (December 1929), where it was surrounded by a set of mugshots of the leading Surrealists – all with their eyes shut, all (more to the point) men. The text of Magritte's paintings reads: '*Je ne vois pas la* [blank] *cachée dans la forêt*': 'I do not see the [blank] hidden in the forest'. And in place of the missing word is a nude woman. Not surprisingly, this image has in recent years become a rallying point for discussions of the place of women in Surrealism: a discussion which might seem doomed to brevity, since Surrealism was, on the face of it, such a chap's club. Breton's notorious remark – 'The problem of

woman is the most marvellous and disturbing problem there is in the world' –
is suggestive of the degree to which the movement was by and for men only.

But the story is not quite so straightforward. Though the most obvious role
played by women in the movement's glory days was that of muse or model, the
various friends, lovers and wives of the founders were often included in
Surrealist activities and 'researches', and as the movement developed, more and
more women artists began to join. Recent scholarship – see, for example,
Whitney Chadwick's *Women Artists and the Surrealist Movement* – has done a
good deal to reclaim the contribution of its female members and fellow-travellers: Eileen Agar, Leonora Carrington, Lee Miller, Dorothea Tanning… and
see below, K is for Kahlo and Z is for Zurn.

I is for Insurrection

Perhaps the single most important quality that any account of
Surrealism, however perfunctory, must strive to make clear is that it was
never originally intended as a mere literary or artistic movement, just
one new brand name among all the others. It was a sensibility, a philosophy, a
creed, a way of life… above all things, a revolution. Surrealism, Breton stressed
from the outset, was in revolt against the church, the family, the army, the state
and every aspect of 'bourgeois' repression, from the sexual morality which crippled erotic drives to the logic which denied the power of the irrational, the
marvellous, the fantastic.

Its two key maxims came from Marx – 'Transform the world' – and from
Rimbaud: '*Changez la vie!*' Hence the titles of two of its main organs: *La
Révolution surréaliste* and *Le Surréalisme au service de la révolution* – the latter
being a product of the Surrealists's short-lived alliance with the French
Communist Party, an affair which was always bound to end in tears, and did so
sooner than most expected. The story of their ructions has a kind of glum
comedy of its own, and includes scenes of Breton howling with indignation at
Communist attempts to censor Surrealist publications in accordance with the
party line; Louis Aragon's defection from the ranks, and the legal wrangle over
his poem 'Red Front', which was accused in the law courts of advocating the

murder of certain public figures; and Breton's eventual partnership with the USSR's most hated bogeyman, Leon Trotsky (see T, below).

The Communists sneered that Breton's brand of revolution was purely verbal; a charge which is at once stinging (the world has yet to see a Surrealist government… not a self-defining one, anyway) and irrelevant: Surrealism is a hunt for bigger and stranger game than a change of political and economic arrangements. 'It's clear to us,' Breton said, 'that the world's real torment lies in *the human condition*, even more than in *the social condition* of individuals.' History brought in a curious mode of revenge for the Surrealist side: during the *événements* of May 1968, the rioting students scrawled many more slogans on the walls from the writings of Breton than from those of either Marx or Lenin.

J is for Humphrey Jennings

One of Britain's greatest film-makers, remembered mainly for his documentaries showing life on the Home Front, Humphrey Jennings (1907–50) was also a key member of the British Surrealist movement. With the poet David Gascoyne and the painter and art historian Roland Penrose (later Sir Roland, founder of the Institute of Contemporary Arts), Jennings was largely responsible for importing Surrealism from across the channel. An excellent French speaker, he got on well with both Breton and Paul Eluard – who later wrote a sonnet about him – and translated a number of Surrealist texts, including a collection of poems by Benjamin Peret. Jennings also wrote poems for the two leading Surrealist publications of the day, *Contemporary Poetry and Prose* and *London Bulletin* – the latter published from E.L.T. Mesens's London Gallery, the unofficial HQ for British Surrealist activities. At the same time, Jennings was painting pictures, taking photographs and making collages, some of which were put on show at the 1936 Surrealist Exhibition, and one of which – a small collage depicting Lord Kitchener – created an outrage among patriots. The quiet irony of this is that within a few years, Jennings was applying some of the lessons he had learned from Breton and company to his films, which are among the most stirringly patriotic depictions of Britain anywhere in the cinema or any other medium.

K is for Frida Kahlo

Today one of the most fashionable, frequently cited and highly regarded of all Surrealists – not to say, the heroine of an Oscar-winning movie starring Selma Hayek – the Mexican artist Frida Kahlo was born in 1910 and died, too young, in 1954. When André Breton visited Mexico in 1938 he was astounded to discover that a young woman who had no direct contact with the movement had been painting images that were as 'authentic' in their Surrealist aesthetic as anything that had been created in Montmartre. Example: a skyscraper shoots up out of an erupting volcano; a strange flower bristles with human figures, either naked or dressed in outdated clothes. Vastly impressed by this 'intuitive Surrealist', Breton wrote enthusiastically in *Le Surréalisme et la peinture* that 'I was witnessing here, at the other side of the earth, a spontaneous outpouring of our own questioning spirit…' He went on to write the catalogue essay for her show at the Julien Levy gallery in New York. Nor did she lack for admirers among her fellow residents of Mexico, temporary or permanent: Leon Trotsky kept her self-portrait in his office; and she was also, as admirers of committed art will know, the wife of Mexico's most celebrated muralist Diego Rivera. Her own art is very different from Rivera's, and draws more on the inner world of dreams than the external world of Mexican traditions of image-making.

L is for Lautréamont

'For us, from the outset, there was no genius that could hold a candle to Lautréamont': Breton, *The Autobiography of Surrealism*. Like other artistic revolutionaries, the Surrealists loved to nominate their heroes and villains, and above all to uncover supposed forebears, both real and imaginary. Some of the nominated Surrealist ancestors are famous – Rimbaud, the Marquis de Sade, the Gothic novelists, Lewis Carroll – and others were either forgotten or chronically unknown. Of all these ancestors, none was more important than Isidore Ducasse, self-styled 'Comte de Lautréamont', whose macabre prose poem *Les Chants de Maldoror* was one of the movement's sacred texts. 'For centuries to come', Breton wrote of *Maldoror*, 'the most auda-

cious things that can be thought or undertaken will find their magic law formulated here in advance.' Breton rescued this obscure nineteenth-century poet
from oblivion by copying out by hand, and then printing, the text of the one
surviving copy of Lautréamont's works in the Bibliothèque Nationale. It was in
the pages of *Maldoror* that the Surrealists found their beloved formula, 'Beautiful
as the chance encounter, on a dissecting table, of a sewing machine and an
umbrella'. Under Surrealist patronage, various sumptuous editions of *Les Chants
de Maldoror* and other works, with illustrations by Dali (1934) and Max Ernst
(1938) were published; and the Surrealist deck of cards featured 'Lautréamont'
alongside such favourites as 'Alice' and 'Freud'. Outsiders had to be wary of
taking the name in vain: when, in 1930, one entrepreneur had the audacity to
open a Montparnasse nightclub called 'Maldoror', the Surrealists showed up in
force while Breton shouted 'We are the guests of the Comte de Lautréamont!'
In the ensuing riot, the club was trashed and one Surrealist, René Char, was
stabbed in the thigh. Lautréamont, one suspects, would have approved.

 is for René Magritte
Salvador Dali's only rival for the title of 'most famous
Surrealist painter', though the Belgian's international fame
came much later than the Spaniard's. As almost everyone
who has stepped into a modern art galley will know, one of the fundamental
ploys of Magritte's art is the spookily matter-of-fact juxtaposition of unrelated
objects or states, or of things related only by a species of visual punning: an old
pair of boots ends in toes; a window overlooking a landscape is obscured by an
easel bearing a painting of (is it? Or isn't it?) precisely that same landscape; a
man (actually, the rich collector and eccentric Edward James, the Surrealists's
most generous English patron), seen from behind, stares into a mirror which
shows not the front but the identical back of his head; bowler-hatted men
plummet from the skies like raindrops; a giant rock floats in mid-air like a cloud;
another bowler-hatted man is obscured by a giant apple (the image which
inspired the Beatles' company, Apple); the image of a pipe is tagged with the
assurance that 'this is not a pipe'. (Of course not: it's a painting.) André Breton

summed it up nicely: 'Magritte… taking his cue from the visual arts as I did from poetry, glimpsed what could result from juxtaposing words with great resonance… with forms that negated them or at the very least, did not rationally match them.'

His life story, which begins in 1898 in Brussels and ends in the same place in 1967, may be quickly told. His mother commits suicide when he is fourteen; he studies art from 1916 to 1918 and then takes a job as a commercial illustrator; he marries his childhood sweetheart Georgette Berger in 1922; is inspired, like so many others, by a glimpse of De Chirico's paintings; helps set up a Belgian Surrealist group; travels to Paris and meets the Breton gang; is published in the final issue of *La Révolution surréaliste* in 1929; returns to Brussels in 1930; paints until he drops.

 ## is for *Nadja*

Breton despised novels, and though *Nadja*, one of his most famous works, appears to be just such a creature, he presents it as though it were a fragment of autobiography. The story goes something like this:

Towards the end of 1926, Breton meets a young woman of striking appearance – frail, vaguely vampiric – near the Rue Lafayette, and starts following her. They fall into conversation, go to a café, and over the next few weeks carry on meeting and talking, though without any obvious romantic or erotic involvement. Nadja, it appears, has no means of support; she claims psychic powers, and seems justified in the brag – at one point, she predicts that a particular window will light up red. It does so. Eventually, they sleep together; but Breton becomes alarmed at her increasing dependency on him, and shuns her. Unable to see him, she sends him odd drawings – drawings which Breton reproduces in the book. Then the letters cease, and he hears no more of her until word arrives that she is now confined in a mental hospital. Soon afterwards, she commits suicide. The text ends with one of Breton's most often-cited maxims: '*La beauté sera CONVULSIVE ou ne sera pas*': beauty will be convulsive or it will not be.

The significance of *Najda* has been the subject of great debate, and not only because of the callousness to which Breton so freely confesses: it seems as if the writer were using Nadja's visionary qualities – or incipient madness – as a royal road to his own unconscious, discarding her when she ceases to fulfil this function. On the other hand, it is by no means clear whether or not this tale is entirely or even partly true: it may be a dream, a fantasy, a fable. What does seem clear is that during the time described in the book, André's rocky marriage to Simone Breton finally broke down in a mess of recriminations and ugly squabbles over property. Whether Nadja was a real muse or an imaginary one, Breton's dalliance with her was as disruptive as any Surrealist might wish. Perhaps demonic forces were at work – see:

is for the Occult

Though Breton was sometimes, and particularly in his earlier years, scathing on the subject, there are deep and demonstrable affinities between Surrealism and certain aspects of the Western Hermetic Tradition. (And even in the movement's earliest days, the similarities between those 'seances' held by the Surrealists and those devoted to contacting the dead were obvious to all; indeed, René Crevel had actually been tutored in mediumistic techniques by a spiritualist.) According to one definition, the whole point of Surrealism was to 'transform the world by invoking powers which had been atrophied through centuries of Greek logic and Christian morality'. A more precise word for those 'powers' might be 'demons'.

A good deal of work has been done on this subject, and a good deal remains to be done. To cite just a few of the occult strands in Surrealism, consider: Breton's fondness for magical objects from Oceania and elsewhere, and his invocation of the name of the fourteenth-century alchemist Nicholas Flamel; the career of Victor Brauner, who collected voodoo chimeras, went in for casting spells, and – notoriously – painted a self-portrait which prophetically depicted him minus one eye; Kurt Seligman, himself rumoured to be an expert sorcerer, writing the scholarly *Magic, Supernaturalism and Religion*, still one of the standard texts; Max Ernst's cultivation of an avian 'familiar', Lop-Lop; and the Surrealists' pervasive interest in all heretical systems of thought, from

Gnosticism to the Kabbalah, which deal in analogy. It has even been maintained that the fundamental tenet of Hermetic thought is echoed in a famous phrase from the second Surrealist Manifesto: 'Everything leads us to believe that there exists a point in the mind from which life and death, the real and the imaginary, the past and the future, the high and the low, the communicable and the incommunicable, will cease to appear contradictory.'

P is for Paris

Paris, the native city of Surrealism, is also the subject of some of its most enduring works: Aragon's *Paris Peasant*, for example. But the Surrealists could be extremely choosy about which parts of Paris were worthy of their attention. Breton, for example, decided to colonise Montmartre at a time when most artists and intellectuals congregated in Montparnasse; and his Montmartre was not that of Maurice Chevalier and the Moulin Rouge, but the quiet, businesslike place where the tourists never wandered and where one could sit undisturbed in cafés all day, using them like offices. He liked to hold court discreetly in the Café Cyrano in the Place Blanche, where the other Surrealists would join him twice a day for policy meetings (those in the know would order mandarin-curaçao) or to write undisturbed in the Batifol, another peaceful café in the Rue Faubourg St Martin.

Seen through the re-enchanted eyes of Surrealism, Paris was like a magic kingdom, where *l'hasard objectif*, objective chance, would lead one into desirable encounters or unforeseeable adventures – Breton's haunted affair with Nadja is a classic instance – or reveal glimpses of the marvellous. Incidentally, of all the leading Surrealists, only one – Aragon – was Parisian by upbringing or birth. A recent collection of photographs by Michael Woods, *Paris and the Surrealists* (text by George Melly) revists many of the once-sacred sites.

is for Raymond Queneau

The polymathic writer, philosopher, encyclopaedia editor and mathematician (1903–76), best known in the UK as the author of *Zazie dans le metro* and *Exercises in Style*, joined the Surrealists as early as 1924 and left, after a blazing row with Breton, in 1929. He went on to associate with Georges Bataille on the bizarre and influential journal *Documents*, to join the College of Pataphysics, and to co-found that extraordinary and admirable body the Oulipo ('Workshop for Potential Literature'), dedicated to the creation of verbal works of art produced in accordance with extreme formal constraints. During his Surrealist period, Queneau was part of the fly-by-night population of possibly the most bizarre shared household in history, a ramshackle place on the Rue du Château – his room-mates included the likes of Jacques Prevert, Yves Tanguy and Benjamin Peret. The decor was calculated to shock or dismay timid souls, and included a lavatory chain with a stolen church crucifix as its handle. After his falling out with Breton, Queneau was one of the ex-Surrealists who joined together to issue an insulting attack on their former leader, *Un cadavre* (*A Corpse*) – the title being a cheeky echo of an attack published by Breton and company at the time of the death of the French Academician Anatole France.

 is for Man Ray

The most celebrated of all Surrealist photographers and, for enthusiasts, the man who re-invented the art from scratch with such technical developments as his *rayographs* or *rayogrammes* (produced without a camera, using just light-sensitive paper to create patterns and textures), and for the technique of solarisation, said to have been stumbled across by accident when his assistant, pupil and lover Lee Miller – herself to become a major photographer in both Surrealist and more conventional modes – startled by a mouse scuttling over her foot, snapped on a light while developing some prints. (Man Ray himself told the story somewhat differently.) Born in Philadelphia in 1890, and named Emmanuel Radnitsky, Man Ray studied architecture, took up painting, helped found a short-lived artists' colony and fell under the influence of his new friend Marcel Duchamp.

He moved to Paris in 1921, already well known to the city's artistic circles, and rapidly established himself as a gifted portraitist of the more flamboyant, scandalous and exotic figures of the age; he also made a name for himself as a lover of beautiful women, including the legendary Kiki de Montparnasse. When the Surrealist Gallery on Rue Jacques Callot opened its doors in March 1926, its first show was dedicated to his work. In these years, he also made or help make a number of films, including the anagrammatic *Anemic Cinema*. He spent most of the 1940s back in the USA, and returned in 1950 to Paris, where he died in 1976. Much reproduced, Man Ray's body of work is among the most enduringly popular legacies of Surrealism; the best of it has an unmistakable signature that has often been mimicked but seldom matched.

 is for Sex

Sex, love, eroticism, the libido, the id, desire, what have you... there is no subject dearer to the heart of Surrealist art and thought, let alone Surrealist life. Consider just a few of the more obvious phenomena: Dali's gallery of fetishes, from soiled underwear to crutches and cannibalism; Magritte's frightening erotic puns, such as *Le Viol* (1934), in which a woman's bare torso stands in for her face – nipples for eyes, navel for nose, pubic triangle for mouth; Breton's *Nadja* and his *Mad Love* (*L'Amour fou*); Man Ray's portraits of Kiki, Lee Miller, and other Surrealist muses; Meret Oppenheim's vaginal *Object* (*Fur Breakfast*) of 1936; Hans Bellmer's disturbing doll scupltures with their flaunted female genitalia; the toe-sucking scene in *L'Âge d'or*; the general craze for the works of the Marquis de Sade... No sex, no Surrealism.

Erotic fantasies and practices were one of the principal objects of Surrealist 'research'; and one of their most famous polemics, 'Hands Off Love' (published in *La Revue surréaliste* in 1927), deplored the fact that their hero Charlie Chaplin was being harassed by lawyers after leaving his wife for another woman. This fascination with all aspects of sexuality was one of the many things about the Surrealists which most annoyed their temporary allies, the Communists. Oddly, Breton himself was somewhat of a prude, who strongly disapproved of homosexuality and even of prostitution… though he tried to justify this latter bias, using Surrealist logic, by claiming that the essence of his disapproval was that brothels reduced the incidence of rape. No one was convinced.

T is for Leon Trotsky

As noted above, Breton's political progress was rapid and unconventional: a member of the French Communist Party for a matter of just a few weeks, and at best a tentative ally of the comrades for the next few years, he finally grew enraged at every manifestation of the Soviet Union and its allies and cast his vote for Trotsky, who, in the eyes of the orthodox, was the Satan who had revolted against the true God of Marxism–Leninism and had duly been expelled from the socialist paradise. (The party newspaper *Izvestia*, by the way, had characterised Surrealism as 'pederasty'.) Breton had his chance to meet Trotsky when he travelled to Mexico in 1938; there is a well-known photograph of Breton and his wife Jacqueline, flanking a dapper Trotsky and an obese, slobbish Diego Rivera. The Bretons stayed in Trotsky's home, the Blue House in Coyaocan, and together the two writers composed a manifesto, *Towards an Independent Revolutionary Art*. Trotsky, it seems, did most of the work. Breton was not disappointed by this meeting with the political leader, who had been a hero for him ever since he had read of his vilification and banishment by Stalin. When the news of Trotsky's assasination reached him, Breton was distraught, and was found sobbing out loud.

U is for the USA

The Surrealists were among that wonderful if motley collection of artists and intellectuals who fled Europe as the Nazi armies advanced, and for the duration of the Second World War, New York became the home of Surrealism in exile. Breton and Masson retreated there, joining the likes of Ernst, Tanguy, Man Ray and Duchamp. New York already knew all about Surrealism – the earliest show had been held there in

1932, at the Julien Levy Gallery, and Dali in particular had been a huge hit. But the new wave of Surrealist arrivals had an impact that was at once quieter and far more pervasive. They exhibited work at Peggy Guggenheim's gallery 'Art of this Century', and published, lectured, and broadcast, both within the United States and back to Europe. Only one young American artist of real note, Arshile Gorky, officially joined their ranks, but they had an enormous if diffuse influence on subsequent artists: Jackson Pollock, for example, was profoundly shaped by his exposure to Surrealism, and the techniques of Surrealist automatism had soon taken root in new soil, giving birth to Abstract Expressionism.

V is for Jacques Vaché

The largely unsung progenitor of the whole Surrealist enterprise, Jacques Vaché was an enigmatic, perversely insouciant dandy whom Breton had met during the First World War in the hospital at Nantes, where Vaché was recovering from a leg wound: he caught Breton's attention by spending hours each morning carefully arranging and re-arranging the objects on his bedside table into the most pleasing pattern. Vaché's combination of nihilistic humour – the quality he called *umour*, and which so greatly impressed the, by nature, largely humourless Breton – and his intuitive originality of outlook was quite stunning. Breton introduced Vaché to his fellow fledglings in Surrealism: Vaché, they said, reminded them of Lafcadio, the blase hero of André Gide's novel *Les Caves du Vatican* (1914).

When Vaché suddenly died, as a result either of a bungled drug adventure or suicidal intent, he unwittingly won immortality. For Breton, it has been said, the whole long progress of Surrealism was at heart an attempt to reincarnate and preserve the spirit of his lost friend.

Hence, in part:

W is for the First World War

It is important, whenever one is tempted to dismiss Surrealism as the hollow plaything of pampered young men, as a joke without wit, or as a revolt without revolution, to recall how formative the experience of the First World War had been for all of its founding members, both in the general sense (as the apologists for both Dada and Surrealism often put it, if the much-vaunted 'logic' and 'humanism' of Western civilisation had led directly to the trenches, then it was time to pull down logic and humanism) and in terms of specific experiences: Breton's friendship with Vaché, for one, but also his encounters with the psychiatric patients who came his way, especially in the hospital at St Dizier. Here, he met a soldier who had developed an astonishingly elaborate paranoid theory about the war, which he held to be a colossal fake, staged by countless thousands of actors using blanks. To prove his theory, the soldier had walked about casually on the trench parapets and for some reason had not been shot – an oddity which gave Breton considerable food for thought. Being Surrealists, however, Breton and company could not allow themselves to rail against the war in the manner of other revolutionary intellectuals. 'War?' Breton wrote in the first Surrealist Manifesto. 'Gave us a good laugh.'

X is for Xenophilia

As enemies of all forms of jingoism, nationalism and chauvinism (with the possible exception of the male kind), the Surrealists were, of course, firmly committed to an admiration of the foreign as well as of the strange. But they went a good deal further than this, and were enthusiastic admirers of what would now be called Third World societies and cultures. This keenness began, in most cases, with a taste for exotic art works: Breton was especially partial to the products of the Oceanic cultures, Max Ernst collected Hopi dolls, and the group as a whole favoured the arts of Africa, the Arctic Circle and Pre-Columbian America over the line of Western art which runs from the Parthenon via the Renaissance to the likes of Poussin. The wittiest and most dramatic emblem of this xenophilia is the 'Surrealist Map of the

World' published in the Belgian magazine *Variétés* in 1929. Among its peculiarities: none of the (then) forty-eight states of the continental USA is visible, though Alaska looms large; mainland Britain is dwarfed by Ireland; Australia is dwarfed by New Guinea; only two cities are marked, Paris and Constantinople – though the rest of France and Turkey are absent; and the Pacific Islands occupy two-thirds of the world. It is a joke, to be sure; but a joke with a perfectly solemn intention.

Y is for Yves Tanguy

Tanguy's paintings underwent a number of metamorphoses, but the works by which he is best remembered are those glossy, enigmatic visions of vast, often featureless 'landscapes' inhabited by vaguely biomorphic forms: they look like visions of some far-off planet (upmarket publishers of science fiction have sometimes used them as cover art) or, perhaps, renditions of life amongst the microbes or on some remote sea-bed. Other artists have learned from and imitated Tanguy's work, but never matched it: these visions, like them or not, are unique. Tanguy was born in Paris in 1900; at eighteen he enlisted on a merchant ship and travelled extensively in South America and elsewhere. After military service, he returned to Paris in 1922 and – inspired by a powerful encounter with De Chirico's *The Child's Brain*, which he had seen from a bus – began to make his first images. He fell in with the Surrealists around 1925 and had his first exhibition under their wing in 1927. He met an American woman, Kay Sage, and in 1941 moved with her to Woodbury, Connecticut, where he worked productively until his sudden death in 1954, and was a major influence on a younger generation of American artists.

Z is for Unica Zurn

One of the most tormented souls of a conspicuously anguished tribe, the German painter Unica Zurn (1916–70) grew up in a house crammed with the marvels that her father, a much-travelled writer, had picked up during his voyages in the Far East. After graduation, she worked for a while as an archivist at the famous German film company UFA, and then set up as a journalist. In 1950s she met and fell in love with the Surrealist Hans Bellmer, who introduced her to the delights of automatic drawing, and she had soon staged her first major exhibition of this work in Paris. Before long, she was taken up by Breton and became friendly with the likes of Man Ray, Ernst, Brauner and others, and was invited to take part in Surrealist group shows.

Sadly, she suffered from mental illness and was diagnosed as schizophrenic. In the last eight years of her life, she spent a great deal of time in various psychiatric hospitals. In 1970, she committed suicide by throwing herself from the balcony of the apartment which she shared with Bellmer; a book of her experiences in asylums was published posthumously. It is an interesting accident – or maybe, Surrealists would say, it was no accident at all, but pure *hasard objectif* – that it is with her life and self-inflicted death that this alphabet now ends, for both the topic and the fact of suicide haunt the movement. The very first issue of *La Révolution surréaliste* launched an enquiry into the phenomenon, inspired by an apparent epidemic of suicides in the Paris of the 1920s, and it has been observed that the heroic years of Surrealism are bracketed by two conspicuous suicides: that of Jacques Vaché and that of René Crevel, who gassed himself in 1935 – partly in despair over a political struggle between the Surrealists and the Communists. Surrealism was, as Breton always stressed, not just a movement but a way of life. It would be no less true to say that Surrealism was, is, also a way of death.

AN
ANDY
WARHOL
ALPHABET

Or, 'From A to B and Onwards...'

A is for 'A'

Many, many forms of 'A': the 'a' he clipped from the end of his family name Warhola, in 1949, to transform himself into Warhol; the 'a' of his tape-recorded 'novel', *a: a novel* (1968); the 'a' of his ghosted credo *The Philosophy of Andy Warhol (From A to B and Back Again)* (1975); the 'a' of asexuality, anomie, anhedonia, anaesthesia, autism, affectlessness and all the other *a*-signalled conditions of conspicuous emotional lack which characterised or became associated with his life and temperament; the 'a' of Andy (he is in that select company of modern artists immediately recognisable by their first name alone – Pablo, Jackson, Salvador...; though the full form 'Andrew', one must admit, brings to mind Andrew Wyeth, a very different American painter); the 'a' of art, and of Artist-with-a-capital-A (was he one?); the 'a' of ambition, and of accomplishment (for all his scrupulously cultivated airs of languor and laziness, he was a strangely driven man, and certainly deserves an A for Effort); the 'a' of A-lists, on discotheque doors and in histories of modern art; the 'a' of albinism; the 'a' of America (is he the most quintessentially American artist?), and of his last published book, *America*; the 'a' of the A-bomb, exploded above the streets of Hiroshima on Andrew Warhola's seventeenth birthday, then picked up twenty years later as the subject for a silk-screen painting, in 1965; the 'a' of AIDS, by which Warhol, who called it 'gay cancer', was horrified to the point of hypochondriacal superstition; and so on.

As the critic Wayne Koestenbaum suggested in his admirable brief life of Warhol (2001), to which this small opening bouquet of indefinite articles is deeply and appreciatively indebted (*gratias ago!*), his life is shot through with 'those *a* words... that... account him Andy'. (Andy was, one might add, something of an Indefinite Article in his own right.)

Further evidence? Well: **A is also for Advertising**.

Warhol's first major career breakthrough came in 1955, when the I. Miller shoe store on Fifth Avenue offered him the then startling sum of $50,000 dollars a year to create ads for the *New York Times*. (He spent his first pay cheque on a hundred identical white shirts; see below, R is for Repetition.) It was congenial work for a dedicated shoe and foot fetishist, and it earned him kudos as well as cash – in 1957, the campaign won the Art Director Club Award, advertising's equivalent to an Oscar. Young Warhol (he was born in 1928) had already made an effortless transition from art student to successful commercial artist. From now on, his relationship with the publicity industries became central to his life's work, and those who dispute or flatly deny Warhol's talent as an artist can scarcely gainsay his genius for advertising.

B is for David Bowie

Warhol had succeeded in made himself a household name by the mid-1960s, well known to amused readers of tabloids as well as to the hip intelligentsia, but his true moment of introduction to the rising Glam Rock generation of the early 1970s was a song by David Bowie on his best-selling *Hunky Dory* album, in which the American artist is said to 'look a scream', hanging on the wall, and to be indistinguishable from a (half-rhymed) silver screen self-portrait. Not, perhaps, as considered a piece of art criticism as Bowie was to offer later in life as a contributor to the highbrow journal *Modern Painters*, but not without point, either. Warhol is said to have squirmed with embarrassment when Bowie eventually played him the song in person, not recognising that it was meant as a compliment; and he would sometimes complain that the whole Glam and Glitter business was a shameless rip-off of his own style inventions. A couple of decades later, Bowie would play the part of Warhol in a biopic of his protegé, the doomed graffiti artist **Jean-Michel Basquiat** – another significant Warhol B.

B is also for b, the uncompleted sequel to *a: a novel*; and for **Boys** (see below, Q is for Queer).

C is for Campbell's Soup

Warhol's calling card as an artist – his *Demoiselles d'Avignon* or *Nude Descending a Staircase*, as it were – was first exhibited to the public in July 1962. The 'Campbell's Soup' series was made up of thirty-two images, representing the full range of flavours Campbell's had to offer the hungry and frugal American consumer, from Tomato to Turkey Noodle; they were on sale for $100 each, and only five were sold at the time. (By the late 1980s, the remaining twenty-seven had been valued at some $10 million.) When a local supermarket tried to ridicule him by pointing out that the real thing cost only 29 cents, Warhol had himself photographed signing cans: the 'joke' shot was reproduced around the world, and Warhol's three decades of fame had begun. By the way, he was genuinely fond of the product, and consumed a great deal of it, though he often declared that his favourite food-stuff was another C: **Candy**.

C is also for *The Chelsea Girls* (1966), the first of Warhol's films to enjoy a commercial release, and then, remarkable fact, to make a little profit. Double-screened, three and a half hours long, the film is populated by a gang of Warhol's female acolytes – hangers-on, hanging out, in the rooms of the raffish Chelsea Hotel. It begins and ends with images of the chill siren, Nico: see N, below.

D is for 'Drella'

The pet name with which Warhol was christened by the denizens of the Factory: a revealing compound of 'Dracula' and 'Cinderella'. (Hence the title of the memorial song cycle by John Cale and Lou Reed, *Songs for Drella*.) It compounds two key myths about Warhol: the idea of the poor little boy who eventually winds up at the prince's ball with all the rich and beautiful people, and the idea of the pale, nocturnal leech on other people's energies and talents.

And for **Arthur C. Danto**, the philosopher and art critic, who has put forward one of the most intellectually formidable cases for Warhol's immense, possibly unparalled importance for modern art, and for culture in general. In *Beyond the Brillo Box: The Visual Arts in Post-Historical Perspective* (1992) and other works, Danto acclaims Warhol not simply as an artist but as a fellow philosopher... and a major one. 'Gee!' as Andy often said.

And for **Dorothy Dean**, one of the very few African-American women to find a place in Warhol's entourage; also one of the few *bona fide* intellectuals – she was an art historian, educated at Harvard.

E is for Elvis

One of Warhol's most powerful insights: fame begets fame. Cast into his own fame on a tidal wave of soup, Warhol consolidated his celebrity in August 1962 by making the first silk-screened paintings of people who were already universally familiar: Elvis, Marlon Brando, Liz Taylor, Marilyn Monroe... and the Mona Lisa. Simple, Brilliant, Simply Brilliant.

E is also for Edie (that is, Edith) **Sedgwick**, a thin-skinned, self-doubting, self-destructive, upper-crust WASP beauty who was recruited by Warhol in 1965, and immediately transformed into one of his leading players: 'Superstars', as they were called, not entirely in irony. (Attempted decoding: Superstars, ostensibly anonymous but indisputably *fabulous*, were both bigger and smaller than the mere 'stars' of Hollywood.) Edie cut her hair and dyed it silver to look like him, he adjusted his posture to look like her. One is reminded of a famous Velvet Underground song; 'I'll Be Your Mirror'. She died on 23 November 1971, at the age of twenty-eight: 'acute barbital intoxication', said the coroner. Warhol did not, would not and almost certainly could not mourn her. Her life is recorded – unfairly to the Factory regulars, some have claimed – in Jean Stein's *Edie: An American Biography* (1982), a book which has done as much as any in sustaining the horror story of Andy the Vampire King.

And so, inevitably, to:

F is for the Factory

There were four Factories in all, but the one everyone thinks of when the name is mentioned is the original place, on the fifth floor of East 47th Street, opened in the otherwise fateful month of November 1963. This version of the Factory lasted for five years, until operations shifted to Union Square West. It was a single room, 100 by 40 feet, with little more in the way of comforts than a couple of toilets and a payphone. Here, Warhol threw himself into an intensely productive period of making paintings and sculptures (Brillo boxes), then, soon, turned to film – more of which in a moment. Meanwhile, a curious chap called Billy Linich – who rechristened himself Billy

Name (see N, below) – began to line the Factory's walls with 'space-age' silver foil, built himself a sort of human nest in one corner, and opened the Factory's doors to a stream of unconventional souls, many of them fuelled by amphetamines. The place became Warhol's Camelot, his commune, his Bauhaus, his Metro-Goldwyn-Mayer…

Because **F is also, definitely, for Films**: *Haircut*, *Kiss*, *Sleep*, *Blow Job*, *Couch*, *Poor Little Rich Girl*, *Vinyl* (see V, below)… He began shooting in 1963, using a 16mm Bolex, and kept on until the very different shooting, by Valerie Solanas, in 1968. The films were removed from distribution in 1972, and until quite recently have been seen by very few; but there are critics (of all levels, sloppy, adequate and dazzling) who regard them extremely highly, and consider them every bit as worthy of consideration as the fine art products, if not more so. For a brief and truly remarkable apologia for Warhol's cinema, see the appropriate entry in David Thomson's magisterial *Biographical Dictionary of Film*.

G is for Nathan Gluck

One of Warhol's most important 'assistants', though that term hardly does justice to his contributions, who worked with him in the crucial decade of Warhol's career from 1955 to 1965. Gluck often signed Warhol's signature to his works when the master himself could not be bothered (Julia Warhola could do the same trick); he also added greatly to Warhol's informal education, generously sharing his considerable knowledge of literature, art and music, and fostering Warhol's development as a collector – which later grew hypertrophied: a kind of mania to accumulate – of all manner of *objets*, from the precious to the downright junky.

G is also for Gossip; and for **Glamour**: the centre of Warhol's universe. 'I was really surprised when I arrived at my office and found a message: "The White House called" – which is really the most glamorous message you can get in the world.' Glamour was Warhol's muse, his obsession, and his Achilles' heel. He was often derided for his slavish and snobbish addiction to glamour, and yet he seemed to regard it, at least potentially, as a democratic wind which blew where it listeth, and which could transfigure anyone at all. This is one of the sentiments which underlies – if that metaphor of depth isn't grossly inappropriate for the man of surfaces – his most frequently cited maxim: 'In the future, everyone will be world famous for fifteen minutes.' (Question: why does the 'world' usually go missing when this is quoted by journalists?) As to the specific form of glamour he usually found most potent:

H is for Hollywood

According to one of his Factory staff, Warhol 'thought Hollywood was heaven and treated stars like saints'. As a sickly child, he had written to Shirley Temple for her autograph, and throughout his adult life he continued to be astonished and enraptured by stars old and new. One of his great regrets was that he never made the crossover into mainstream movie-making, the kind that had real stars instead of Warholian 'Superstars'.

I is for *Interview* Magazine

Or, in its orginal form, *inter*/VIEW magazine: possibly the most lightly edited, uncritical and fawning publication in the history of journalism; at any rate, a strong contender. One of its lowest points was a hypnotically dull conversation with Nancy Reagan, which prompted the radical political columnist Alexander Cockburn to write a scathing parody for the *Village Voice*, in which Andy and his fellow interviewer put the same breathless questions about interior design and the frothy like to one Adolf Hitler. It seems that even some of the *Interview* crowd thought this jape was quite funny. Astonishingly, the magazine also – by accident? – managed to publish a number of genuinely well-written, thoughtful and influential articles: see below, T is for Truman Capote. From 1970 onwards, its executive editor was Bob Colacello, later the author of *Holy Terror: Andy Warhol Close Up* (1990), one of the superior memoirs of its kind.

I is also for Iran. See K, below.

J is for Julia Warhola

The artist's mother, and the most important figure not only in his childhood but, one can plausibly argue, in his entire life. She was born Julia Zavacky, 17 November 1892, in Mikova. (See below, W is for Warhola.) Andy's father, Andrej Warhola – born 28 November 1889 – was also a Mikovan. She came to America in 1921, to join her husband who had landed a job as a construction worker in Pittsburgh. Several years earlier, she had given birth to a daughter, Justina, who died in infancy of a bowel disorder; in America, she bore three sons: Paul (1922), John (1925), and Andrew (1928). Unlike his brothers, little Andrew was a sickly child – among other juvenile ailments, he suffered badly from chorea, which made him shake uncontrollably – and a classic mommy's boy, doted on and indulged to the limits of the family's meagre income. Julia was often in poor health herself, and underwent radical surgery for bowel cancer.

Andrej Warhola died, reputedly from drinking contaminated water, in 1942, when Andrew was only just in his teens. He left enough money for one of his three sons to have a college education; the lucky ticket fell to Andrew, acknowledged as the artistic one, most likely to benefit from a funded escape from the blue-collar world. Andrew attended the Carnegie Institute of Technology, graduated in 1949 and moved to New York; Julia followed him not long afterwards, and mother and son set up unconventional home together in a sparsely appointed apartment, which they shared with about two dozen reasonably fastidious (i.e., non-smelly) cats. The odd couple continued to live together – though in much more comfortable circumstances, on the Upper East Side – throughout the wildest, headiest, druggiest years of the Factory, from which Warhol would always retreat at bedtime. Apart from her beloved son, the primary comforts of Julia's ageing life were the church (Andy also attended Sunday services) and, increasingly, alcohol. After her death in 1972, at the age of eighty, Warhol – never very brave when it came to confronting mortality – was so reluctant to admit her absence that would always tell unwitting people who enquired after her health that she was 'shopping in Bloomingdales'.

J is also for another important woman in his life, **Jackie (Kennedy) Onassis**. His first association with JFK's widow – one of the women he most admired – came shortly after November 1963 when he created a sixteen-panel piece, in blue and grey, based on newspaper portraits made just after the assassination: it was praised highly by sympathetic critics. In later years, they became friends: her first words to Warhol were 'So tell me, Andy, what was Liz Taylor like?' (Answer: 'Oh gee. She was great...')

K is for Ayatollah Khomeini

Who, in January 1979, put paid to Warhol's long and careful courtship of the Shah of Iran and his empress, and to cosy dinners at the Iranian Embassy on Fifth Avenue. (Andy and his entourage also enjoyed hobnobbing with Imelda Marcos: the 1970s were his time for cultivating chic dictators.) Warhol had made himself into a sort of court painter to the Shah, and fantasised greedily about installing a print of the Shah's portrait in the home of every rich Iranian. He was about to attend the Shiraz Arts Festival in September 1978 when it was cancelled by riots; then Khomeini made his triumphal entrance into Teheran. The short-term loss to his business was $95,000 – the price of two studies of Princess Ashraf and three of the Shah. Nothing damaged Warhol's reputation among the liberal intelligentsia more profoundly than his soft spot – was it due to cynicism? ignorance? sheer greed? – for wealthy tyrants. In the words of his biographer Victor Bockris: 'People associated with the Factory were looked upon by left-wing elements as the dregs of humanity.'

L is for *Lonesome Cowboys*

Warhol's gay cowboy epic (1968), shot in Arizona by the Factory-in-Exile while the local police looked on with hostile eyes... and eventually drove them away, to finish the shoot in New York. Unusually for a Warhol production, it was filmed in colour and intended to have a story-line; part of its significance in Warhol's film-making career was that it was in the course of its troubled shoot that Warhol gradually handed over all directing duties to:

is for Paul Morrissey
Who directed all the best-known 'Warhol' films from this point onwards. Morrissey was not quite the sort of chap you'd have expected to meet at the Factory in those louche days: he was a right-wing Irish Catholic and self-styled 'square' who revered John Ford and John Wayne and despised intellectuals, liberals, drug-takers and other forms of degenerate. Among the films loosely ascribed to Warhol over the next few years, but in fact executed by Morrissey, are *Flesh* (1968), *Trash* (1969), *Heat* (1972), *Women in Revolt* (also 1972), *Andy Warhol's Dracula* and *Andy Warhol's Frankenstein* (both 1974).

M is also for Max's Kansas City, a bar-restaurant-club near Union Square, which became a favoured watering-hole for the Factory gang after its opening in 1965.

And for **Mao Zedong**, subject of a series of deadpan, oddly haunting portraits begun in 1972.

And for **Money**, which Warhol always loved dearly, and pursued with great and undisguised eagerness long before avarice became chic.

 is for Narcissism
Chronically worried about his looks, and seldom happy with his appearance until he took up disciplined weightlifting and macrobiotic food in middle age, Warhol was a narcissist of the anguished rather than the complacent kind. His image of himself was no doubt unduly harsh: he looks perfectly all right in the photo albums of his youth. Still, his anxieties were far from groundless. As a child, he suffered from unsightly blotches over his face and neck; most of his hair had dropped out by the time he graduated in 1949, driving him to adopt his trademark wigs; he had his nose altered, and tried to build up his scrawny fame in short-lived visits to gyms, with no great success.

And for **Nico**, *née* Christa Paffgen, former model and Fellini star, actress in Warhol's factory movies (see *The Chelsea Girls*, C is for Campbell's Soup), and lead singer – 'chanteuse' is the favoured word in most histories – for the Velvet

Underground (see V, below). Her loud, deep, heavily accented, creepily inexpressive voice, unkindly referred to by one of her later backing musicians as a 'foghorn', is one of the strangest noises in all rock music: once heard, never forgotten (however much you might wish to). It gave an other-worldly, and sometimes nearly self-parodically doom-laden quality to such songs as 'All Tomorrow's Parties' and 'Femme Fatale' – a chill which has kept them fresh for four decades and counting. Her post-Warhol years, mainly squalid and heroin-sodden, ended in an entirely predictable early death, and have been well detailed in a mordant memoir, *Nico: Songs They Never Play On The Radio*. Highly recommended.

And for **Billy Name**, *né* Linich. A sometime waiter at a fashionable restaurant Warhol patronised, Linich/Name impressed Warhol greatly by his part-time work as a lighting designer, and by the ingeniously simple decor of his modest flat, which he had lined with silver foil. Warhol invited him to come and live in his loft, and to replicate his tinfoil scheme there: the birth of the Silver Factory. Mr Name appeared in several Warhol films; his own moody, high-contrast photographs of the 'Silver Factory' have been published in *Andy Warhol's Factory Photos* (1996) and *All Tomorrow's Parties: Billy Name's Photographs of Andy Warhol's Factory* (1997).

is for Oral

Oral history, that is. (What else?) Warhol discovered the joys of tape recording early, became unbreakably addicted to recording his phone conversations when he was in hospital in 1968, and, once the small portable versions came on the market, was hardly ever to be seen without 'my wife, Sony'. The editorial policy on *Interview* magazine was simply to transcribe tapes direct, with every 'um' and 'ah' and *non sequitur* left intact; and, as noted above, his 'novel' *a* was a product of four marathon tape sessions between 1965 and 1967, totalling twenty-four hours. Its purported subject is twenty-four hours in the life of Ondine, one of the more articulate members of the Warhol tribe.

is for Pop

Roy Lichtenstein, yes; Claes Oldenburg, absolutely; Jasper Johns, well, sort of... but in the eye of the great tabloid-browsing public, Warhol was always the King of Pop Art.

And for **'Andy Paperbag'**, the name he toyed with adopting in his hungry years.

is for Queer

'To ignore Warhol's queerness is to miss what is most valuable, interesting, sexy and political about his work': so say the angry editors of *Pop Out: Queer Andy Warhol* (1996), who maintain that despite the fact that the artist was almost universally known or assumed to be homosexual, the vast bulk of commentary on his work systematically 'de-gays' him; moreover, that many of the hostile accounts of his work and life – such as those by the art critic Robert Hughes, no fan – are written in gay-bashing code. Warhol, they insist, was '...a fabulous queen, a fan of prurience and pornography, and a great admirer of the male body'. There is a good deal of justice in this line, though it would be intellectually dishonest to claim that only homophobic bigots were dismayed by him: see above, K is for Khomeini. Warhol himself, it should also be added, was fairly coy about the subject of his sexuality, and liked to refer to homosexuality as 'problem', asking friends with discreet excitment whether or not some newcomer had 'a problem'.

is for Repetition

Repetition Repetition Repetition
Repetition Repetition Repetition
Repetition Repetition Repetition...

Is an essential component both of Warhol's work and of his life. There is a great deal to be said about this, not all of it repetitious: one cute story sees the origins of the practice in his childhood, when he helped his mother in her obsessive task of sticking thousands of green savings stamps into books.

S is for Valerie Solanas

Author of the notorious (and surprisingly well-written) SCUM *Manifesto* – the acronym standing for 'Society for Cutting Up Men' – as well as of the unproduced screenplay *Up Your Ass*. On 3 June 1968, she became Warhol's would-be assassin. Two bullets from her .32 pistol cut through his stomach, liver, spleen and both lungs. He nearly died – at one point during surgery, was actually pronounced clinically dead – and remained seriously wounded for the rest of his life, though he may have found more comfort than most other victims would in the likelihood that this violent and much-publicised event had helped secure his fame for good. (There are cynics who have said that death would have been an even better career move; and at least part of this flip suggestion is well-founded: with a couple of exceptions, little of the work Warhol produced after the attack, such as his 'Society Portraits', has been found worth of sustained critical attention. Warhol himself seems to have suspected at times that he had lost his spark.) The incident has been dramatised in Mary Harron's film *I Shot Andy Warhol*, which takes a far more tolerant – indeed, at times all but admiring – view of Ms Solanas than will be found, say, in the scathing track about her on *Songs for Drella*.

T is for Truman Capote

As with many other young gay men of the day, Warhol's fascination with Truman Capote began when he saw the provocative author's photograph on the back cover of *Other Voices, Other Rooms* and was immediately smitten. But where those others mostly wanted Capote, Warhol wanted to *be* Capote, and set about that task with a dedication that bordered on the frightening. More than bordered: Capote was understandably alarmed by this stringy oddball who wrote to him literally every day ('Happy Monday', 'Happy Tuesday…', on paper covered with watercolours of angels and butterflies), who pestered him on the phone, who lingered on the street outside Capote's apartment until the writer's mother begged him to stop. But as Warhol's fame grew, Capote eventually came to find him acceptable, and took him up as a member of his swanky set. According to witnesses in George

Plimpton's *Truman Capote* (1997), the two had a good deal in common, from a certain persistent childishness to a genius for social manipulation. In later years, a time of *rapprochement* when the two would socialise together at Studio 54 and other night spots, Capote became a regular contributor to *Interview* magazine: an arrangement which gradually evolved from Warhol's hobby of following him everywhere with a tape recorder. Capote's pieces – including a much-discussed feature about a day spent with a New York cleaning lady as she goes from empty apartment to empty apartment – were well received, but his conduct towards what he began, ominously, to call 'our' magazine began quite high-handedly and soon developed into full-blown tyranny. Many of the pieces collected in Capote's *Music for Chameleons* were originally published in *Interview*.

U is for Ultra Violet

Née Isabelle Collin Dufesne, sometime convent girl: Superstar, and thus sister-in-art of Baby Jane Holzer, Candy Darling, Holly Woodlawn, Viva (see V, below) and all the other Superstars, female and not indisputably female, bred by the Factory.

V is for the Velvet Underground

For ardent fans of their piquant, polymorphously perverse and at times painfully loud brand of rock music (our name is Legion, for we are many), Warhol's sponsorship of the Velvet Underground was far and away the most important act of his varied career. The classic line-up: Lou Reed, John Cale, Sterling Morrison, Maureen Tucker… and Warhol's contribution to the recipe: Nico. He 'discovered' them at New York's Café Bizarre late in 1965, saw potential in their uncomfortable repertoire, offered to finance them provided they would take on Nico, and became a mentor to the band's main song writer, Lou Reed. (One of Reed's earlier mentors had been the distinguished poet Delmore Schwartz, sadly out of fashion today, but still eminent in the early 1960s. Reed commemorated their master–pupil relationship by dedicating the song 'Pale European Son' to Schwartz.)

The Velvets served as the house band for the Exploding Plastic Inevitable, a mind-numbingly loud multi-media show which soon became revered by New York's hippest, who flocked to the events to dance, be deafened and receive abuse. (Jackie Kennedy, see J, above, was one of the enthralled dancers.) Predictably, the relationship between Warhol and his protegés soon went sour, though from time to time Lou Reed could still be heard declaring that Warhol was not only the greatest artist of the twentieth century but the greatest artist of any century.

V is also for Viva, one of the Superstars: *née* Susan Hoffman, notable for her Pre-Raphaelite hair, brutal frankness and almost entirely affectless voice. Warhol said of her that he had never guessed that a voice could express such tedium. Her childhood and later adventures are documented, though not for those who blush readily, in her novel *Superstar* (1970).

And for the film **Vinyl** (1965), loosely – not to say imperceptibly – based on Anthony Burgess's *A Clockwork Orange*, to which Warhol had bought the rights for $3,000. Those who have sat through the film report that it shows the Factory regular Gerard Malanga as a captured juvenile delinquent named Victor (not, as in the novel, Alex) being tortured with hot wax and force-fed with (probably) amyl nitrate. The action was not faked.

W is for Warhola

The full, ancestral version of Warhol's family name: they originally came from an obscure sometime fragment of the Austro-Hungarian Empire called Ruthenia, in the Carpathians, north of Translyvania. More handy ammunition for those who considered Warhol a kind of avatar of Count Dracula. (A conceit soon to be given a new lease of life, or Un-Death, in Kim Newman's forthcoming novel *Johnny Alucard* – in which Warhol, all appearances to the contrary, emerges as one of the very few noctural denizens of the Factory who is not, in fact, a full-blooded vampire.) Unlike Count Dracula and his kind, however, Warhol(a) was not ultimately despatched by stake and garlic and daylight, but died in hospital from complications after routine gall bladder surgery, on 22 February 1987. He was buried in the St John the Baptist Byzantine Cemetry, Pittsburgh, next to the graves of Julia and Andrej Warhola.

 is for Xerox
Not merely one of Warhol's most important working tools, but a resonant symbol of his art and 'philosophy'. He famously said that he wanted to be a machine: and what better kind than a machine for making exact reproductions?

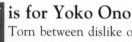 **is for Yoko Ono**
Torn between dislike of her personality and awe for her fame, Warhol had a complicated relationship with Mrs John Winston Lennon. When she ranted to him about the male establishment's suppression of struggling women artists, he pointed out to her that her family owned a bank; when she tried to wheedle him into attending one of John's birthday bashes, he said that he would only go if she told him the size of Lennon's penis – a standard conversational ploy. Even so, he was happy to go to her parties and let her ramble at agonising length in the pages of *Interview*.

 **is for ZZZZZZ...**
The likely reaction of anyone who seriously sets out to watch, for example, the six uneventful hours of *Sleep* (which shows a man – John Giorno – sleeping) or any of Warhol's other uncompromising Underground films from 1963 to 1968. 'I like boring things,' he pronounced in 1968; and there is a sense in which everything he did was either an escape from, a perverse indulgence in, or a cartography of boredom. Was it a worthy enterprise, a good use of a life and a talent? No, says – among others – Robert Hughes: in the end, boredom became boring. Let us modify that to a slightly gentler verdict: one of the most generous aspects of Warhol (and the alleged Vampire

Zombie Sex Fiend could be a very generous host; thoughtful, too) was his democratic willingness to let each and every one of us join in his patented, paradoxical game of finding the banal beautiful, the mass-produced unique, the normal exotic, and the boring somehow... *fabulous*.

A MARGUERITE YOURCENAR ALPHABET

is for Académie Française

It is too soon, no doubt, to say whether Marguerite Yourcenar (1903–87) will prove to be an immortal, but her status as an 'Immortal', or *Immortel(lle)* – that is, a member of the Académie Française – is an undisputed fact of history. She was the first woman member admitted to the ranks of that cautious institution, and it should surprise no one that her candidacy met with violent, if varied, forms of opposition: from the right-wing academicians, on the grounds that she was a woman, and a known lesbian to boot; from the left-wing academicians, who considered her a die-hard political conservative, and in some cases believed the (groundless) murmured slanders that she was an anti-Semite to boot; and from the structural anthropologist Claude Lévi-Strauss on the amusing technical grounds that the Académie was, is, a tribe, and one simply does not changes the rules of a tribe. Despite all the objections, her candidacy was approved: Yves Saint-Laurent designed her pioneering Lady Academician's gown, and in lieu of the traditional sword bestowed on male authors, she was presented with a coin from the era of the Emperor Hadrian: a thoughtful allusion to her most famous book, *Memoirs of Hadrian*.

A is also for the novel some consider her most substantial and personal achievement **The Abyss** (English translation, 1976): see Z is for Zeno; and for her very first novel, written half a century earlier, **Alexis ou le traite du vain combat** (1929).

is for Buddhism

Towards the end of her life, Yourcenar became increasingly preoccupied with spiritual questions, and though her learning encompassed aspects of many faiths, she grew particularly attracted by the religious traditions of the East. This preoccupation shaped her creative work as well as her private thoughts: she was pleased, for example, when an unusually erudite critic noted that a number of Zeno's meditations in *The Abyss* were in fact Buddhist meditations on water, fire and bones. Elsewhere, she contended that Buddhism was the only religion which had evolved 'a truly profound psychology', and admired its ability to address so broad a sweep of the human condition without hardening into dogmatism – 'a very rare feat'.

The texts read for her funeral service, on 16 January 1988, at Northeast Harbor's Union Church, included (as well as the Sermon on the Mount; I Corinthians 13; the 'Canticle of Living Creatures' by St Francis; two passages from Chuang-Tzu; and a poem by a Japanese nun, Rye-Nen) the Four Buddhist Vows:

> Sentient beings are numberless,
> > I vow to save them all.
> Delusions are inexhaustible,
> > I vow to end them all.
> The gates of the *Dharma* are manifold,
> > I vow to enter them all.
> The Buddha-way is supreme,
> > I vow to complete it.

The third of the Four Vows was, she considered, the highest spiritual expression achieved by the human soul. Her ashes, held in an Indian basket of sweetgrass, were covered with a scarf embroidered with the Buddhist emblem of flying cranes, and buried.

B is also for the Blues: Yourcenar, an ardent supporter of the American Civil Rights movement, was also a warm admirer of African-American music and its accompanying lyrics; she was particularly moved by spirituals and the blues. Her translations of the former were published in the volume *Fleuve profond, sombre rivière* (1964); In this context, it is also worth recalling another important B in her life: **James Baldwin** – a close, if rarely visited friend of her later years. She translated his play *The Amen Corner* into French in 1982.

C is for the Crayencours

'Yourcenar' is a pseudonym, and a near-anagram (see Y, below): our author's true family name was Crayencour, and her ancestry was Belgian. Her father, Michel de Cleenewerck de Crayencour, seems to have been a somewhat feckless character, much given to the pleasures of gambling. On the positive side, he was entirely free of his age's conventional wisdom about the place and destiny of young ladies, and not only financed his daughter's private studies but heartily encouraged her early literary career. He died on 1 January 1929; a publisher had just accepted her debut novel *Alexis*, which was eventually published in the November of that year.

For the most part, she had little to do with the other Crayencours. When she finally grew internationally famous, and was elected to Belgium's own Académie, they condescended to seek her out – advances she treated at best with cool courtesy, at worst with open contempt.

D is for Dreams

Yourcenar was fascinated by dreams, and recorded her own in *Les Songes et les sorts*, orginally published in 1938 by Grasset, and then – posthumously and in revised form – for the Pléiade edition in 1991. (It is this later text which has appeared in the United States as *Dreams and Destinies*, translated by Donald Flanell Friedman, 1999.)

D is also for *Dear Departed* – in French, *Souvenirs pieux* (1974) – the first part of her three-volume family memoir.

E is for Essays

She was a wonderful essayist, one of the twentieth century's finest exponents of the form; at her best, as in the collection published in English as *The Dark Brain of Piranesi* (in French, *Sous bénéfice d'inventaire*) she displays a rare combination of lucidity, forcefulness, grace, profound historical imagination and considerable but never clumsily ostentatious learning. She would deserve a considerable reputation had she never written in any other genre.

E is also for her play *Electre ou la chute des masques*. She began writing it in the summer of 1943, during her first full-length stay on Mount Desert, as she began to recover from depression and the unwonted fatigue that came of holding down her first-ever real job. (See below, S is for Sarah Lawrence College.) *Electra* was first staged by a local amateur troupe in 1944, and – though published in France as early as 1947 – did not receive a professional staging until ten years later, at the Théâtre des Mathurins in Paris. This was, to put it gently, not a happy event. Yourcenar took angry exception to many aspects of the production, from the casting of Electra and Orestes to the producer's failure to honour a 'try-out clause' in their original contract. She let her unhappiness be made public, and the reviewers seemed to agree: the critic for *Le Monde* went gleefully to work with his hatchet, and declared the production an absolute mess. Strengthened in her opinion that she was being travestied, Yourcenar ordered her lawyer to file a suit against the producer. The case went to court in March 1956, and Yourcenar won. She was awarded 500,000 francs in damages. Another verdict, of a different order, was equally cheering: Thomas Mann, who had just read the play's published text, wrote her a letter praising it extravagantly, lamenting the fact that it was not considered one of her finest achievements, and hinting that he thought it even more admirable than *Memoirs of Hadrian*.

F is for Frick

The most important person in Yourcenar's life: Grace Frick, her lover, housemate, housekeeper, protector, and general spouse-equivalent for forty years, as well as the principal translator of Yourcenar's works into English. She is a slightly cloudy figure, who left little to the world save her (far from negligible) gift to those who cannot, or prefer not to, read Yourcenar in the original. A few bare facts: the daughter of an affluent family from Kansas City, she studied at Wellesley, taking her BA in 1925 and a Master's in English Literature in 1927. She decided on an academic career, and began by teaching at Stephens College in Columbia, Missouri from 1927 to 1930. In 1931 she moved to New Haven, where she attended courses at Yale for the next two years, before setting off for extensive travels in Europe. In 1936, she took a teaching post in England; in 1937, during a visit to Paris, she met Yourcenar. From the next four decades, they were seldom parted for more than a few days at a time.

After a long and painful struggle against cancer, Grace Frick died on 18 November 1979.

F is also for Yourcenar's editor of the 1930s, **André Fraigneau**, one of the few men the predominantly homosexual Yourcenar ever loved; and for *Feux* (1936), nine lyrical prose pieces inspired by Greek myths. Hence:

G is for Greece

Greece, both ancient and modern, was a constant source of fascination and nourishment throughout Yourcenar's adult life; never more so than in the years from 1932 to 1939, when she was 'centred on Greece' with all her soul, and spent several months of each year living there. (She favoured the Petit Palais hotel in Athens.) Though she always poured cool water on suggestions that her work was 'Hellenic' in nature, the persistence of Greek themes – and especially of themes derived from Greek mythology – is quite undeniable.

This tendency begins at least as early as 1926, when she was twenty-three, and wrote a book-length biographical essay on Pindar. It was originally rejected by Grasset, the house to which she sent it, until in the summer of 1929 a young intern – name of André Fraigneau – discovered the manuscripts in a cabinet full of 'discards', immediately saw its quality and set about the difficult task of tracking her down. By the time he did so – she had since moved to Lausanne – Yourcenar had all but forgotten about the manuscript. The book was published in 1931, and Fraigneau remained her editor throughout the 1930s. In later years, Yourcenar came to disparage this early exercise in Hellenism, and refused to let it be reprinted as one of her collected works; but other readers have judged it less harshly, seeing in it evidence both of a precociously mature style, heavy with aphorisms, and also of a prophetic self-portrait of the artist as the old woman she would become. Her essay ends: 'The only lesson we can learn from this life, so distant from our own, is that glory after all is nothing more than a temporary concession.' Shortly afterwards, in 1932, she engaged in a friendly literary game with Fraigneau and the author 'Gaston Baisette' (a pseudonym), in which each produced a short text on a topic derived from Greek myth. When the subject of the Labyrinth came up, Yourcenar produced a sketch entitled *Ariane et l'aventurier*, which later became the basis for her play *Qui n'a pas son Minotaure?*

Among the many other manifestations of her Hellenism are her translations and edition of Constantine Cavafy, often regarded as the greatest Greek poet of the twentieth century, who had died in 1933. She was introduced to his *oeuvre* by a friend, Constantine Dimaras, who became her – sometimes reluctant – collaborator on the project. (Dimaras was in profound disagreement with her philosophy of translation: he wanted word-for-word accuracy, she sought beautiful French.) Their work began in 1936 and was complete by the summer of 1939, though only small extracts from it reached the public until 1958, when Gallimard published the translations with her long critical essay. She eventually made a literary pilgrimage to Cavafy's Alexandria in 1982. Her work on Cavafy led her onwards, or backwards, to translations of much earlier Greek poets; these translations were eventually published as *La Couronne et la lyre* in 1979. A bulky volume, 480 pages long, it included extracts from 110 poets, starting with verses from the seventh century BC and continuing into the reign of Justinian, c. AD 520. Yourcenar had assembled the original texts mainly between 1948 and 1951 – years when she was at work on *Memoirs of Hadrian* – and she claims to have translated them, in the first instance, purely for her own enjoyment.

Nor was her love for Greece purely a matter of myth and literature. Her Hellenophilia took on her a personal dimension in her relationships with, among others, André Embiricos (1901–75): a charismatic, fiercely handsome and magnificently eloquent Surrealist, Communist, psychoanalyst and *éminence grise* of modern Greek literature. The precise nature of their relationship remains hazy. Though obviously passionate, it may not have consisted of anything more carnal than long walks in the Greek countryside and intense conversations. Some memoirs have painted him as a kind of Pygmalion to her maturing talent;

others deny the suggestion. For Yourcenar's other Greek passion, see below, K is for Lucy Kyriakos.

H is for Hadrian

The emperor, the novel. The French publication of *Mémoires d'Hadrien* (1951) (translated as *Memoirs of Hadrian*, 1954) when she was nearly fifty, brought Yourcenar the first real fame she had ever known, and launched her on her path from impoverished, all but forgotten minor writer of the inter-war years to literary lioness of the post-war period and national treasure.

I is for Italy

Though her involvement with Italy was less profound than that with Greece, Yourcenar loved the country, relished travelling to its cities and would generally go there whenever time and money allowed. Her first major Italian trip, taken with her father, was to Venice, Milan and Verona in 1922. Here, she witnessed the March on Rome at first hand, and met a number of Roman men and women involved in underground anti-fascist activities – experiences which inspired her novel *Denier du rêve* (translated as *A Coin in Nine Hands*), 1934. Using the (rather eighteenth-century) conceit of a ten-lira coin which circulates between the main characters, the novel describes – in partly realistic, partly symbolic terms – an attempted anti-fascist assassination in the year XI (1933) of the dictatorship. This novel was entirely rewritten in 1959; her public explanation was that she had made an artistic botch of the first version, and yielded to the temptations of the grotesque. This is something of a half-truth. André Fraigneau, angered by this emollient version of the story, insists that the real motive of Yourcenar's revision was to make the book more politically acceptable, since the the first version had lacked any perceptible note of anti-Mussolini sentiment, an abstention which reflected the fact that Yourcenar had been perfectly comfortable with her life in fascist Italy.

The other outstanding Italian trip took her to Rome in 1924. She discovered the (soon to be vulgarised) charms of the Villa Adriana, where she had a moment of inspiration comparable to Gibbon's imperial epiphany, and resolved on the project which, twenty-seven years later, would emerge as her novel on Hadrian.

J is for Japan

Though she did not realise her ambition of travelling to Japan until 1982, just five years before her death, Yourcenar had been enthralled by the nation and its literature for much of her adult life. When asked what woman novelist she most admired, Yourcenar would nominate Muraski Shikibu, who wrote in the eleventh century – the period, Yourcenar believed, when Japanese civilisation had been at its zenith. Describing Murasaki as the Marcel Proust of medieval Japan, a consummate portrayer of social class, love and tragically thwarted ambition, she would conclude that 'nothing better has ever been written in any language'. Besides Muraski, she adored the poetic reflections of Sei Shonagon, the haiku and travel narratives of Basho, and the Nō dramas, saying that she ranked them every bit as highly as the great Greek dramas – they 'constitute one of the two or three triumphs of universal theatre' – and was eternally grateful that she had happened across the medieval Japanese dramas *Atsumori* and *Sumidagawa* at the same time that she first read the *Antigone*. (The influence of her early reading of Nō plays may be found in her one-act drama *Le Dialogue dans le marécage*, 1930.) Among modern Japanese writers, Yukio Mishima was her particular fascination: she wrote a book-length study, *Mishima: A Vision of the Void*, and – having begun the study of Japanese in her seventies – translated his *Five Modern Nō Plays*, published in 1984.

K is for Lucy Kyriakos

The young Greek woman, by many accounts an exceptional beauty, with whom Yourcenar had a discreet but highly passionate affair in the late 1930s – a liaison cut short by Yourcenar's departure for the United States in October 1939. Kyriakos did not have long to mourn her lost love: according to one well-informed source, she was killed shortly after the outbreak of war, in the bombardment of Janina, Turkey (Easter 1940; though other accounts put her death in 1941 or 1942). Yourcenar kept faith with her lover's memory in a quiet private ritual: for many years afterwards, she would underline the date of St Lucy's Day in her calendars. In 1942, she wrote a poem, 'Epitaphe, *Temps de Guerre*', inspired by Lucy's death.

And for **'Kali décapitée'** – 'Kali Beheaded' – an early short story which was the first published evidence of her interest in authors from the Far East.

 ## is for *Le Labyrinthe du monde*

The original title for the second volume of her three-volume family memoirs, later used for the trilogy in full. The definitive version now stands as:

Le Labyrinthe du monde:
I   *Souvenirs pieux* (1974); in English, *Dear Departed*, 1991
II *Archives du nord* (1977); in English, *How Many Years*, 1995
III *Quoi? L'éternité* (1988); in English, *Eternity Regained*, 2003

 ## is for Maine

To the incredulity and occasional indignation of the French, the north-eastern American state was home to this profoundly French artist for many years, and became her burial place. (The fact that Maine has long been home to a substantial number of citizens descended from French settlers – a demographic oddity well known to neurologists, thanks to a rare but spectacular disorder whose principal symptom is clearly implied in the quaint term 'the Leaping Frenchmen of Maine' – had nothing to do with her life decision.)

She and Grace Frick moved from place to place in their early Maine days, before finally settling for good in Mount Desert – an outstandingly beautiful part of a state not lacking in natural glories. They christened their modest house Petite Plaisance; it has been preserved as museum, open to visitors in summer months.

M is also for Thomas Mann, a devoted fan of Yourcenar's work, which he characterised as 'poetic and full of erudition'; he expressed his enthusiasm in at least one elegant letter to her.

N is for *La Nouvelle Eurydice*

Her second novel, published by Grasset in 1931 in an edition of 5,000 copies, concerns an amorous triangle. The narrator, Stanislaus, is friendly with a couple, Thérèse and Emmanuel. Stanislaus falls in love with Thérèse, but she persists in doting on Emmanuel despite his obvious preference for men. For the most part, the critics were harsh, and Yourcenar did not include it in the Pléiade edition. Twenty-five years after its first appearance, it had sold no more than 2,667 copies, though its failure to find a popular audience was nothing remarkable: none of her early works published by Grasset sold even that insignificant number, and one, *Les Songes et les sorts*, barely scraped past the 1,000 sales mark.

O is for Charles Orengo

Her publisher, regular correspondent and friend of twenty-three years (from *Hadrian* to *Dear Departed*) until his death from cancer in 1974 at the age of sixty-one; he devoted himself tirelessly and disinterestedly to her needs and wishes, and admired her as 'one of the great minds of the century'. It seems, however, to have been rather an undemonstrative friendship, and the surving correspondence, though bulky, is largely devoted to practicalities.

O is also for the *Oriental Tales*, first published in 1938 by Gallimard, and dedicated to André Embiricos – see G, above. (They are available in a typically felicitous English translation by the Argentinian-born novelist and critic Alberto Manguel.)

P is for the *Pléiade*

Alongside the formidable likes of André Malraux, Saint-John Perse and René Char, Marguerite Yourcenar was one of the very few French authors ever to be honoured by being published in the august Pléiade edition during her lifetime. She broke with convention by insisting that there be no critical apparatus.

Q is for *Quoi? L'éternité*

The third volume of her family memoirs; death interrupted her work on its final chapters. It has been published in English as *Eternity Regained* (Aidan Ellis Publishing).

R is for *Reflections on the Composition of the Memoirs of Hadrian*

A short, aphoristic and intensely revealing essay, constructed in the form of apparently independent paragraph-fragments, which is one of the most eloquent and thought-provoking productions of her total *oeuvre*. Its contents, well worth the effort even for those who have never read her novel and do not intend to read it, touch on matters which often seem to be at a great remove from its ostensible subject:

> The sorcerer who pricks his thumb before he evokes the shades knows well that they will heed his call only because they can lap his blood…

R is also for À *La Recherche du temps perdu*. She often lectured on Proust, notably during her years at:

S is for Sarah Lawrence College

Through a combination of good luck, frugal habits, inherited funds and tolerant publishers, Yourcenar managed to avoid the disgusting fate of having to work for a living until she was almost forty. Her only period of more or less regular employment began in September 1942, when she was forced by the harsh economic realities of emigré life in the United States to seek some kind of paid employment. She found it in a part-time teaching post at Sarah Lawrence College, about twenty miles north of New York. Teaching mainly French language and civilisation, as well as some courses in Italian, she remained on the faculty until June 1950, when she took a long leave of absence, finally returning to fulfil a contractual obligation by completing the academic year 1952–3. *Memoirs of Hadrian* had restored her cherished financial independence.

Sarah Lawrence was a women's college, modest in size (about 350 students), and enjoying a reputation for its progressive educational policies. Yourcenar taught her classes punctiliously but without much warmth, and maintained stringent standards; she shunned informal contact with students and lecturers alike. To them, she seemed an impressive figure, curiously dressed (by their lights) in monkish outfits of capes and shawls, usually of dark but exquisitely judged hues – an exotic, perhaps an eccentric, who stood out even in a milieu with more than its share of 'characters' both natural and contrived.

T is for *That Mighty Sculptor, Time*

A major collection of essays (English version 1992; from *Le temps, ce grand sculpteur* 1983). Explanation (partial) of title:

Escaping from chaos by way of the artist's conception and his chisel, the stone returns to chaos little by little by way of the violence of nature and of men: yes, time has reclaimed its rights.

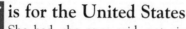

U is for the United States

She had, she once said, not given so much as one second's thought to the United States before the age of thirty-four – 'Greece had become my centre and I imagined that it would continue to be.'

V is for the Vietinghoffs

The aristocratic Dutch family which played a major part in her life from infancy onwards. The Baron Egon de Vietinghoff, a painter – whose father served as one of the models for her male protagonist in *Alexis ou le traite du vain combat* – recalled playing with her on the Dutch beach of Scheveningen in the summers of 1905 and 1906; she sometimes referred to him – archly? – as her 'first boyfriend'. Egon's mother, Jeanne de Vietinghoff, was idealised – perhaps idolised – by Yourcenar, who commemorated her under false names ('Monique', etc.) in several books, and in an essay of 1929 'En memoire de Diotime: Jeanne de Vietinghoff', later republished in *That Mighty Sculptor, Time*. Jeanne and Yourcenar's mother, Fernande, had first met when they were pupils at a boarding school in Brussels. Yourcenar speculated that their friendship may well have been a love affair, or at least a romantic infatuation. In a sense, Yourcenar had two mothers – one real, one elected – and she later learned that the two young women had taken a vow that, in the event of one dying prematurely, the survivor would look after any children. Hence the generous letter Jeanne sent to M. de Crayencour in 1905, when she heard, belatedly, of Fernande's death; hence the beach holidays together.

V is also for *La Voix des choses*, the last publication to appear in her lifetime: a book of photographs and texts, the latter chosen by Yourcenar, the former shot in Kenya by:

W is for Jerry Wilson

For a period of six years, in the lonely time after the death of Grace Frick, Jerry Wilson – a young, talented, gay American, who spoke excellent French – restored pleasure to Yourcenar's widowed life by becoming her regular travelling companion: part of the delight she took in him was that she felt starved of the chance to speak and listen to French in her everyday American life. He died, at the Laennec Hospital in Paris, of AIDS, on 8 February 1986. He was thirty-six. She often thought of herself as an avatar of Hadrian; her loss of Jerry Wilson was, to her, an echo of the loss felt by the Emperor on the death of Antinous. She lived on alone, for almost two years, and died on 17 December 1987.

W is also for Virginia Woolf, and for ***The Waves***, which Yourcenar translated as *Les Vagues*. Yourcenar, who met the English novelist for just two hours on 23 February 1937, considered Woolf one of the four or five great living virtuosos of the English language, and hoped that there would be minds sensitive and subtle enough to appreciate her craft in the year 2500.

X is for 'Cousin X'

A family member who seduced her when she was pubescent – an event she looked back on with a degree of equanimity that many, today, would find shocking.

X is also for her inveterate Xenophilia, which found its fullest expression in the many exotic travels she undertook in the last few years of her life, after the death of Grace Frick.

Y is for 'Yourcenar'

As noted above, under C, this celebrated name is in fact a pen name – a near-perfect anagram of 'Crayencour', which she arrived at in the course of an evening spent with her father, arranging and rearranging the letters of their family name. She adopted it in 1920; more exactly, she began her literary career signing herself 'Marg Yourcenar', and maintained that *nom de plume* for about a decade. 'Marg' is not only a weird first name in France, but a sexually indeterminate one, so that readers of her early volumes would have had no hint that their author was a young woman. The first publication credited to 'Marg' was *Le Jardin des chimères*, in 1921: the author was eighteen. When asked about the resonances of 'Yourcenar' – again, a strange, exotic-sounding name in French ears – she would say it was chosen 'for the pleasure of the Y'. 'Marguerite Yourcenar' finally became her legal name when she took on American citizenship.

Z is for Zeno

The hero of what may be her greatest work, *The Abyss* (*L'Oeuvre au noir*, 1968; English translation by Grace Frick and the author, 1976.) Among Zeno's most heartfelt sayings: 'Who would be so besotted as to die without having made at least the round of this, his prison?' Hence the title of Yourcenar's travel book, *Le Tour de la prison*.

Finally, **Z is also for Zen Buddhism**: a Zen *koan* appears as the epigraph to *Dear Departed*:

What did your face look like before your mother and father met?

INDEX